Sabine Ickler & Katrin Klink

Fun with Gelli Plate Prints

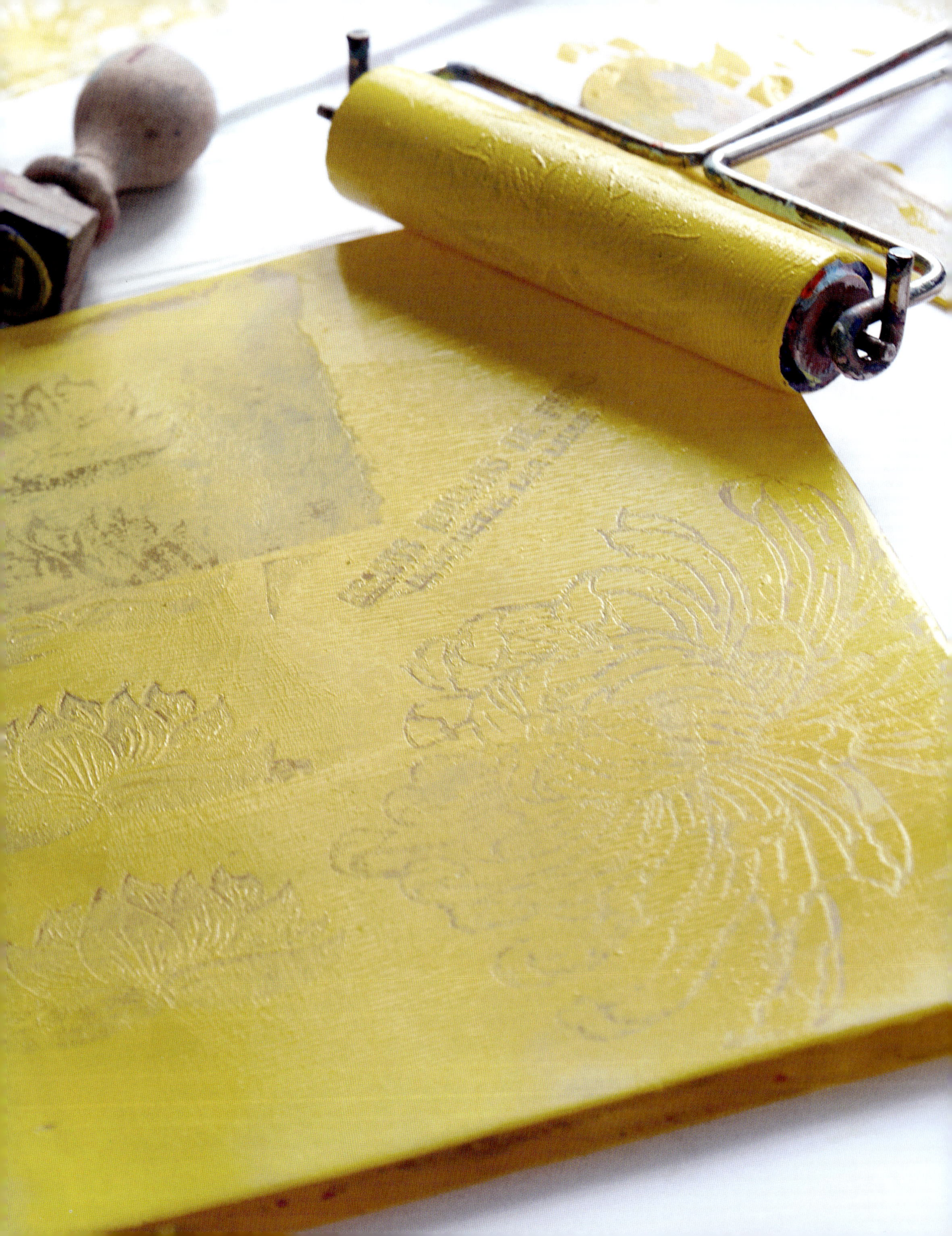

Sabine Ickler & Katrin Klink

Fun with Gelli Plate Prints

Easy mixed-media printmaking

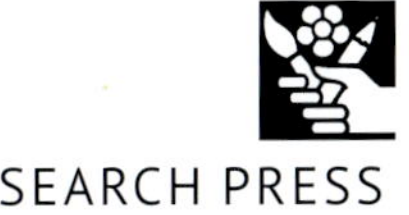

SEARCH PRESS

Introduction

We think that gelli printing, or gel printing, is one of the best techniques for unleashing your creativity in surface design – on paper, fabric, collage materials, lampshades and much more. 'Gelli' is derived from 'gelatine', and you can easily create gelli plates yourself with little effort and using just three materials (see page 19 for the recipe).

Gelli printing is essentially a monoprinting technique. Monoprints have been around for centuries and they are created using a smooth surface such as glass, applying paint and designing with it. You can remove or cover parts of the paint using the back of a brush, natural materials, stamps or stencils. Afterwards, the designed paint is printed onto paper.

Gelli printing is almost everyday monoprinting – a version that you can create on your kitchen table – you don't need an artist's studio, you can use almost any type of paint, a gelli plate is easy to clean, and you end up with a plethora of creative results.

Normally, the most challenging aspect of getting creative is being faced by a blank sheet of paper and having to think about how to use colours and surfaces. Gelli printing turns this process on its head, and so it is wonderfully intuitive and experimental. With materials you have to hand, or even household objects, paint is dabbed, stamped, textured or patterned on to the gelli plate; then you simply place a blank sheet of paper on the gelli plate and rub down with your hand or the back of a spoon – and you will have a monoprint, a unique print. It is incredibly easy and this printing technique is suitable for paint enthusiasts of all ages. Gelli printing can be addictive – you fall into a printing and colour frenzy!

Keep even those prints that seem less successful at first glance; there are many techniques for printing multiple layers on top of each other. The final layer then takes centre stage, and misprints can become wonderful supporting actors.

One of the peculiarities of gelli printing is that we can essentially use two different printing techniques in one; we call them passive and active. Active printing is familiar from stamping: we press our stamp on to an ink pad and then on to a sheet of paper. This is active printing, meaning the motif is printed in the chosen colour.

However, if we press a stamp on to the gelli plate rolled with ink, we have two processes:

a) paint on the stamp, which we can print on to a surface as an active print, and
b) a negative impression on the gelli plate, namely where the stamp has removed the ink.

If we then place a sheet of paper on top and make our monoprint, the motif does not appear in colour, but as a white negative on a coloured background. Two for the price of one, so to speak!

In this book, we later combine simple gelli printing with other printing techniques, such as potato printing or stamping. Firstly, the desire to embellish paper and fabric continues to grow. Secondly, a gelli plate can serve wonderfully as a colour palette where you can mix your own colour combinations, or as a kind of paint pad for acrylic or fabric paint. Of course, you could do this without a gelli plate, but not with the two-in-one effect and, to be honest, it's a lot less fun.

It has never been easier to design papers and images, so next comes the challenge: what can we do with stacks of printed papers? You can cover sketchbooks with them, create collages or bind junk journals (books stitched together from self-designed or other salvaged papers), but at some point, you will want more. That was the moment when we came up with two things: designing on fabric and everyday items. In the second part of the book, we have compiled some projects, which are all wondefully easy to make, and a lot of fun. So, let's get started: step into the cheerful, colourful world of gelli printing!

Sabine & Katrin

1

Materials, paints & techniques

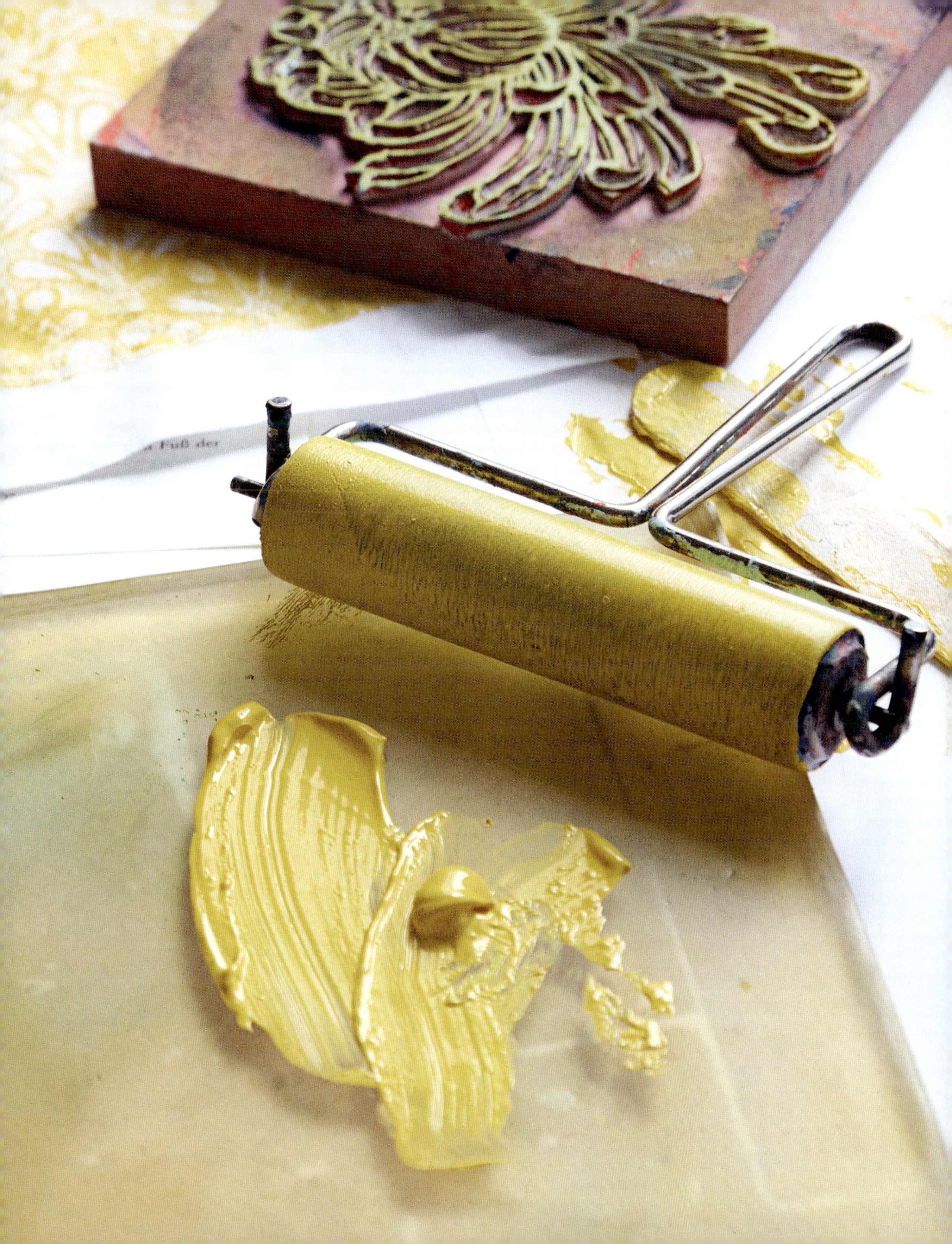
Fuß der

Materials

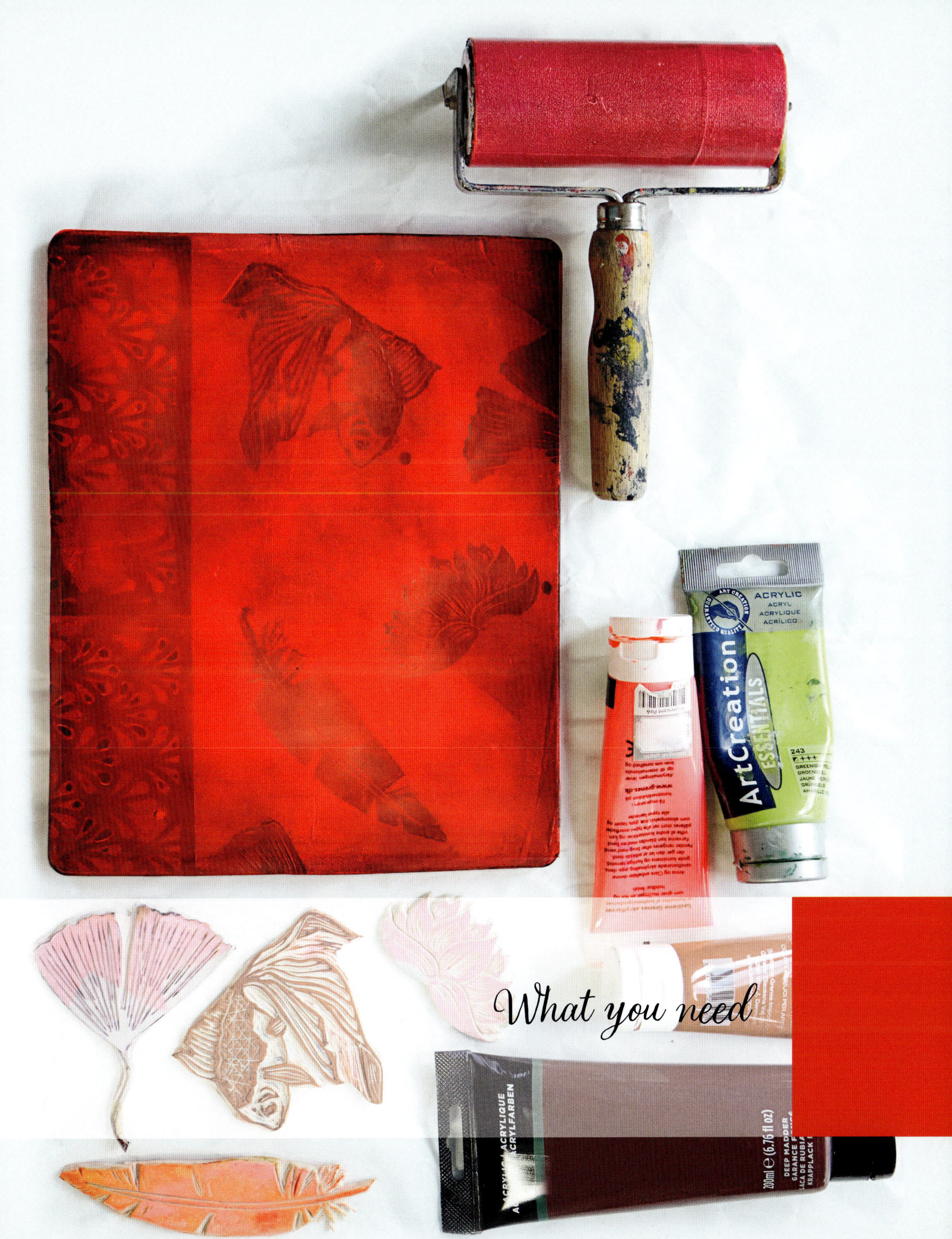

What you need

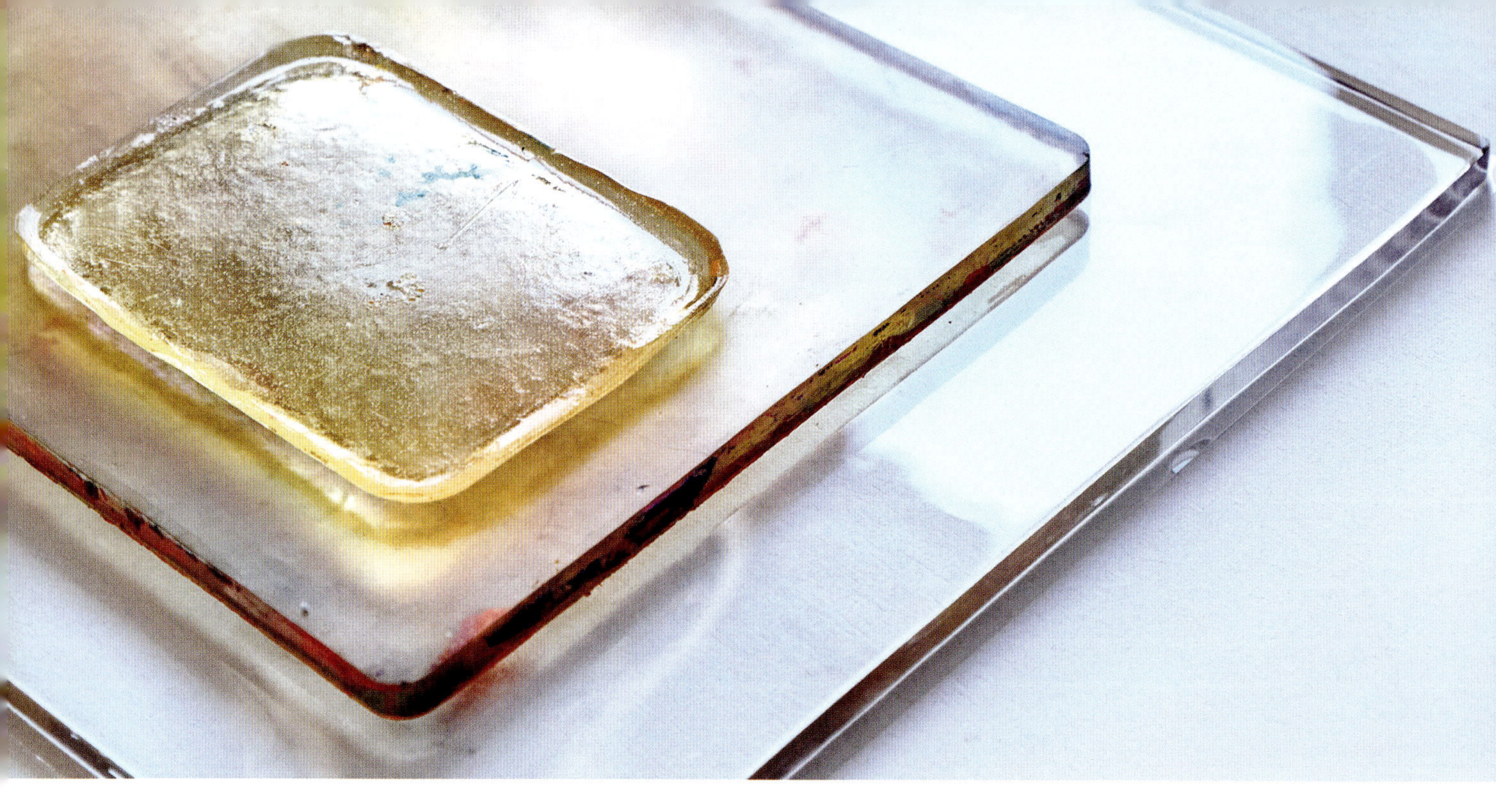

You need four things for gelli printing: a gelli plate, paint, paper (or fabric) and a brayer. In this book, we have taken care to use resources as sparingly as possible. Most of the fabrics used are old linen cloths from second-hand stores, or antique linen sheets from flea markets, often with imperfections and patches. Using unique fabric and resources can make your creations even more special, and you can begin gelli printing using items you already have at home or ones you can obtain inexpensively. Even stubborn stains on a favourite dress can be beautifully overprinted! You can also make the gelli plate yourself – find a recipe for this on page 19.

GELLI PLATES

It is important to know from the outset that gelli plates are robust and not fragile in any way. They are very forgiving, even with dried-on paint if the printing process is interrupted. What they don't like are sharp objects, so never use a knife or scissors near gelli plates. As long as you avoid these, they will last for years.

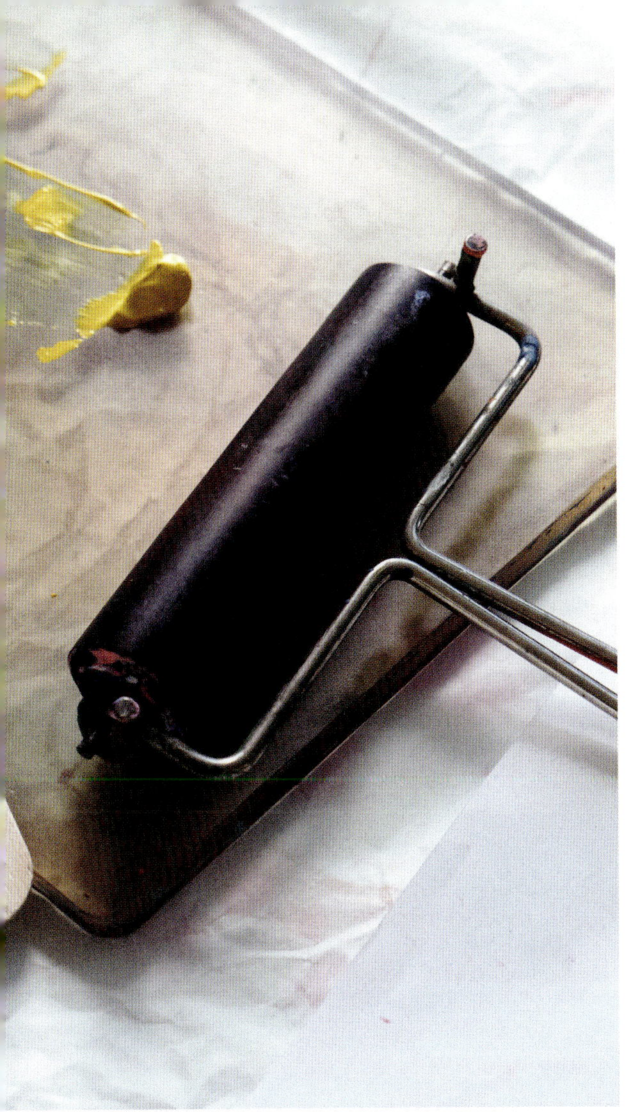

In the picture to the far left, you can see a new gelli plate in its full glory. Over time, the plate will get darker; this does not affect its ability to print in any way. Gelli plates that you make yourself, like the top plate in the picture, have the advantage that you can determine the size yourself. It is sometimes easier to use small gelli plates for smaller projects. Self-made gelli plates are usually somewhat more porous or may contain a few small air bubbles.

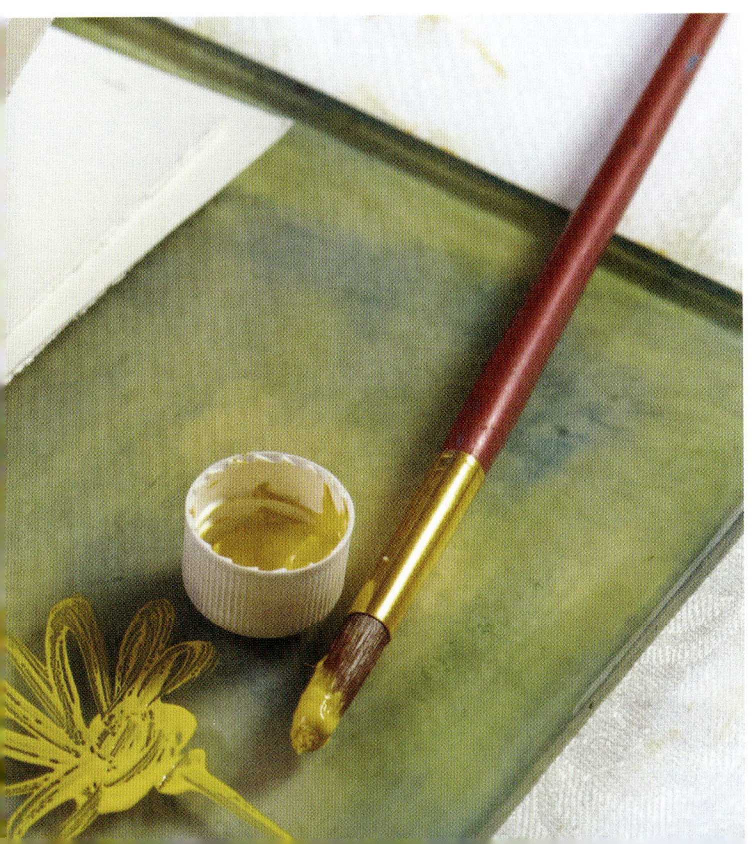

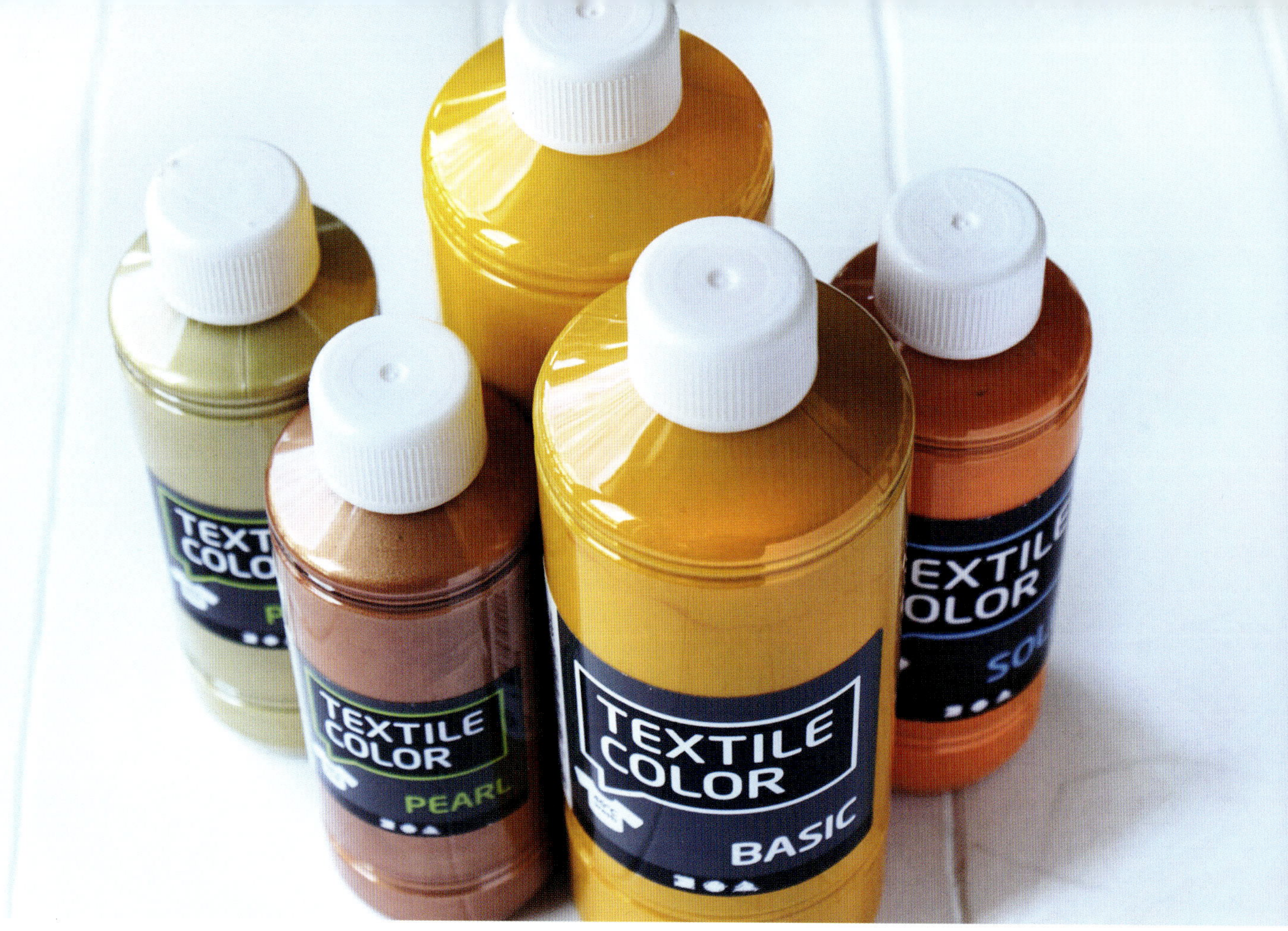

PAINTS

In this book, we mainly use fabric and acrylic paints. You can achieve wonderful results printing on paper with fabric paints and on fabric with acrylic paints.

If the fabric is to be washed later, you can add in a 'textile medium', which makes the acrylic paint washable and, more importantly, softer, so that it adheres better to the textile fibres for longer.

Fabric paint still usually needs to be fixed, most commonly by ironing the reverse side of the fabric. Each paint will have its own method, but as it is essentially about applying heat, fabric paints can theoretically be fixed in an oven.

Fabric paint is usually expensive. The small 50ml (1¾fl oz) pots in craft shops certainly are, but there are also 250ml (9fl oz) bottles from various manufacturers, which only cost a little more and are available in lots of wonderful colours. Most of them can be ordered online.

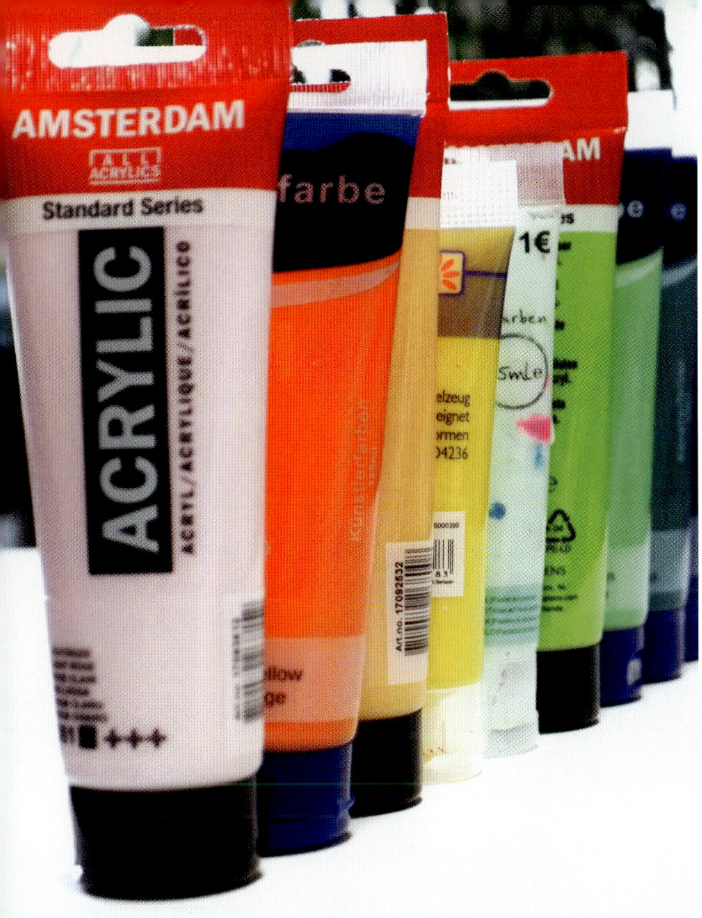

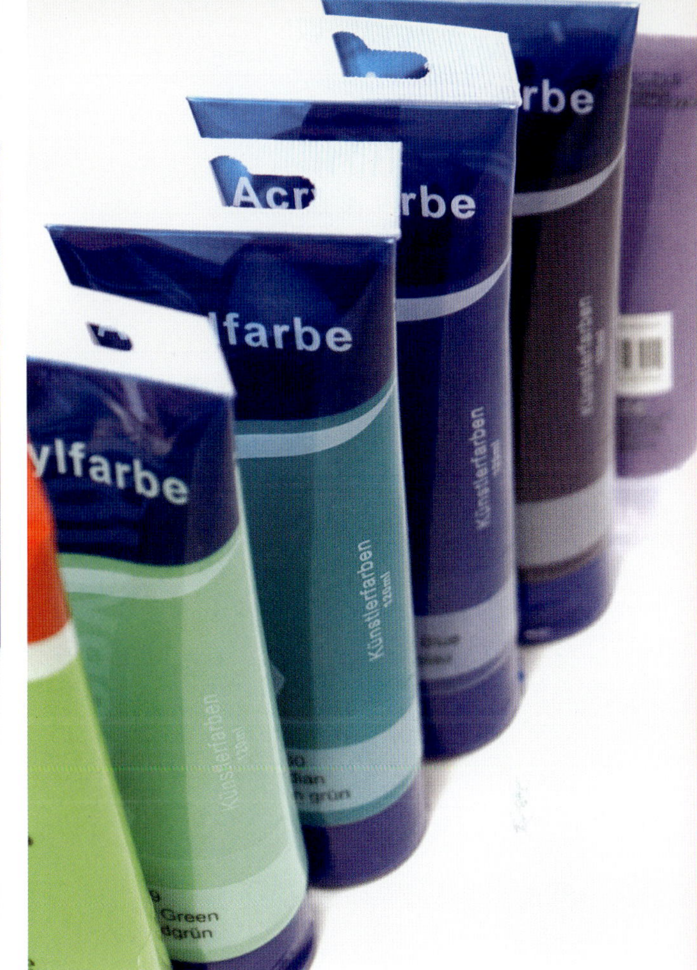

Acrylic paints are available to buy in various qualities and prices, from student to artist quality. Artist-quality acrylic paints contain more pigment: that is, more colour particles, giving them more opacity. However, you may want to achieve a more transparent effect, or use something less opaque to tone down a bright paint application. The cheaper paints with less pigment are perfect for this. Try them out and see which you prefer.

Paints are really important. Favourite colours give you immediate results which make you happy. If you are not happy with the result of a press, the colour is always the prime suspect. Is the shade wrong? Was the paint too fluid or not pigmented enough? Try it with other colours. Fabric paint ranges from fluid to gelatinous, and essentially, the thicker a paint, the more opaque it is, and the easier it is for you to control the print result. After all, you can always dilute the paint.

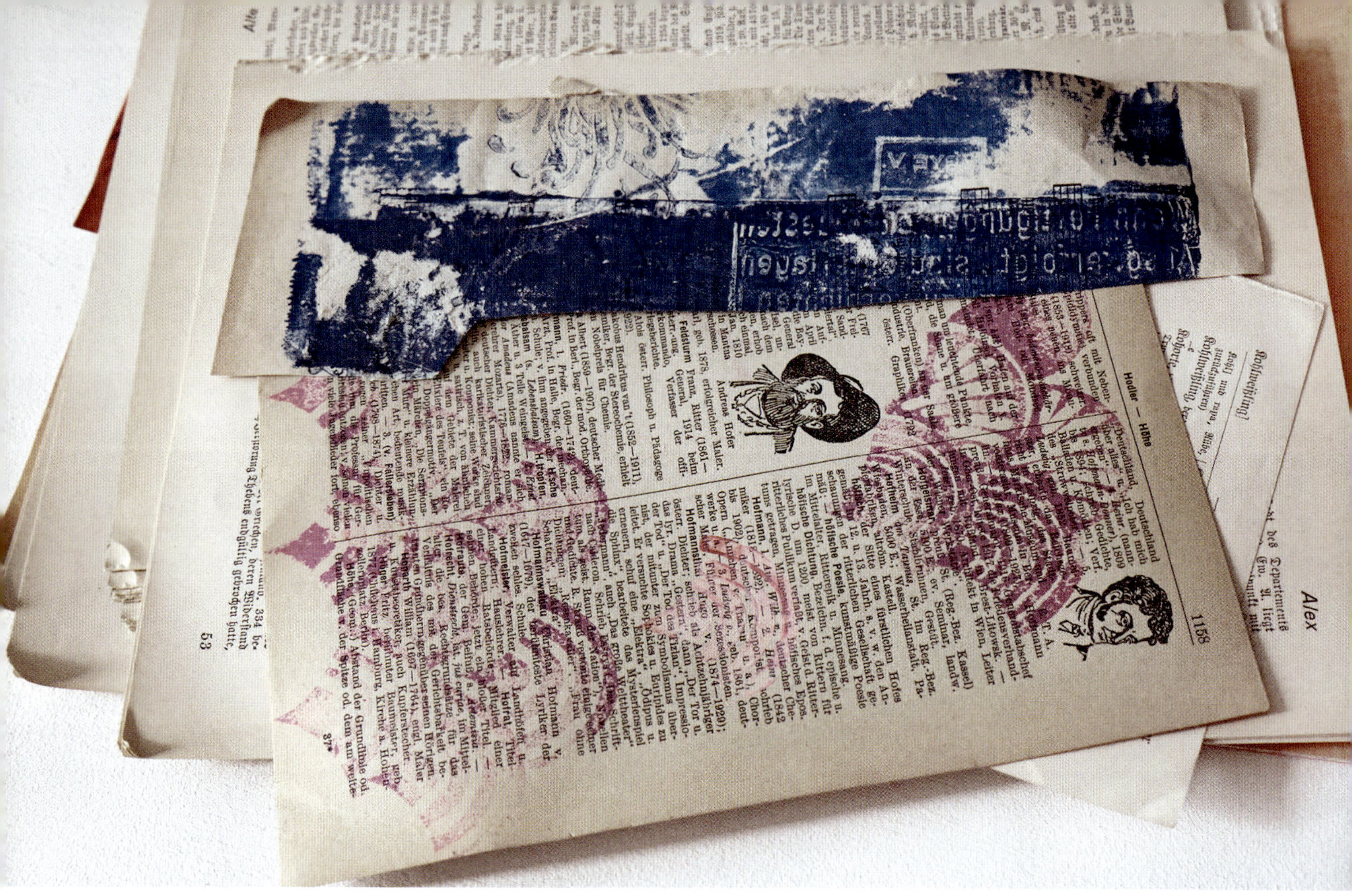

PAPER AND FABRIC

When it comes to paper, there's not much to say except that, here too, you can use resources sparingly. You can roll the brayer on scrap paper to remove excess paint. This saves you the time-consuming work of cleaning the brayer when changing colour and reduces the amount of paint going down the drain when cleaning up. Both acrylic and fabric paint are 'plastic paints', and we should minimize the amount of microplastic particles that end up in water. The resulting scrap paper is, incidentally, a wonderful base material for further prints or collages.

We don't just use white (cartridge) paper but also old book pages, sheet music and so on, and, of course, you can also use coloured paper. The thinner the paper, the more likely it is to adhere to the paint when peeling it off the gelli plate, and possibly tear. This can also happen with older paper, such as book pages, or if you wait too long to peel off the paper. Otherwise, paper produces clear, rich prints and is very easy to use.

When it comes to fabric, there are more factors to consider. The coarser the fabric, the more paint it absorbs and the more uneven the application. The printed result looks 'fuzzier' at the edges, which can create interestingly textured surfaces, and adds to the design and style. For projects involving fabric, you should consider how thick it is, and possibly make some test prints. In general, try to use fabric containing natural fibres. The fabric should not be treated and should be washed before printing.

As with paper, the following rules apply: colours stand out better on light-coloured fabric, whereas highly pigmented colours are needed for dark backgrounds.

Fabric can be printed on before cutting, which is the experimental/intuitive approach. However, if you really want to create a design with motifs placed in a certain way, it is easier to cut the fabric first to give you more precision when printing.

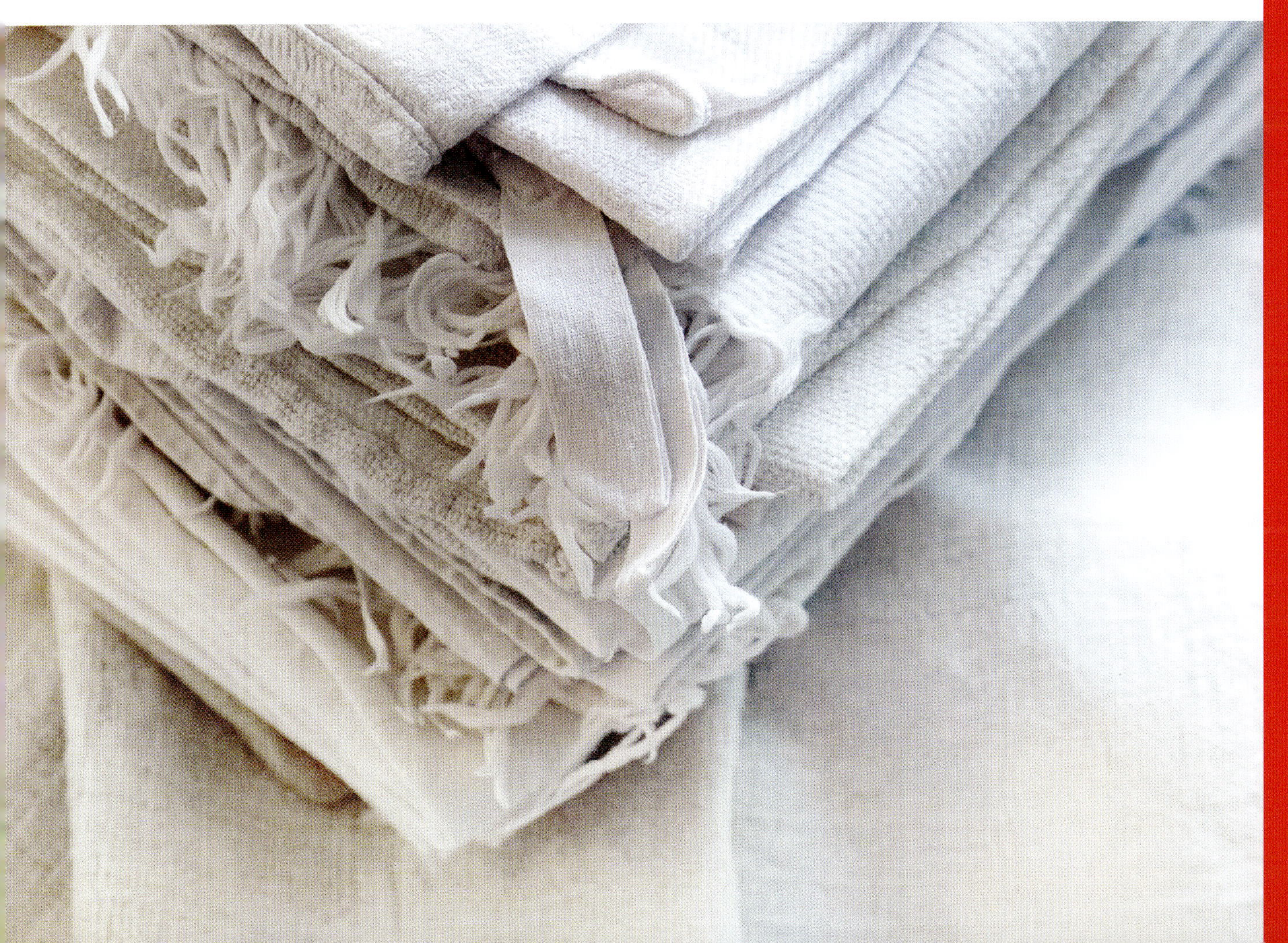

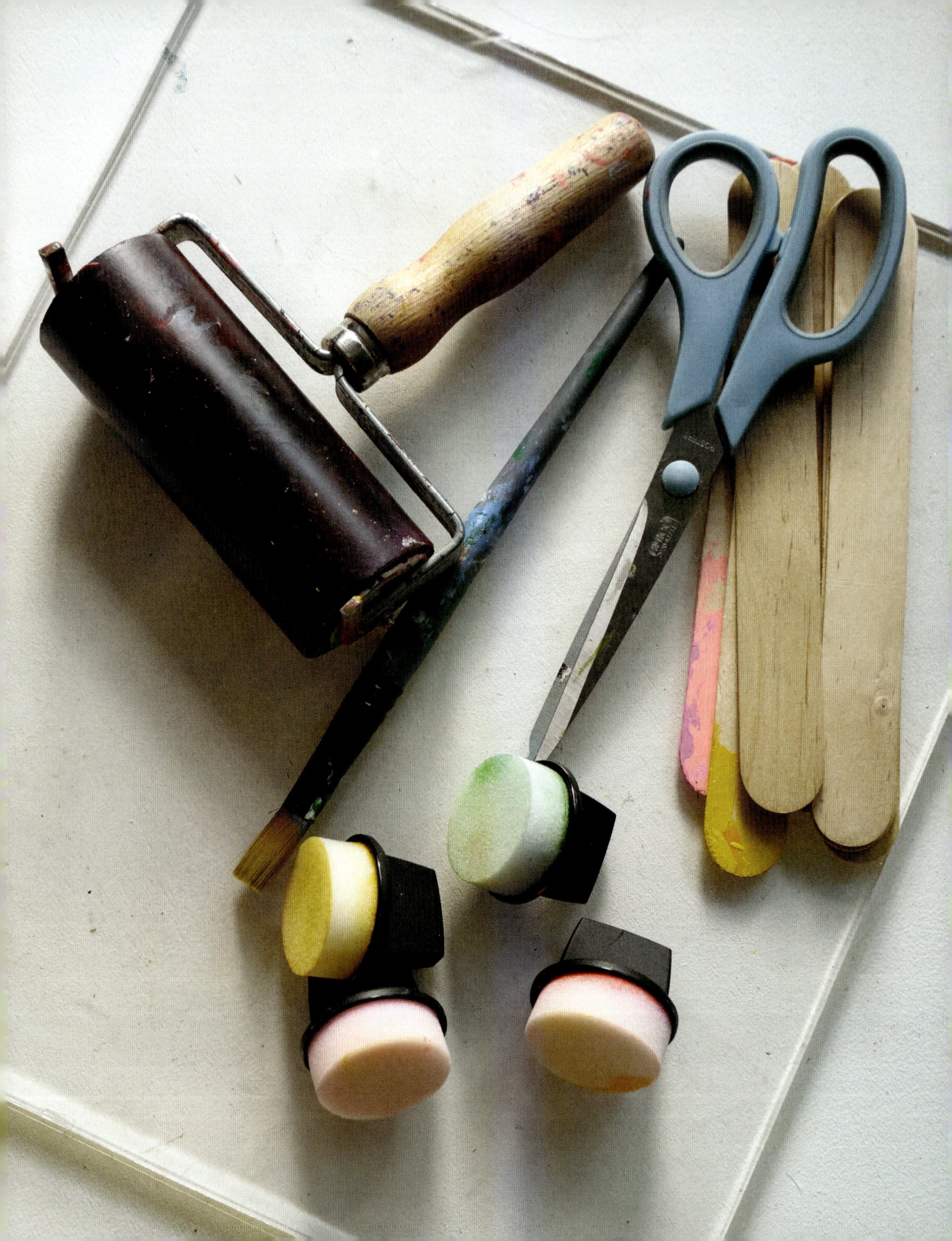

TOOLS

You can apply the paint in lots of ways, for example with a brush or using your fingers. Using a paint spatula or a flat wooden spatula, you can mix colours and remove excess paint from the gelli plate if you have applied too much or if you have some paint left over. Some printing techniques require a brayer, which will give a more even, quicker and thinner application.

Scissors and sticky tape are always good to have around. Likewise, sponges of all kinds, for removing or applying paint – for example, when using stencils. In the picture on the left, you can see some small sponges bought from a craft store, but you can also cut basic dish sponges to the size you want.

Suitable for cleaning, dishcloths also mostly come with some interesting textures, letting you create some great patterns. Then there are wet wipes (baby wipes). They naturally produce waste, but they are brilliant for cleaning gelli plates, the brayer or stamps between stages. You can also do this with a dish sponge and some washing-up liquid, but then the paint ends up in the wastewater. Some paints, mostly the darker ones, leave stubborn stains on the gelli plate that are almost impossible to remove with water and washing-up liquid. However, wet wipes which contain emollients work wonders.

Generally, it is best to lay out all of your equipment to hand so that you do not have to interrupt your printing if something is missing.

RECIPE: HOMEMADE GELLI PLATE

Stir 9 sachets of gelatine powder (not instant or quick-gelatine powder) with 250ml (9fl oz) cold water in a pan and leave it to soak for 10 minutes. Heat slowly until the mixture becomes runny. Remove the pan from the heat, let it cool slightly, then carefully stir in 125ml (4fl oz) isopropyl alcohol and 125ml (4fl oz) vegetable glycerine. Pour the mixture through a sieve into your chosen moulds, at least 1.5cm (½in) thick. Gently shake the mould back and forth to remove any air bubbles. Leave it to set firm; this can take a few days. The finished gelli plate can be cut into pieces or even reheated and recast. Store flat.

If you'd prefer to make a large gelli plate, use double the amounts above and sieve into a baking tray, at least 1.5cm (½in) thick.

You could experiment with making a gelli plate using Agar-Agar if you'd prefer a vegan alternative, but please note that we have not tried this method.

Caution: the alcohol evaporates. Do not leave to set near children or in a very small room!

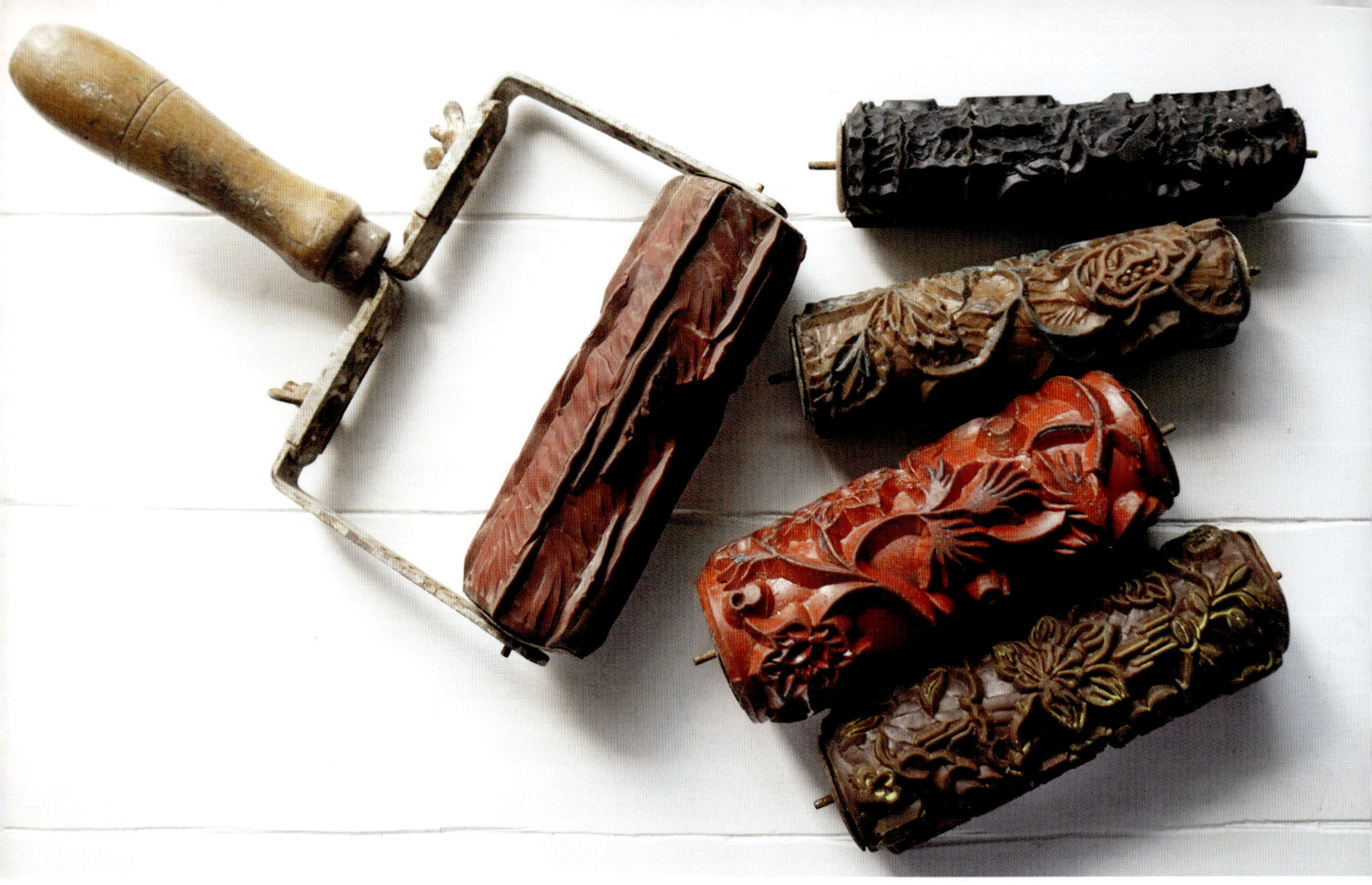

STAMPS

There are lots of varieties of stamps – bought and homemade. We are both graphic artists and love anything to do with typography, which is why you'll often find letter or character stamps in our work. Our collection came from flea markets and local adverts, where you can also sometimes find old school stamps. These are mostly old maps that were used to create teaching materials before printers and photocopiers were commonly used.

The rollers in the picture above are old paint rollers. They are also called textured rollers, used to apply patterns to walls. You can also buy these new, sometimes featuring sensational designs. Rollers have the advantage of being able to create unlimited patterns, making it easy to decorate large areas with little effort.

You can also use an old rolling pin (or in smaller format, a lint roller) to achieve similar effects. The simplest variation is to wrap elastic bands or threads around the roller. Even small motifs – made out of foam rubber, for example – are possible (see page 54).

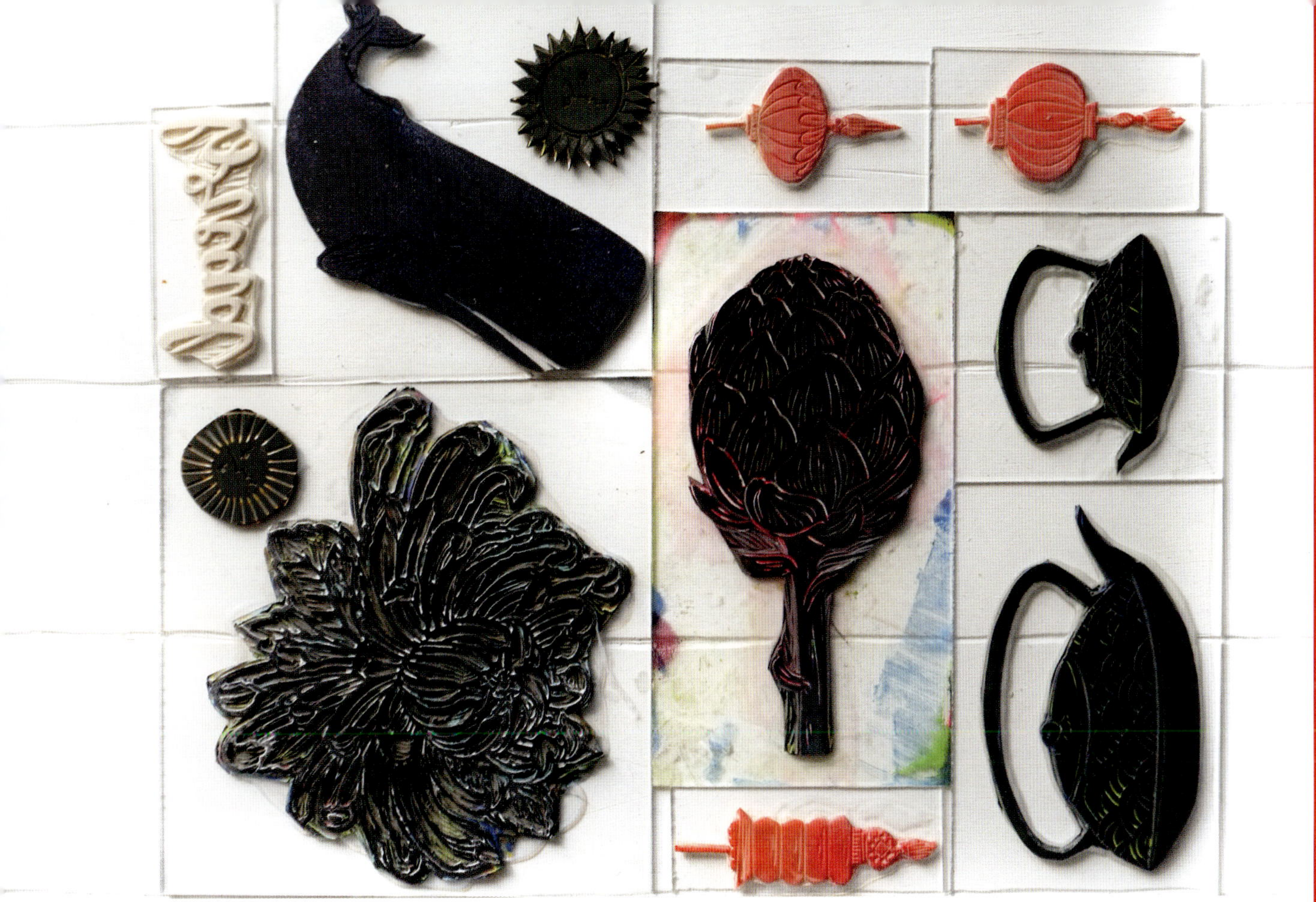

We mostly use hand-carved lino stamps, which are also simple to make. You can find 'soft lino' in craft stores which is easy to carve and cut. However, you can also find a huge variety of beautiful, individual stamps at craft fairs or online. Gelli printing offers endless possibilities and uses a wide variety of items: from 'specialist tools' to household objects. For example, some greeting cards come with 3D lettering, such as the 'Birthday' greeting below. They are inexpensive, and the lettering can be carefully removed and glued on to a more solid surface. When making your own letter stamps, always consider whether they will appear the right way round in the finished print.

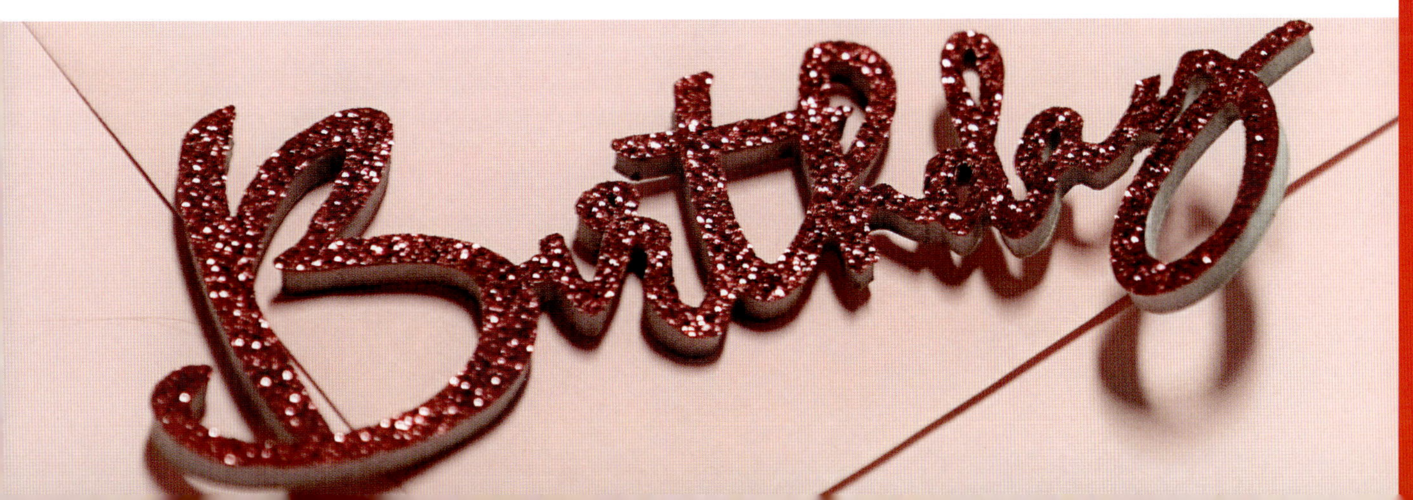

Colours

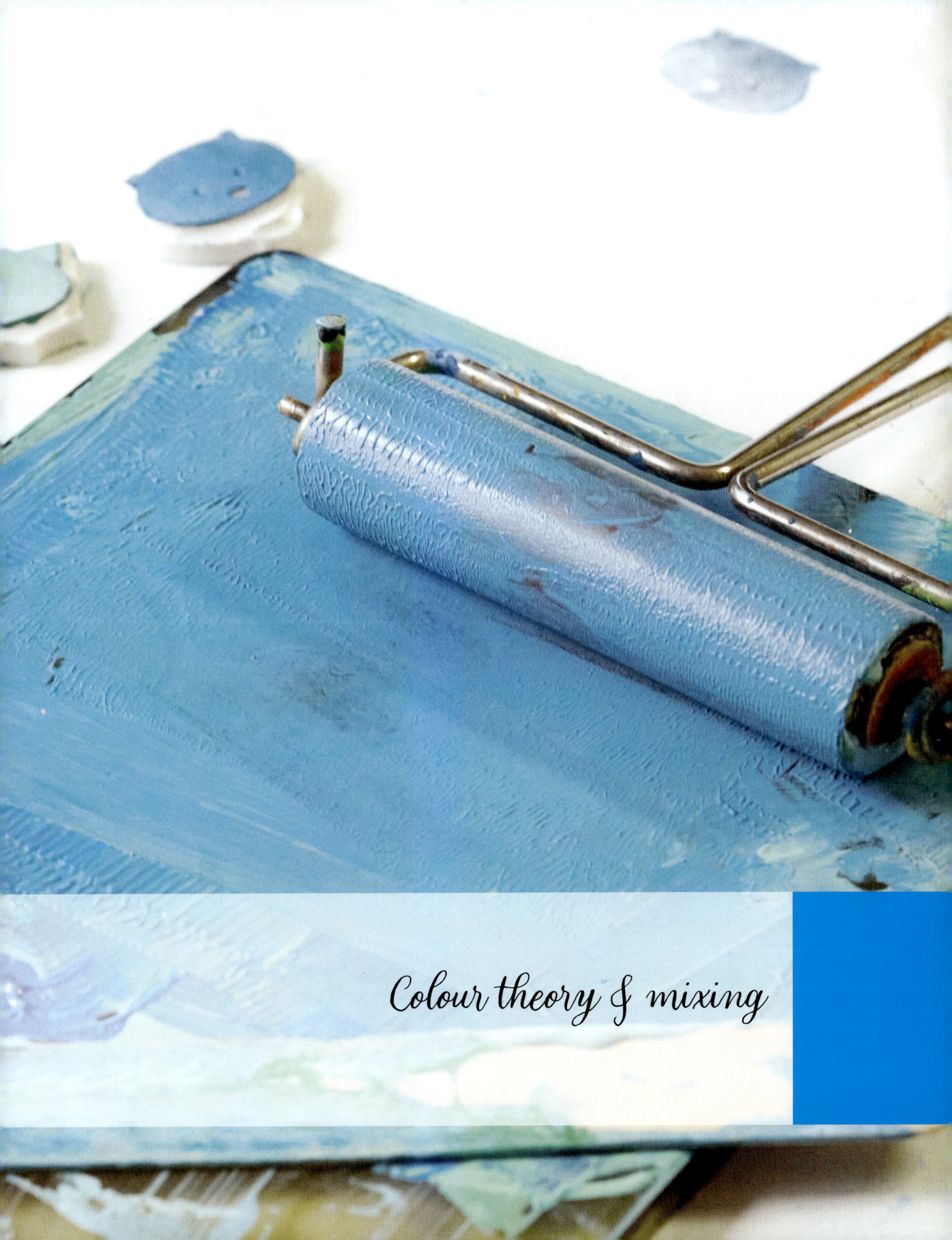

Colour theory & mixing

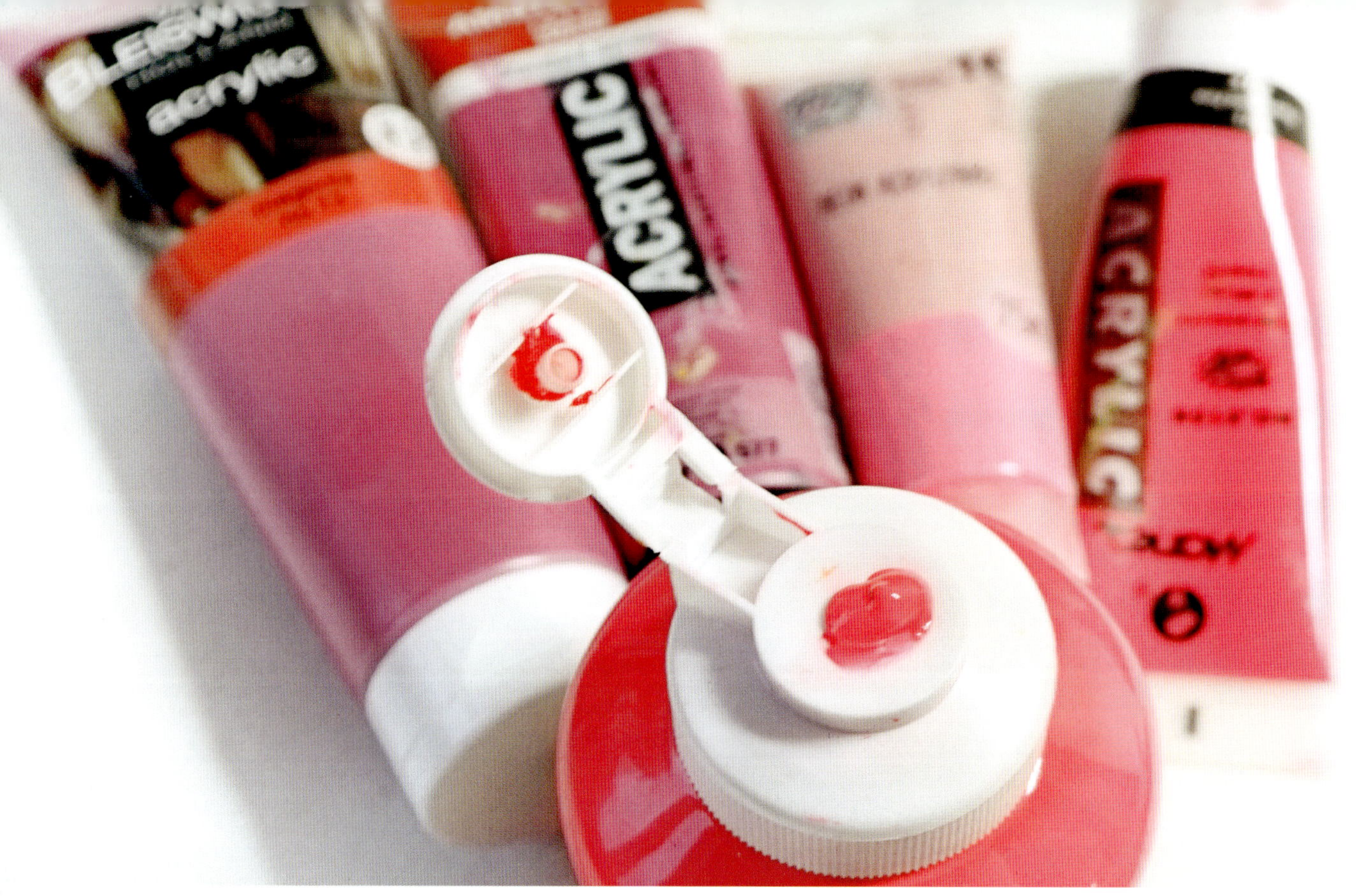

UNDERSTANDING AND MIXING COLOURS – THE COLOUR PALETTE

Everybody has their favourite colours. To see which colours someone is drawn to, all it usually takes is a look in their wardrobe. Colours are a crucial element of gelli printing, and the same technique or motif can have a completely different effect depending on the colour used. If you print with one of your favourite colours, it is likely that the printed result will make you happy. If this turns out not to be the case, try it with a different colour!

Blues and greens are 'cold' colours, while yellows and reds are classified as 'warm'. Colours also have a psychological effect on our mood: warmer colours are generally seen as cheerful and positive; by contrast, cold colours are seen as calming and more reserved. However, if your favourite colour is green, you may still find it cheerful and appealing.

Vibrant colours such as pink and turquoise are harder to mix and are better purchased as pre-made colours.

Colour is a vast topic that could fill an entire book, but we will share with you the four most important concepts here.

THE COLOUR WHEEL

Perhaps you still remember the colour wheel from school. It illustrates the relationships between individual colours. In theory, almost all colours can be mixed from the primary colours: red, yellow and blue. Black and white do not count as colours, but we will come across them again when discussing colour saturation, see page 27).

The colour wheel shows how colour mixtures can be created. In practice, it is easier when you buy your favourite colours and use them straight from the tube; however, this can be expensive. The alternative is to buy the primary colours, conduct a few colour experiments and then mix your favourite colours. You can prepare and store them in plastic containers or jars with screw-on lids. The same is true of leftover paint, which you can store to use later, but be careful: acrylic paint dries quickly and cannot be reactivated again. Most fabric paints, on the other hand, can be diluted again with water and reactivated to use again.

For anyone who wants to go deeper into mixing colours, there are affordable colour wheels with mixing instructions available, which make the colour relationships very easy to understand.

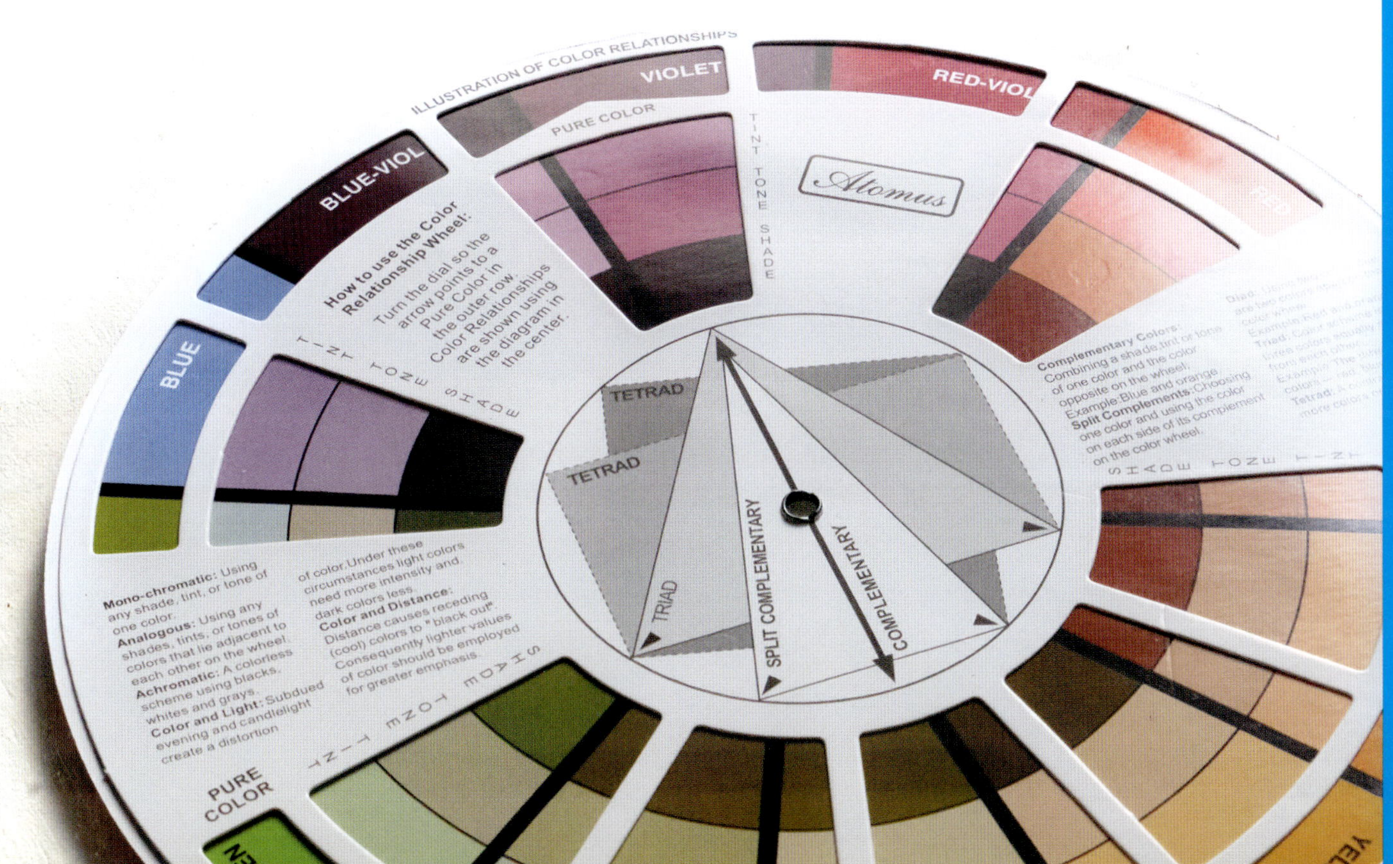

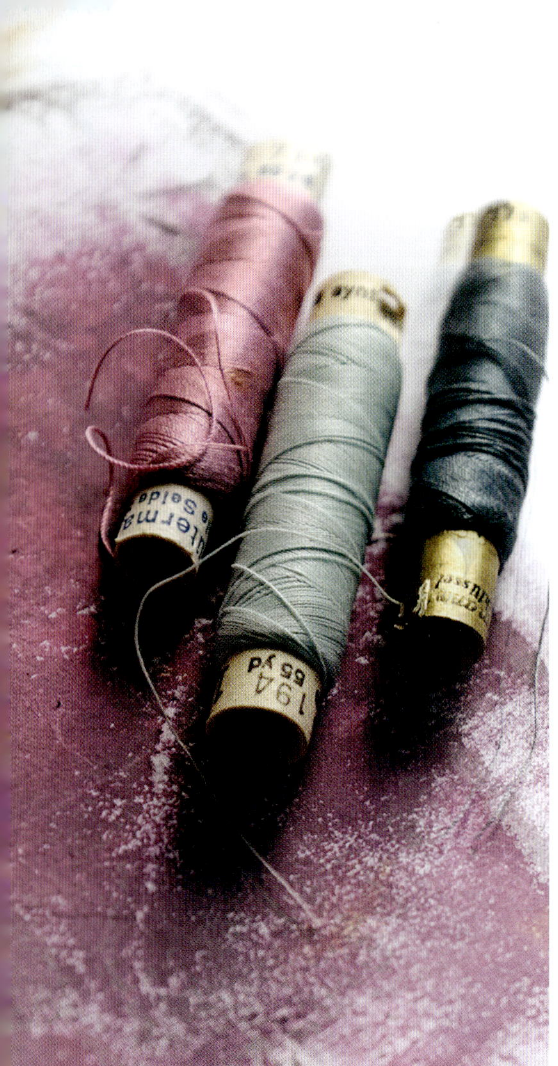

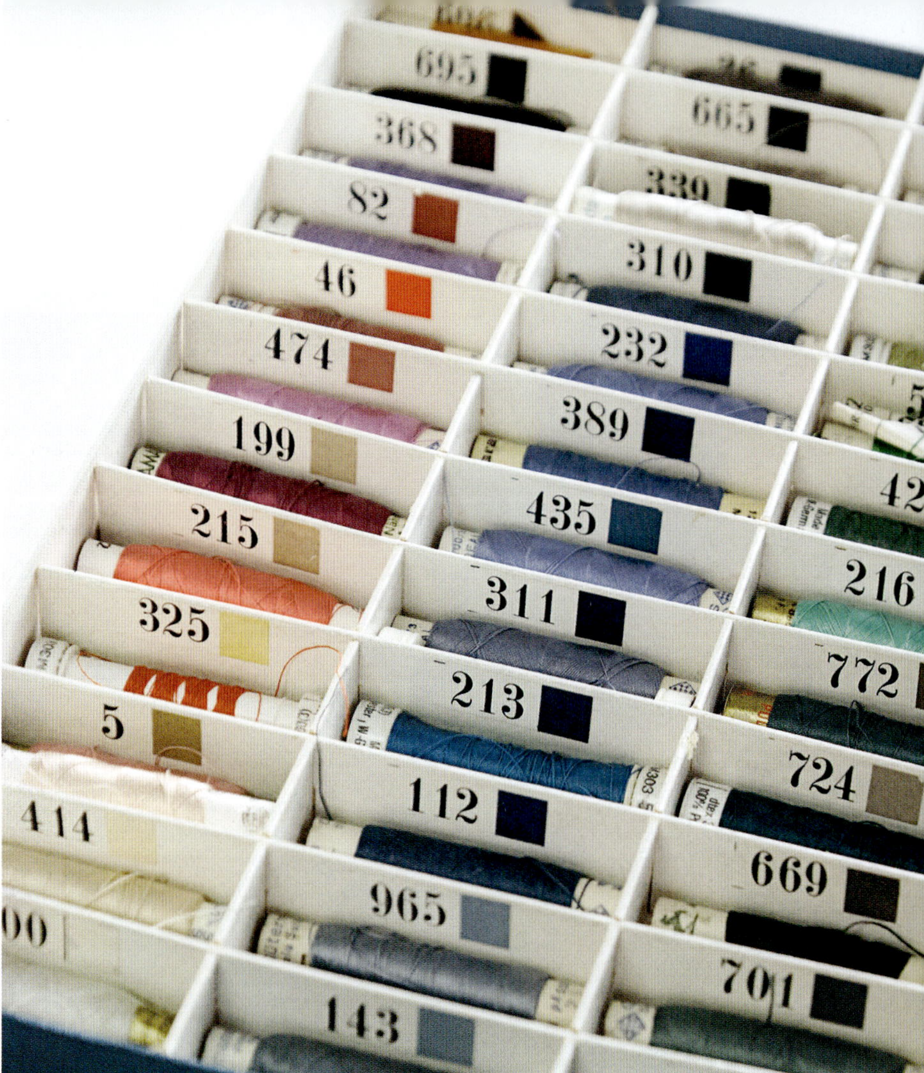

COLOUR GRADATIONS

In theory, millions of shades, i.e. gradations or hues, can be mixed from the primary colours. If you look at the sea, you will find an infinite number of different shades of blue, green or silver. If you use several of these gradations or hues, these colours always go well together, creating a harmonious impression without competing with each other.

SATURATION

In addition to the nuances resulting from mixing primary colours, there is another aspect of colour design: saturation, or intensity. By adding black or white, you can develop your own unique colour palette.

Colours lose intensity or vibrancy in this process. This is not meant to be a judgement: if you reduce the saturation or intensity, the colours become softer and more delicate. In the home, for example, we often unconsciously use softer colours than in our clothes, as colours that are overly bright can be unsettling. The more black or white (or both) we add to a colour, the more the colour tends towards grey.

Reducing the intensity and vibrancy can be used as a design element. Colours tinted with black and a little white, for example, are typical of the 1950s (or a mid-century style) and create a beautiful vintage effect. However, tinting colours can eventually make them look dull or gloomy. This may mean that a contrast, such as pure black or white, is missing for balance. Alternatively, you can use what is called a complementary contrast, which we explain on the next page.

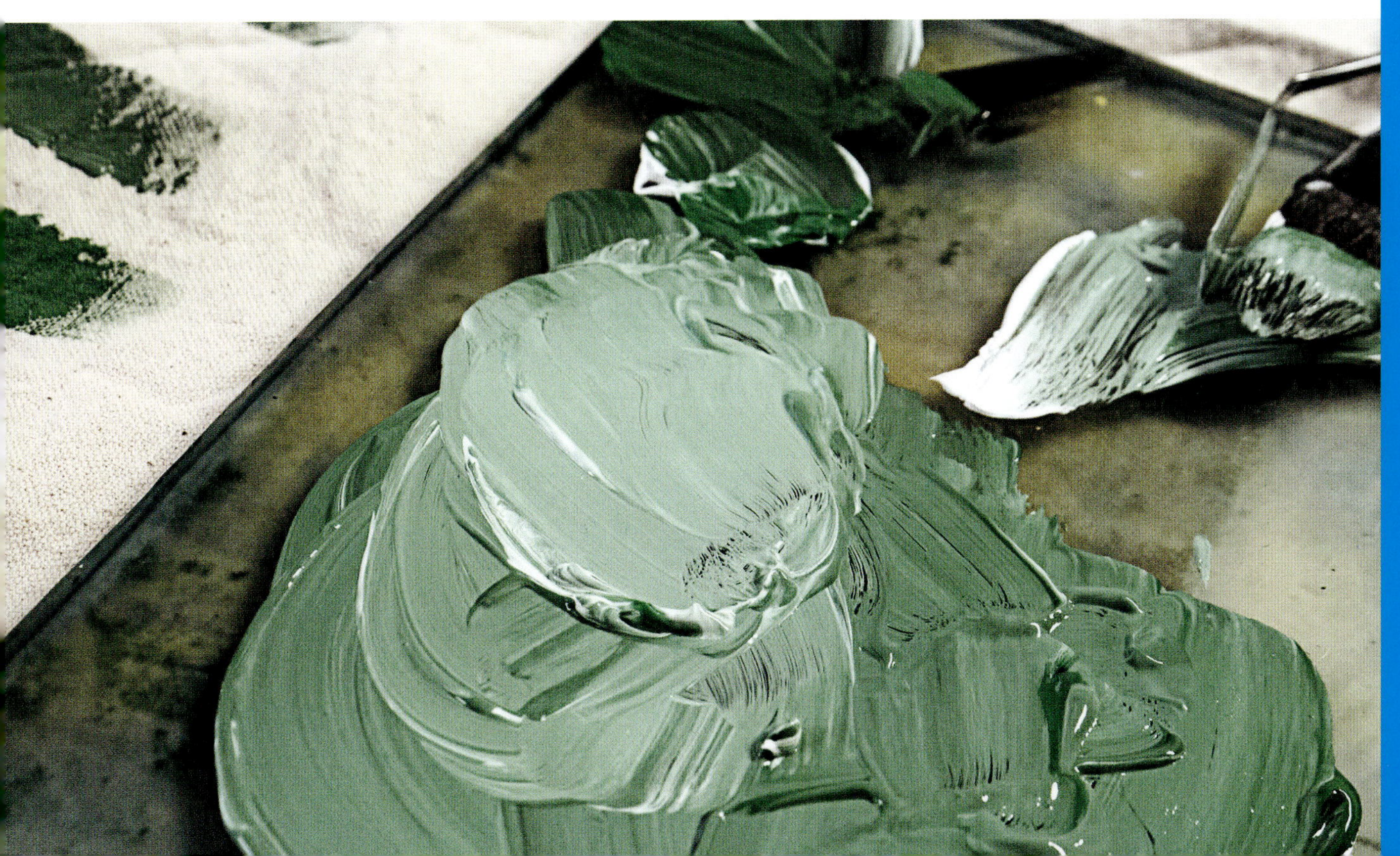

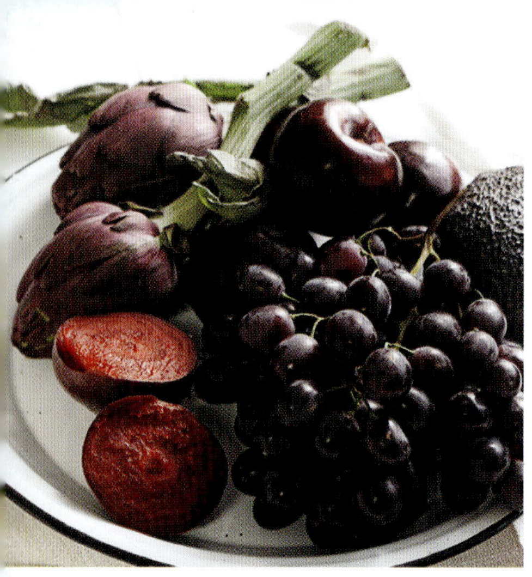
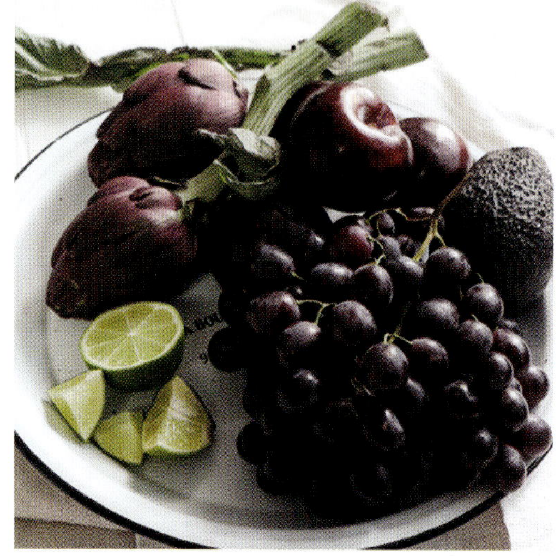
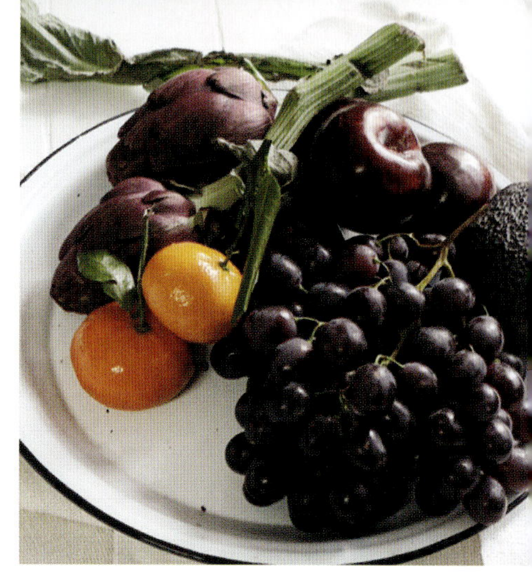

COMPLEMENTARY COLOURS

You don't need to conduct lengthy experiments with your tubes of paint to experiment with mixing colours. Colours are all around you every day, in the form of food, everyday objects, jewellery, or colour patterns from the DIY store.

In principle, there is no right or wrong way of using colours. What matters is what you like – but our four principles can help if you're ever unhappy with a printing result and need to understand why that is.

The three pictures above show you what it's all about. In the left-hand picture, you see colours from a colour family: shades of violet, a hue associated with the cold spectrum. The (also cold) green of the artichoke stems doesn't form a strong contrast. The biggest contrast is in the slices of red beetroot. Red is typically considered a warm hue, but this red is very dark and almost leans towards violet. Overall, the colours create a harmonious, subdued impression.

In the second picture, we have replaced the red beetroot with a sliced lime. Compared with the artichoke stems, this green shines much more brightly, partly due to the higher yellow content of the unsaturated colour, and partly due to the contrast in brightness. The lime green is significantly lighter than the surrounding colours.

An even stronger colour contrast is shown in the right-hand picture with the mandarins. Colours that lie directly opposite each other on the colour wheel provide the greatest contrast, and are referred to as complementary colours. Yellow and orange are directly opposite blue and violet on the colour wheel. We can use complementary colours whenever something needs to glow, stand out, or to achieve a bold effect.

COLOUR IS ALL AROUND US

We are constantly surrounded by colours. Our wardrobe reveals the colours we love and feel comfortable in. Every visit to the weekly market or the paper section in the stationery store tempts us with new colour combinations. The acrylic paint aisle in the art and craft store is a promise in itself, as are the colour sample cards in the paint section of any hardware store.

Collect colours and colour combinations that catch your eye and that draw you in. One simple way is to take a photograph – as we always have our phones with us these days – then bring those colour combinations to life on your gelli plate.

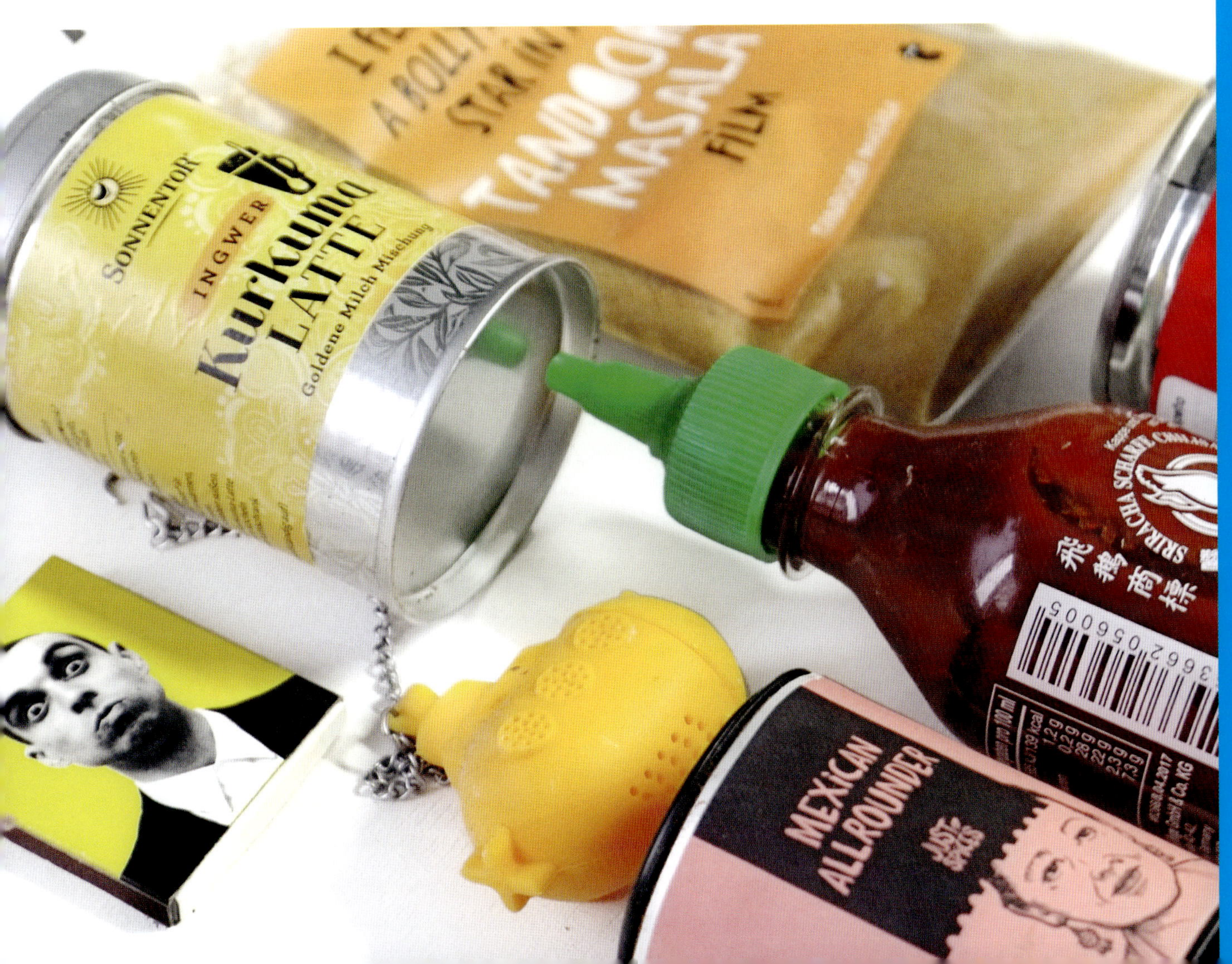

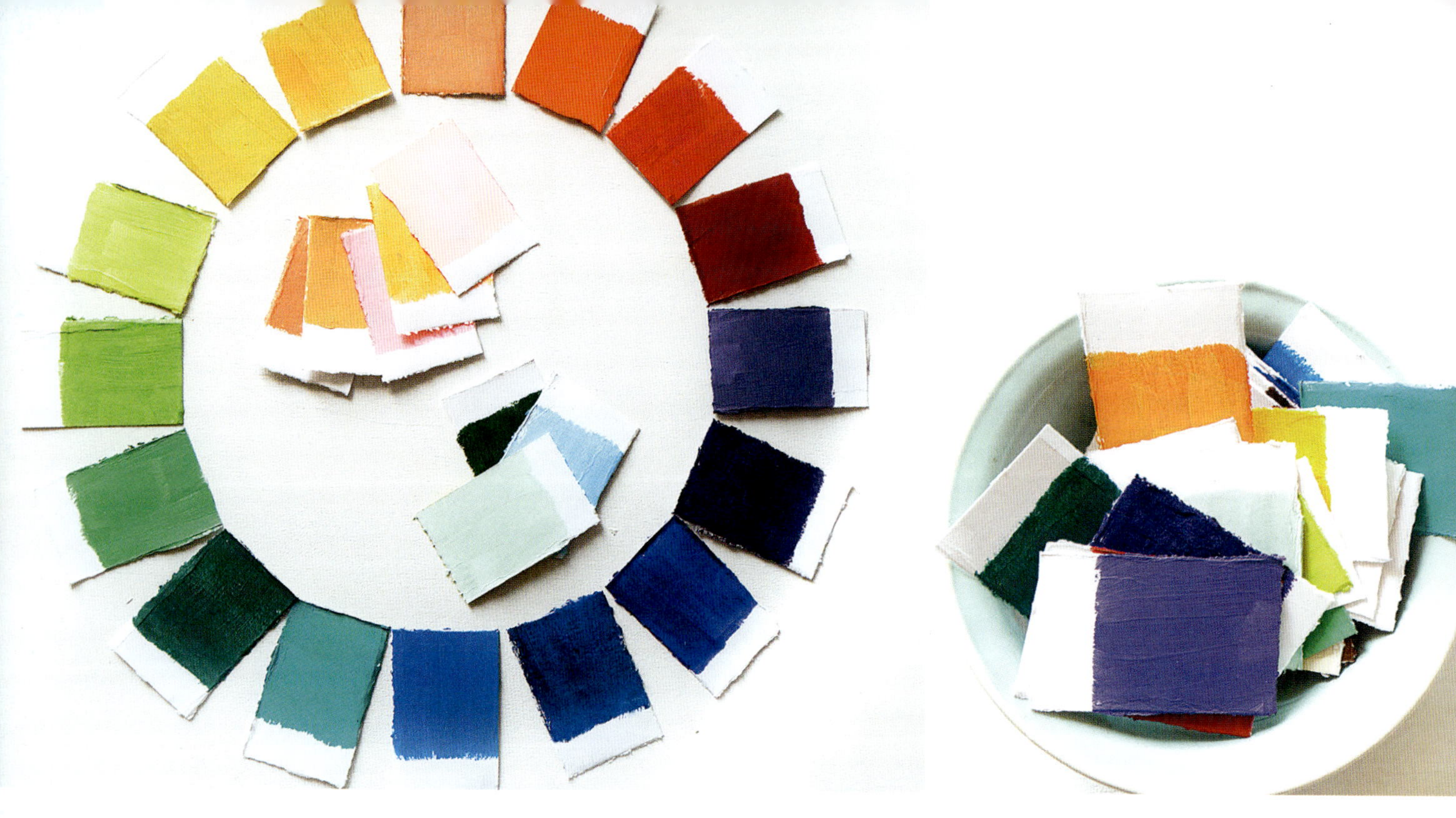

DEVELOP YOUR OWN COLOUR COMBINATIONS

The previous pages have shown how diverse and almost limitless colours can be. In practice, however, we will always print with our favourite colours, or those colours we have at home, and with all the colours that can be mixed from these. That is why it is better to get to know the colours you have around you better, and the best way for us to do this is with the following exercise.

CREATING COLOUR SAMPLES

When it comes to multi-coloured printing later on, colour composition is really crucial for good results. You can, of course, do this intuitively and simply experiment, but if you want to minimize your disappointments, it's useful to compile and test the colours beforehand. It doesn't matter so much if your colours go wrong when printing on paper, but if you're printing on fabric or want to print on a limited resource like a lampshade, colour mistakes can be costly and frustrating.

Cut or tear paper strips – the ones shown here are about 4 x 6cm (1½ x 2¼in). Try out all the colours you have available. Leave a white strip along one edge so you can write notes on it later – e.g. the colours mixed. This may sound boring at first, but it's wonderfully meditative work, especially if you listen to music while you're doing it.

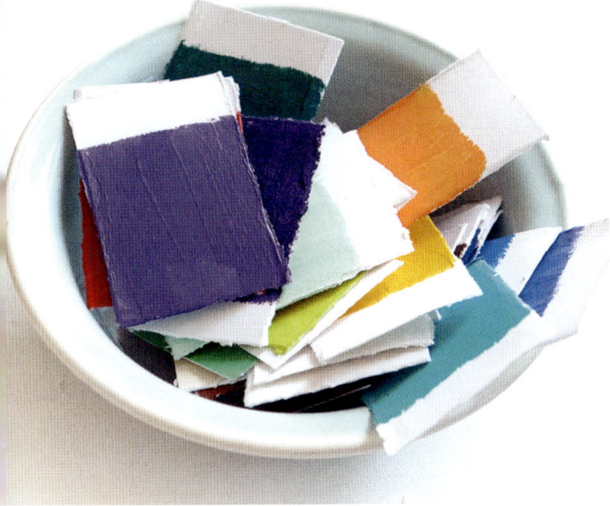

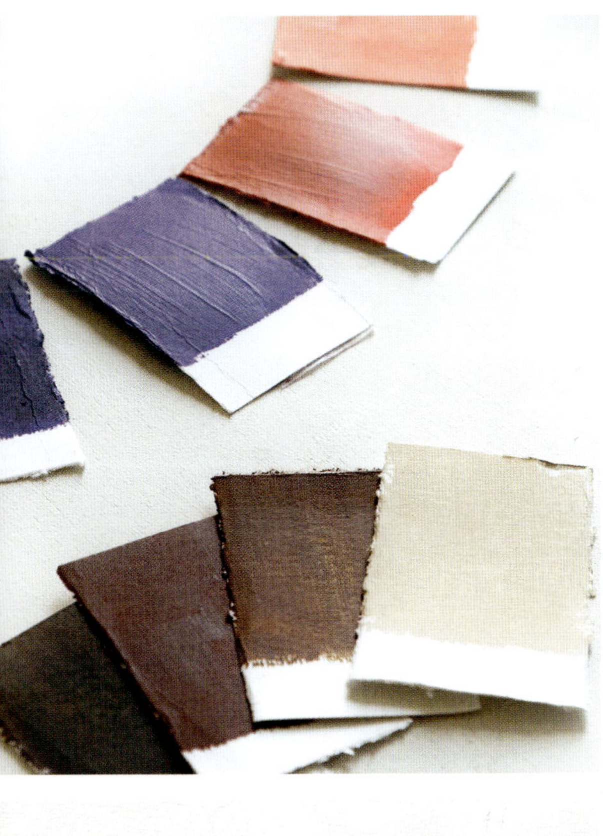

1. First, arrange your colour samples to create your personal colour wheel, starting with the primary colours – red, yellow and blue – and then their immediate mixtures, green, orange and violet (see picture on the far left). If you have all these colours available or can mix them, then you have made a good start.
2. Expand your colour wheel by categorizing all of your colour samples, for example, 'grass green' tends more towards yellow, while 'mint green' leans more towards blue.
3. If you find you don't have enough colours, start to mix your paints and experiment. The blend will vary according to the quantity of each colour you use. For example, an orange made up out of one part yellow and two parts red will be darker than an orange created out of two or three parts yellow and one part red, which will be lighter and brighter. You can concoct an almost endless array of intermediate shades. Write the mixing ratio on your colour sample so that you can reproduce it again.
4. Pay attention to the sensory experience of the colours as you paint them. Colours that evoke particular joy will please you again when you later print with them.
5. Your colour palette may contain colours such as grey and brown. These do not slot directly into the colour wheel, and they are referred to as 'neutral colours'. They can temper bold colour combinations by introducing a sense of tranquillity.
6. Colours like neon pink or orange are also special cases. The more vivid a colour, the more carefully it should be used so that it doesn't overwhelm the other colours. However, these distinctive colours provide excellent accent colours.

Printing

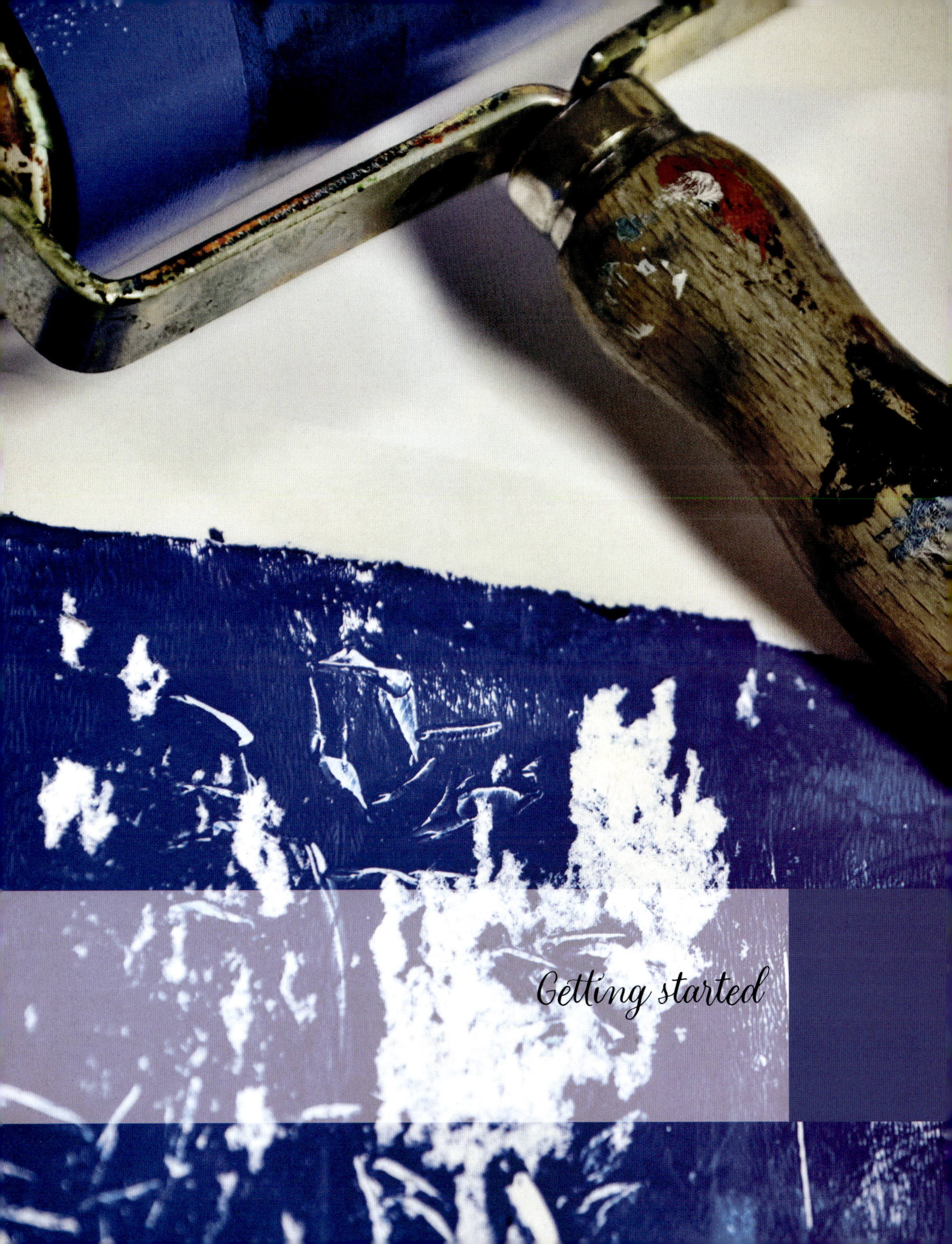

Getting started

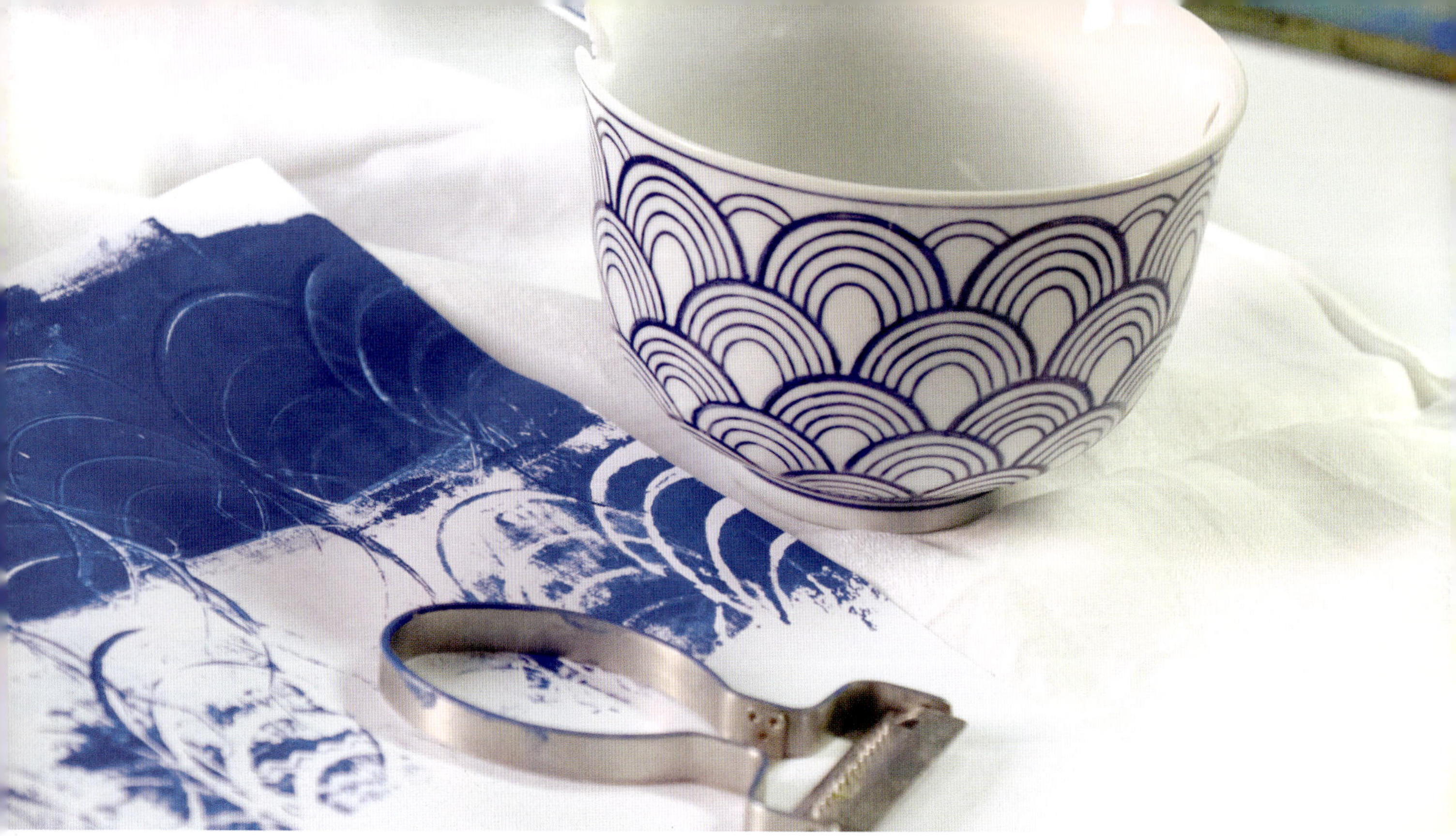

PRINTING WITH SIMPLE HOUSEHOLD OBJECTS

It is best to start gelli printing with a project. You can't go wrong! The principle couldn't be any more simple: apply paint to the gelli plate, create texture, place a sheet of paper on top, and rub your hand over the paper to transfer the paint. Everything else is just variations of this process. To start with, we took inspiration from Japanese bowls, and rummaged through our kitchen drawers for objects (without points or sharp edges) with which we could create similar patterns. Now you can get started!

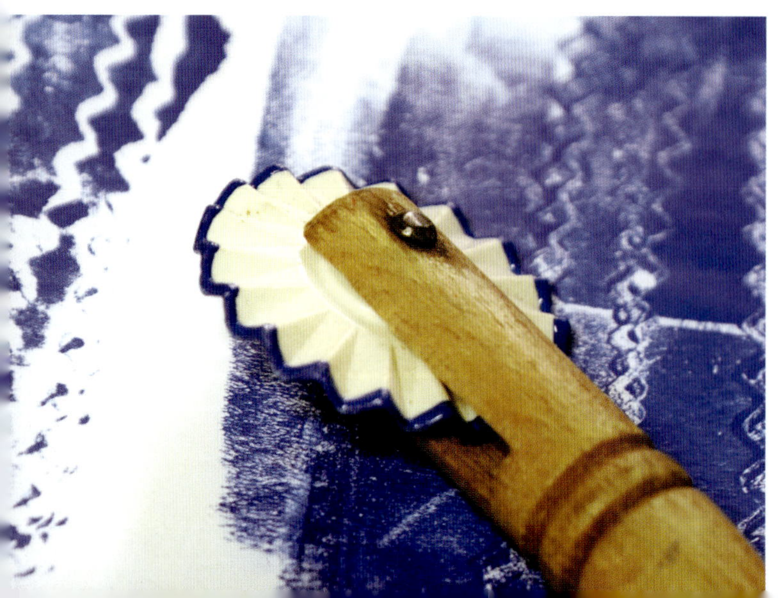

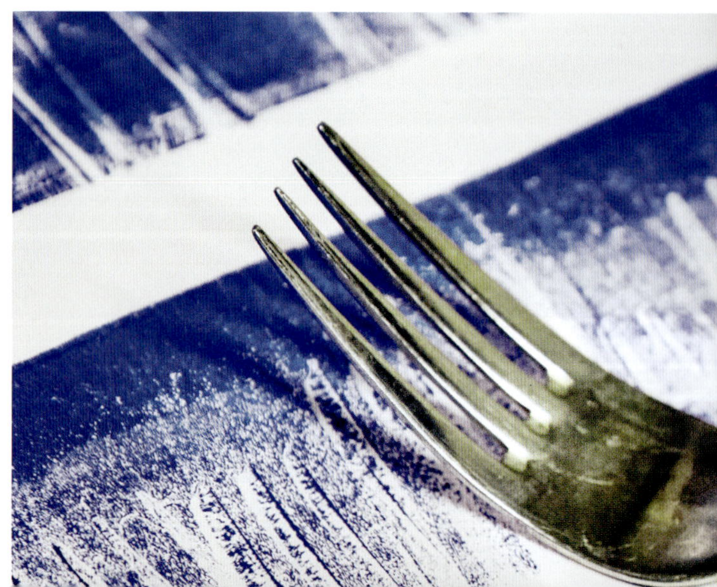

1. Look in your kitchen drawers (or in the toolbox or among children's toys, for example) for objects that leave marks or impressions. The objects need to be washable.
2. Lay out everything else you need for printing: gelli plate, paint, brayer, enough paper, newspaper to protect your surface and old cloths or papers to rest the brayer on or to clean the objects.
3. Roll the gelli plate evenly with paint and start to make marks on it with your chosen object. Don't think about it too much, just do it.
4. Then place a piece of paper on the still-wet paint and smooth over it with your hands. Peel the paper off slowly. Next, make a ghost print (see page 41) and surprise yourself!
5. You can then clean the gelli plate, or carry on without thinking about it. The next application of paint will loosen the remaining paint on the gelli plate and cause it to print off. Experiment with the resulting effects – and have lots of fun trying things out!

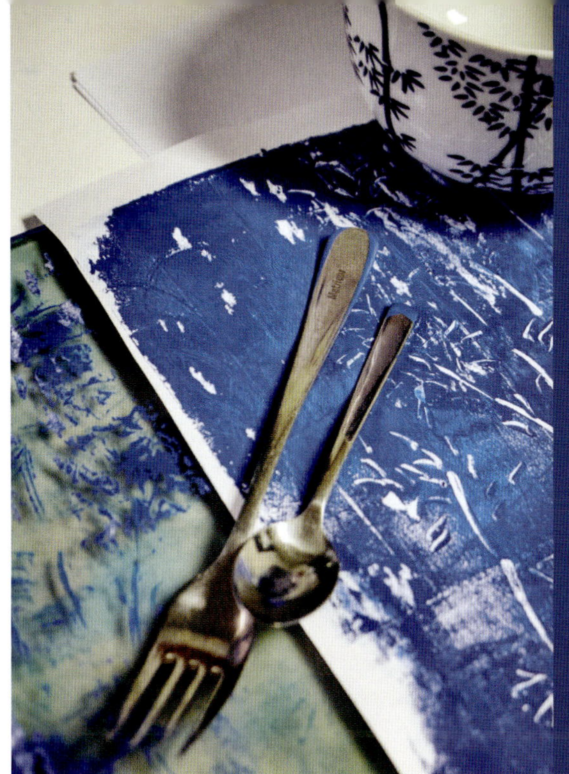

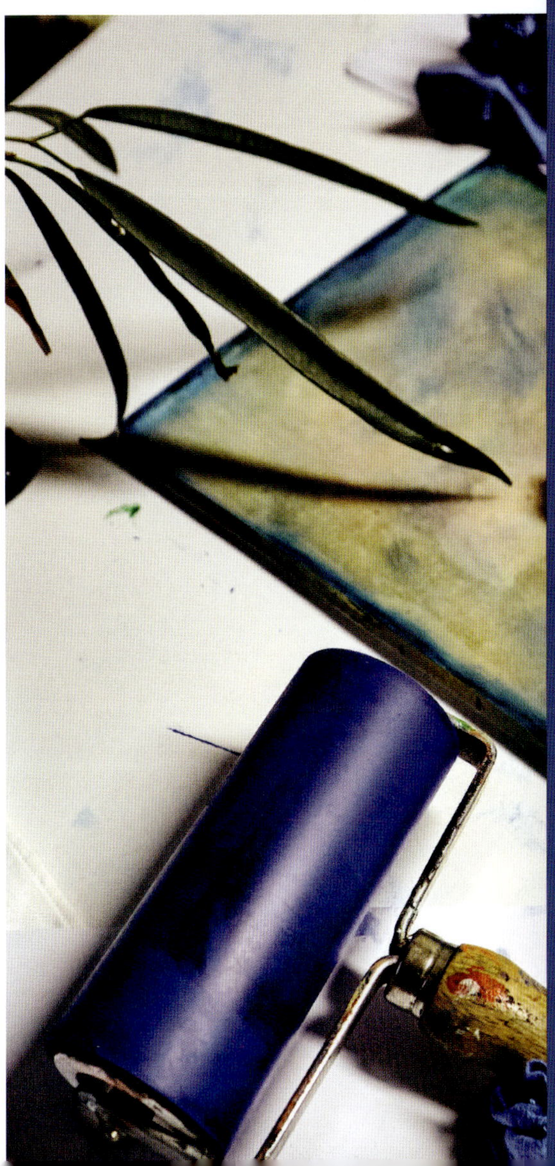

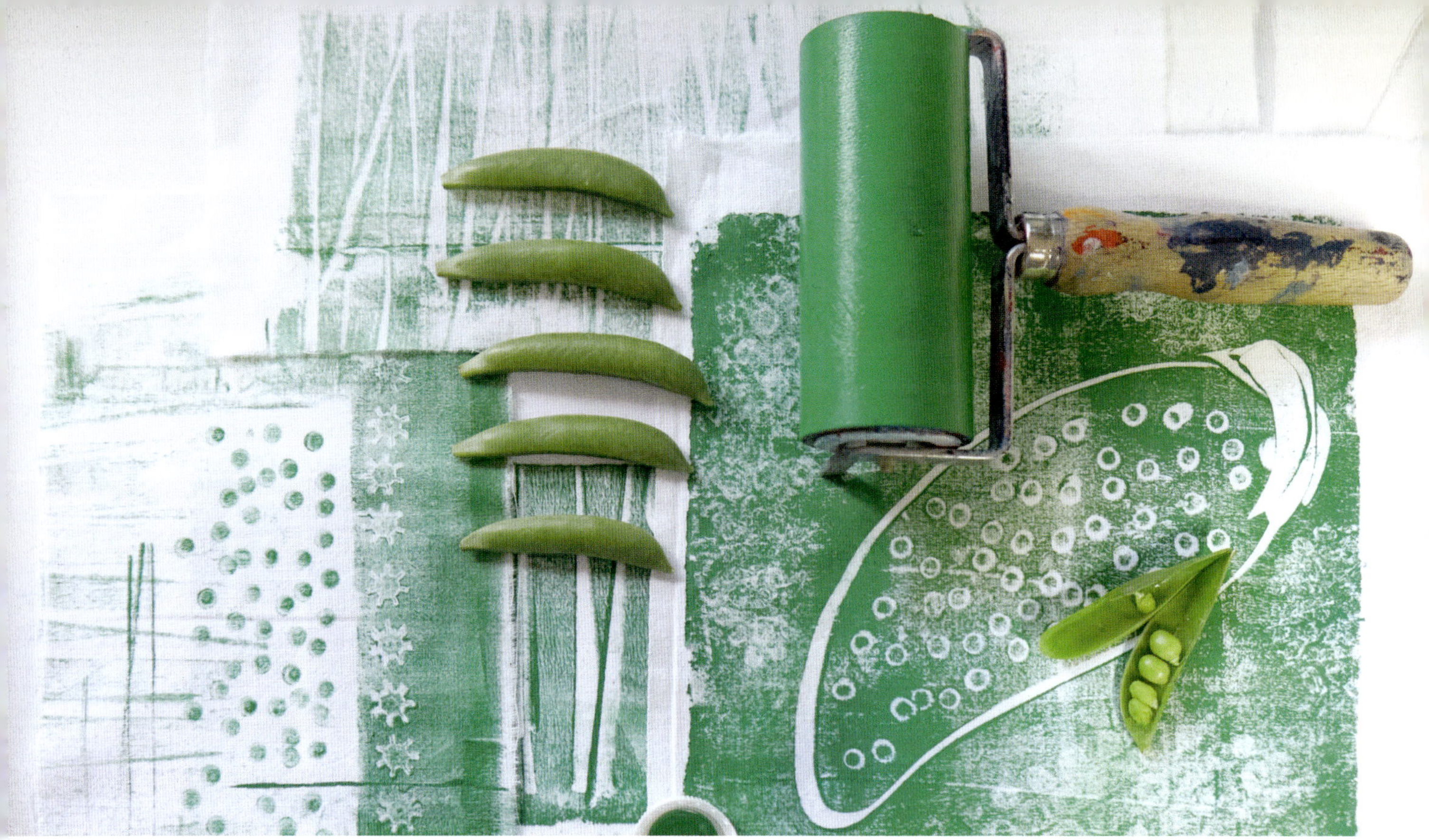

PRINTING SIMPLE SHAPES

The next step, after making patterns with objects from your kitchen or toolbox, is to make our own designs to print. Pea pods were our inspiration here. To start, we have the round peas themselves, which can be reproduced perfectly using various lids to make printed circles and ovals. Then there are the shapes of the elongated pods, which were cut out of paper.

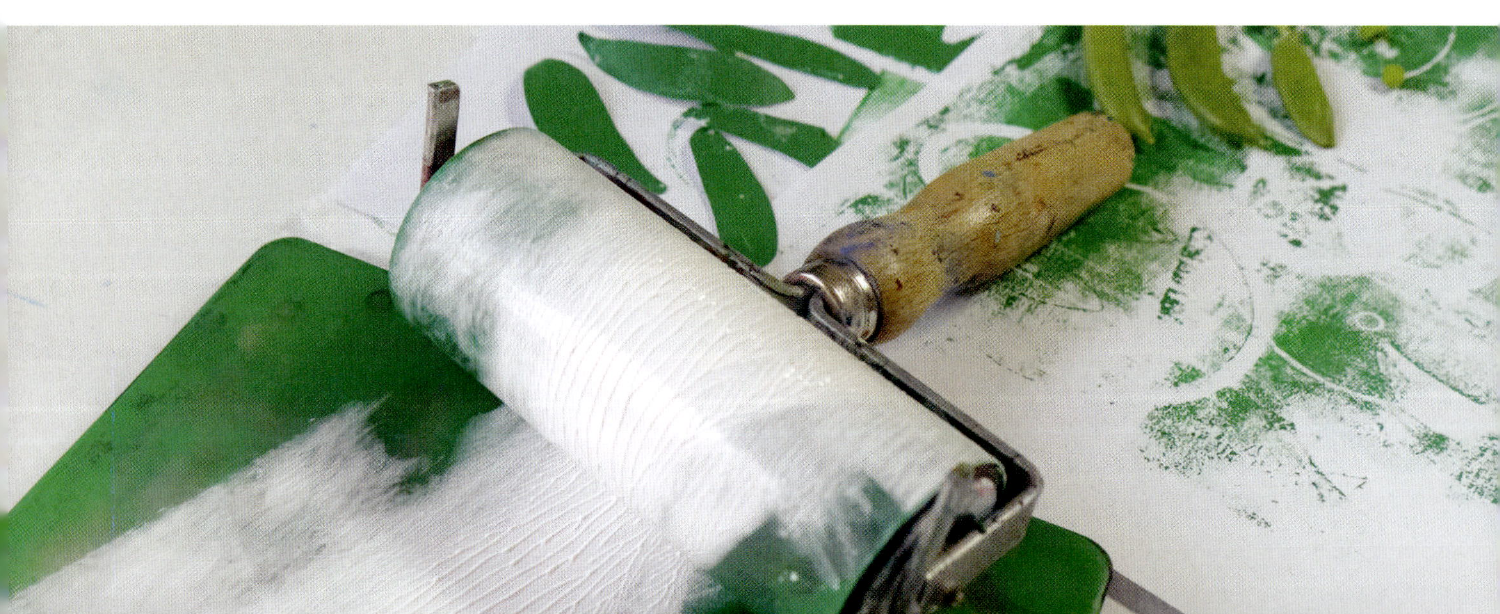

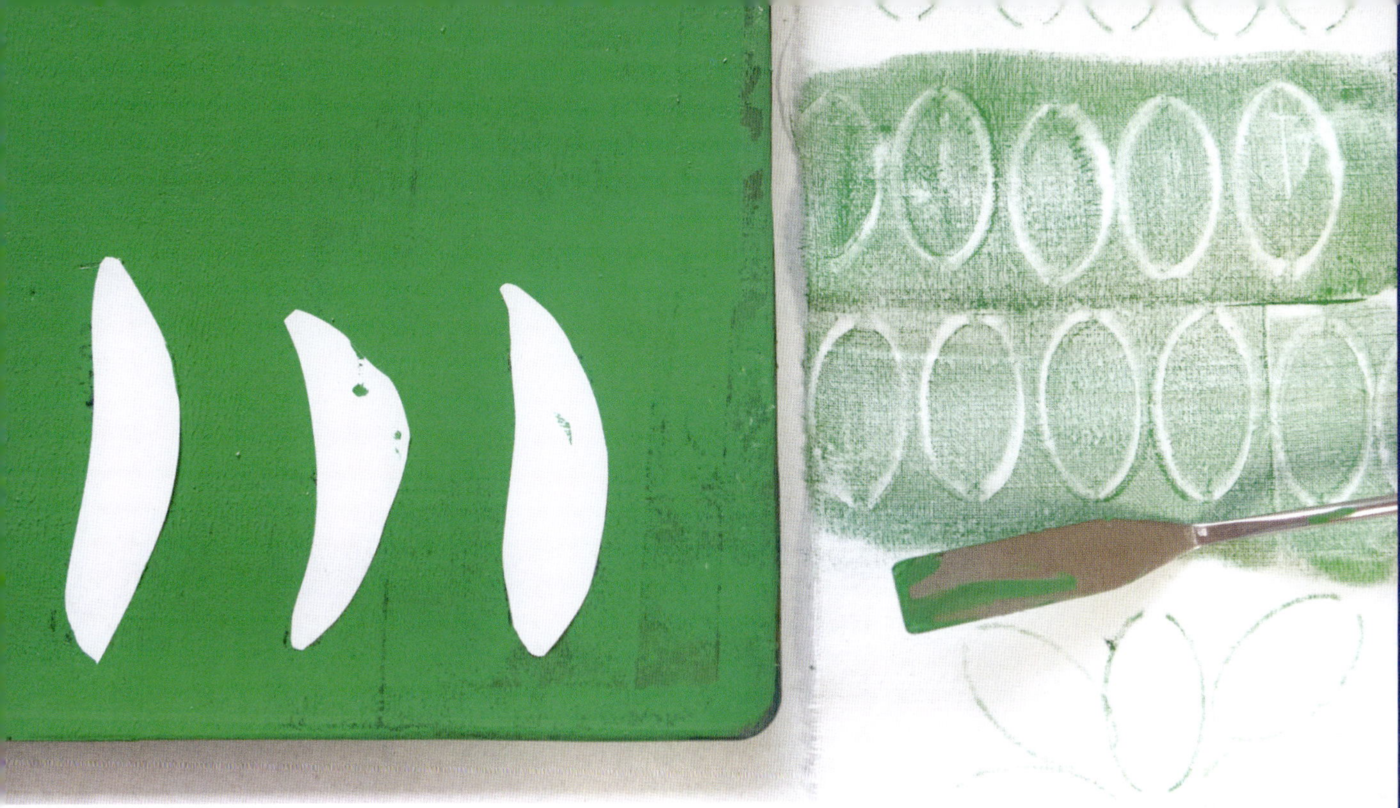

You can create white spaces in two ways:

a. Place the cut-out paper shapes direct onto the gelli plate, roll paint over them, then carefully remove the shapes – the area underneath on the gelli plate will not have any paint on it.
b. First, apply the paint to the gelli plate, then place the paper shapes on top so that it prevents the paint underneath it from printing off.

With both options, you can still add structure to the painted area using stamps or other objects. Afterwards, why not turn your first papers into a mini book (see project on page 96)?

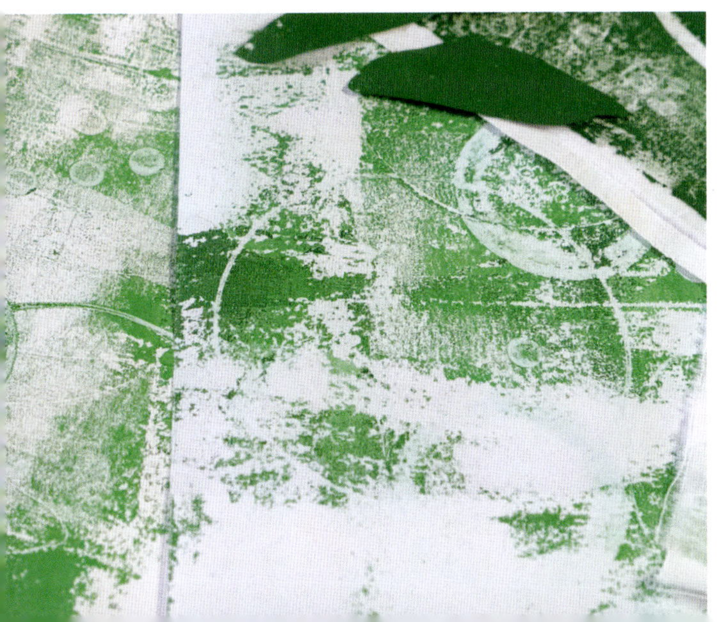

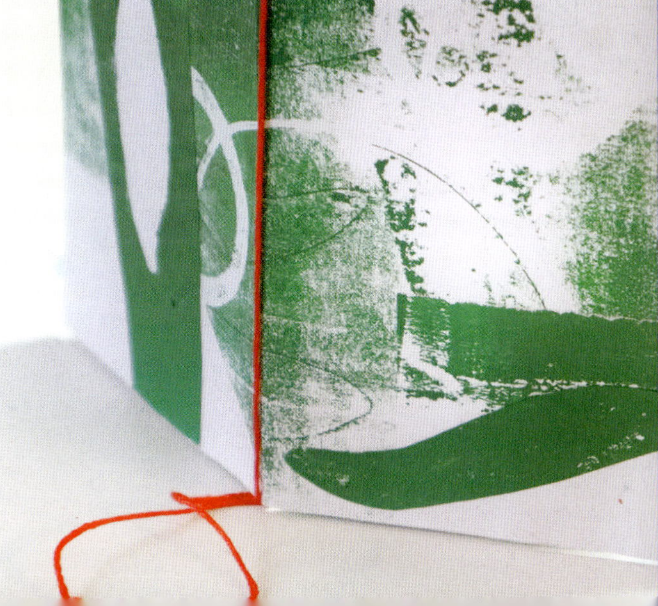

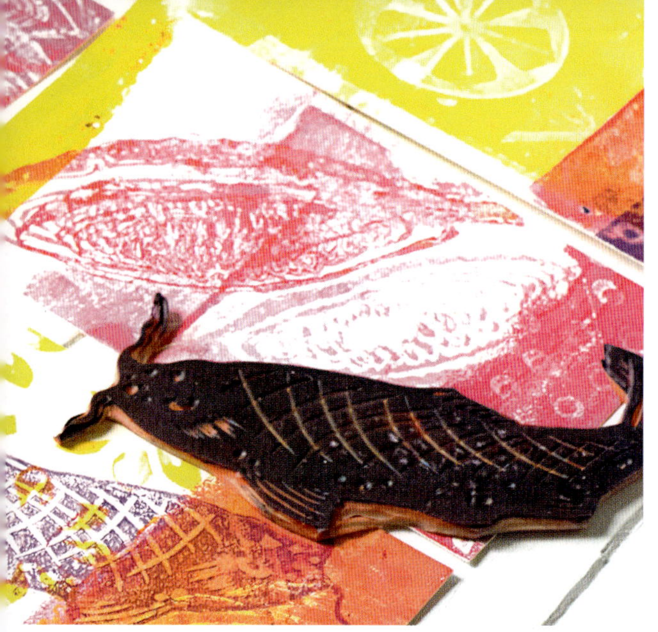

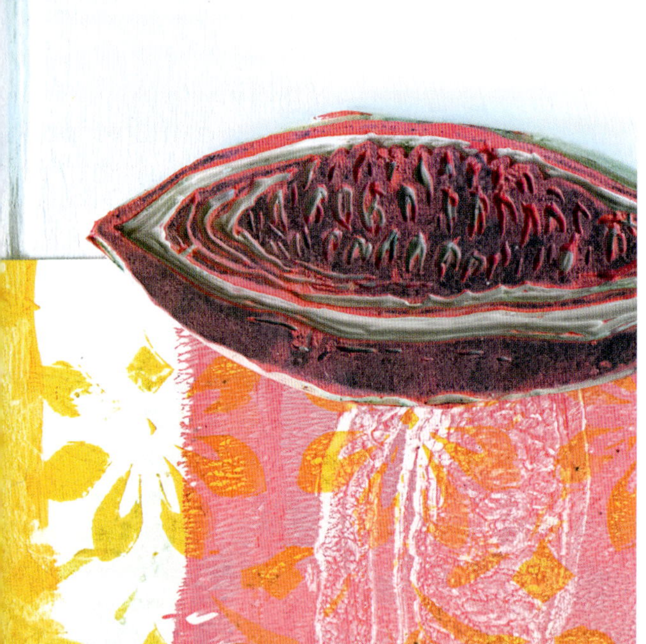

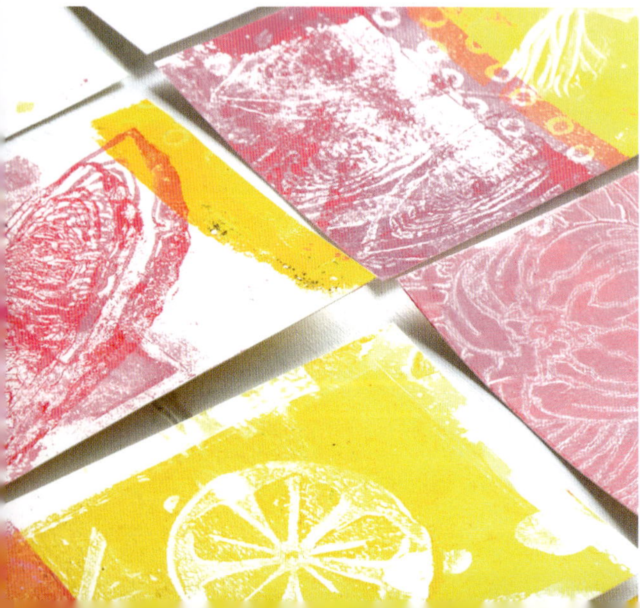

MULTI-COLOURED PRINTING

Gelli printing invites experimentation. So, the next step is about printing a whole series – you'll be surprised with the results. This time, we will dive straight into a project without much explanation.

1. Choose three or four colours; more colours can quickly become overwhelming. They can be similar colours, or colours that create contrasts. You can see the difference in our postcard series, shown here: pink, yellow and red are warm colours and thus in the same colour family. Violet, on the other hand, comes from the cooler end of the spectrum and creates a stark contrast, making the colours pop. If you want to use green and blue shades, for example, then orange, pink or similar colours would create a strong contrast.
2. Roll a thin coat of paint on your gelli plate and texture the surface. Remove some of the paint from the gelli plate using different stamps, so that a motif appears on it as a negative.
3. If, like us, you want to make postcards, cut your sketch or watercolour paper to the desired size, or use some ready-made index cards (available in postcard format, without lines).
4. Start by placing parts of the paper on to the gelli plate and transferring the paint. You do not always need to use a piece of paper that is larger than the plate to cover the entire gelli plate, you can instead make partial prints.
5. If you want clear lines between the areas, mask off the gelli plate with some tape before applying the paint, and remove it before printing, or place paper strips over the painted surface to cover it.
6. Print a second or third colour, so that the colours are overlapping or next to each other. Don't think about it too much, just enjoy the results.

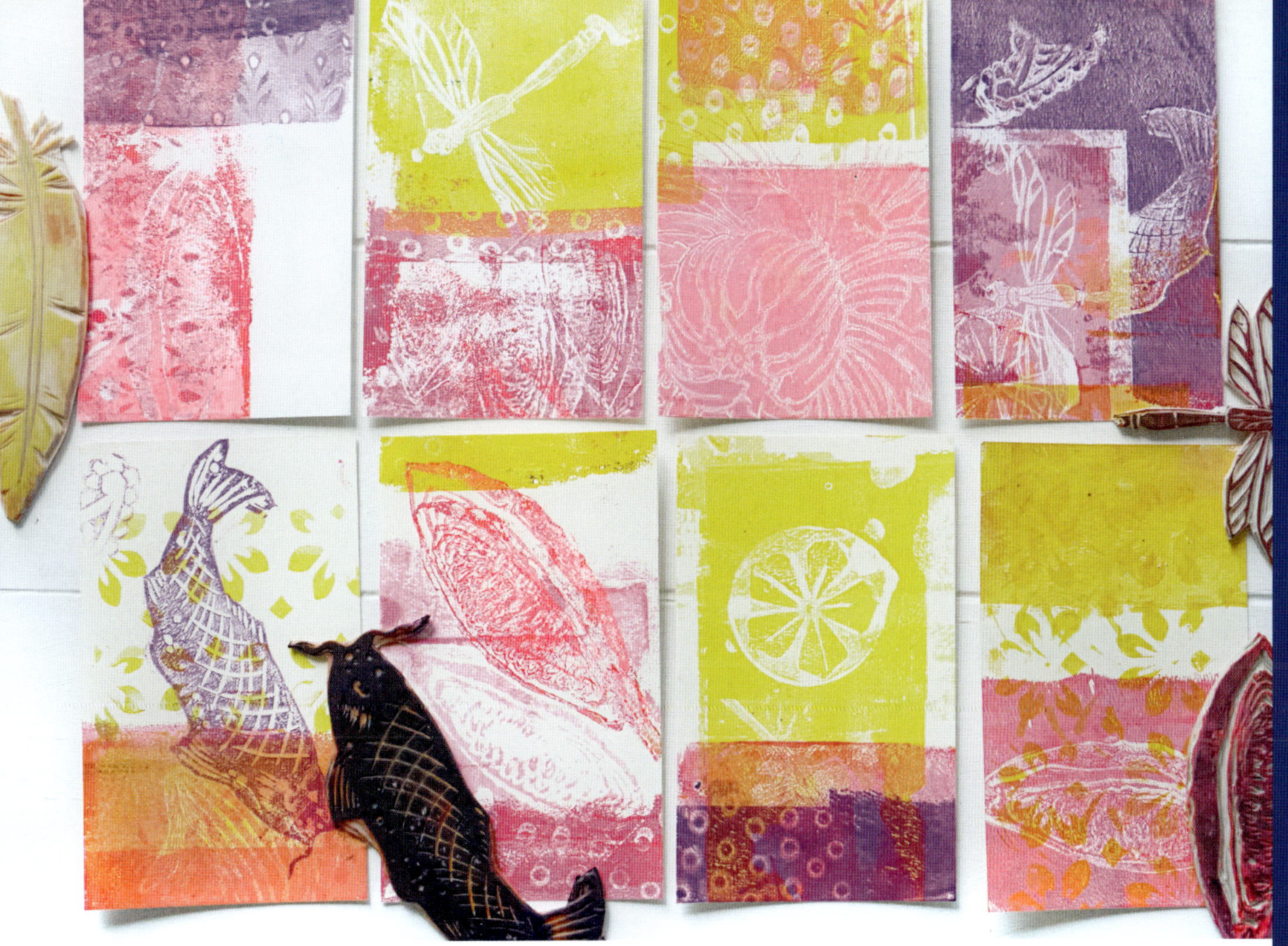

7. Use a negative–positive effect: each time you stamp to remove paint from the gelli plate, you can also stamp this directly on to one of the pieces of paper.
8. Lay out your prints to dry. Pick out any that look 'finished' and set them aside.
9. Analyse the remaining prints. What's missing? A shape, a colour, a connection between individual elements, texture, or maybe just a few small accents? In the next round of gelli printing, you can add all of these; or use some of your discarded misprints – cut the successful elements out and collage them, as in the sketchbook project on page 50.

Pink with a light structure not printed on the whole area.

Yellow-green with a very light grunge effect and a stamp impression.

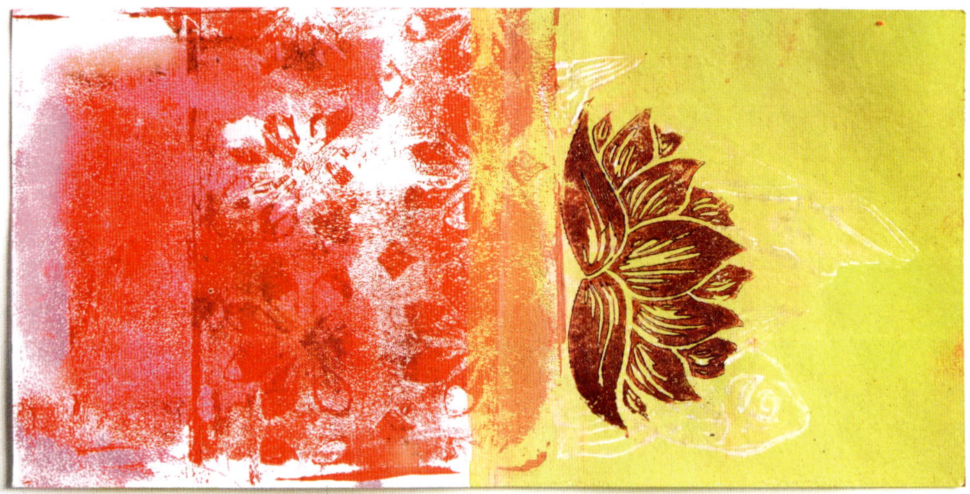

Bright red, not over the whole area.

Stencil pattern, in slightly darker red, overlapping the yellow-green area.

Positive impression in a dark red: stamp pressed into a saturated gelli plate.

Grunge effect: pink rolled on, with dried remnants of red underneath.

Negative prints (red rolled on to the gelli plate, motif stamp pressed on).

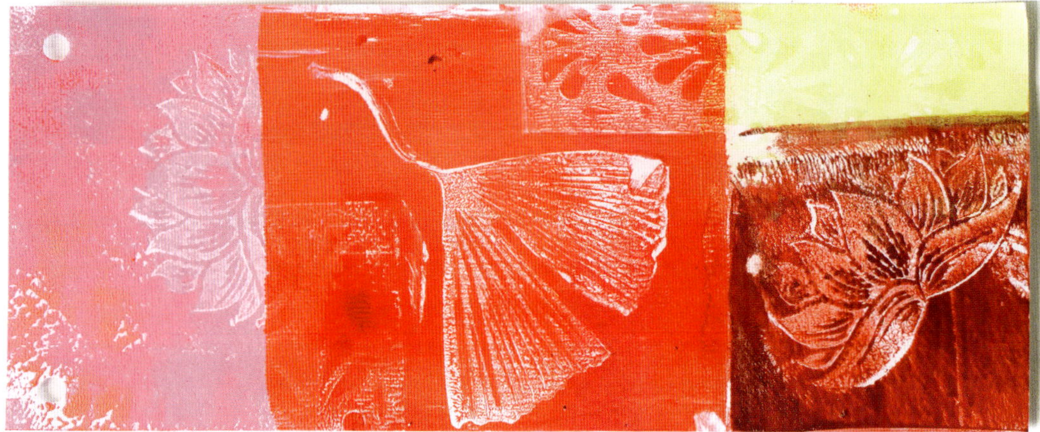

Pink negative print.

Light red, not fully covered.

Stencil on gelli plate, dark red.

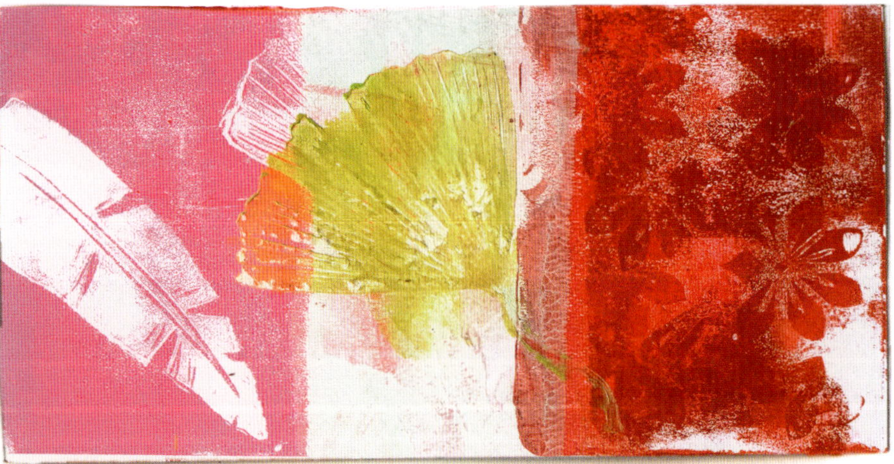

Grunge effect print in very light turquoise, overlapping here with the red area.

Positive print with leaf stamp in yellow-green.

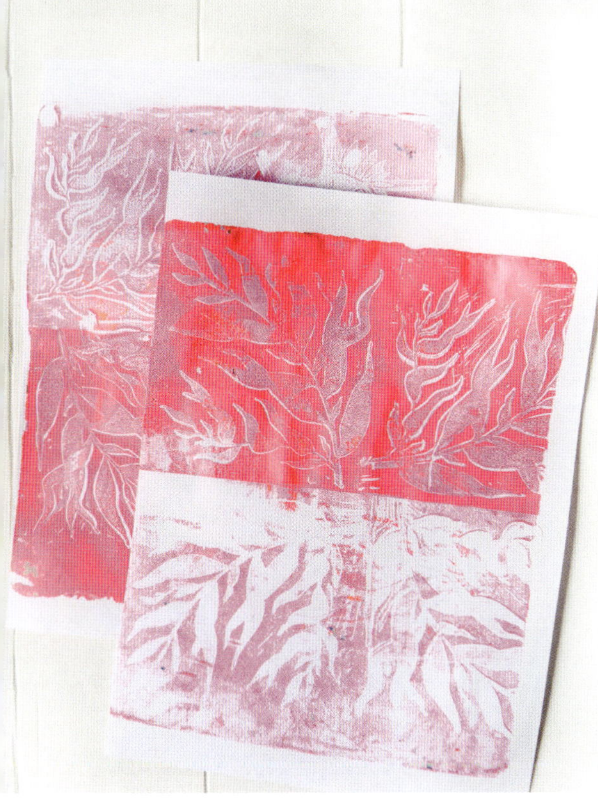

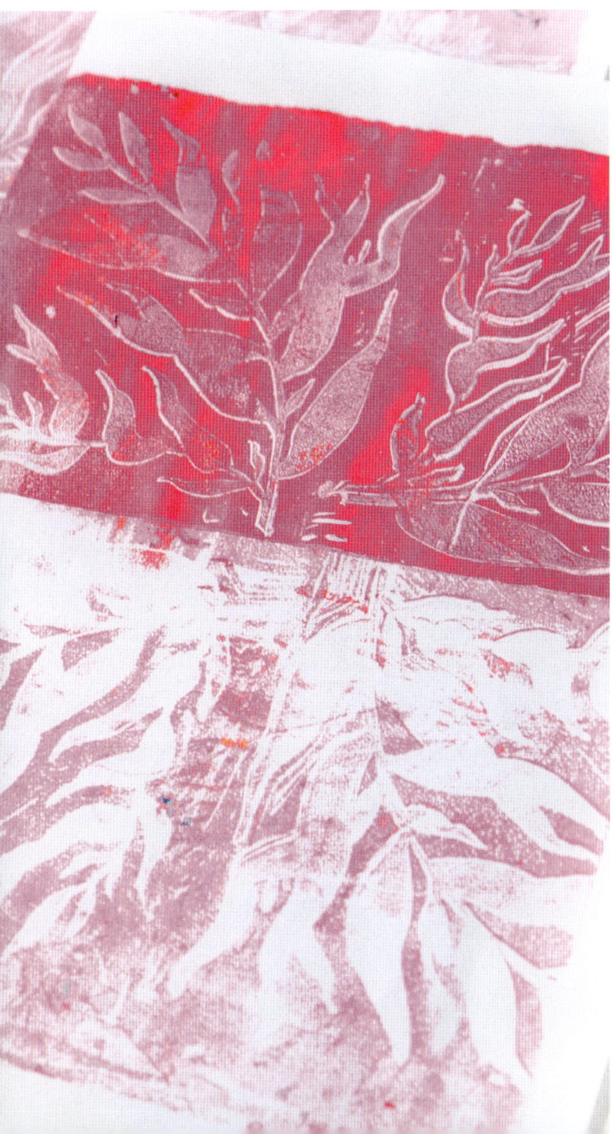

GHOST PRINTS

We can generate two print results with one printing process: the positive print, when we remove ink from the gelli plate with a stamp and then press the stamp somewhere; and the actual gelli print, when we place paper or fabric on to the gelli plate and remove the ink from the design-bearing surface.

Since there is usually ink residue left on the gelli plate, there are two additional printing variants:

a. With the ghost print, if you work quickly and the remaining ink is still wet, you can make a second print directly after the first print. This will appear very delicate and as an indistinct motif, like a ghostly shadow of the first print. In the picture on the left, the darker areas represent the direct, first print, and the light, delicate structures represent the ghost print of the same motif.
b. If you let the ink dry on the gelli plate, it will be reactivated and printed off along with the new ink the next time it is used. This is called a grunge effect. Just experiment with it! You will learn how to use grunge effects as a deliberate design element in the next section (see page 44).

Stencils & stamps

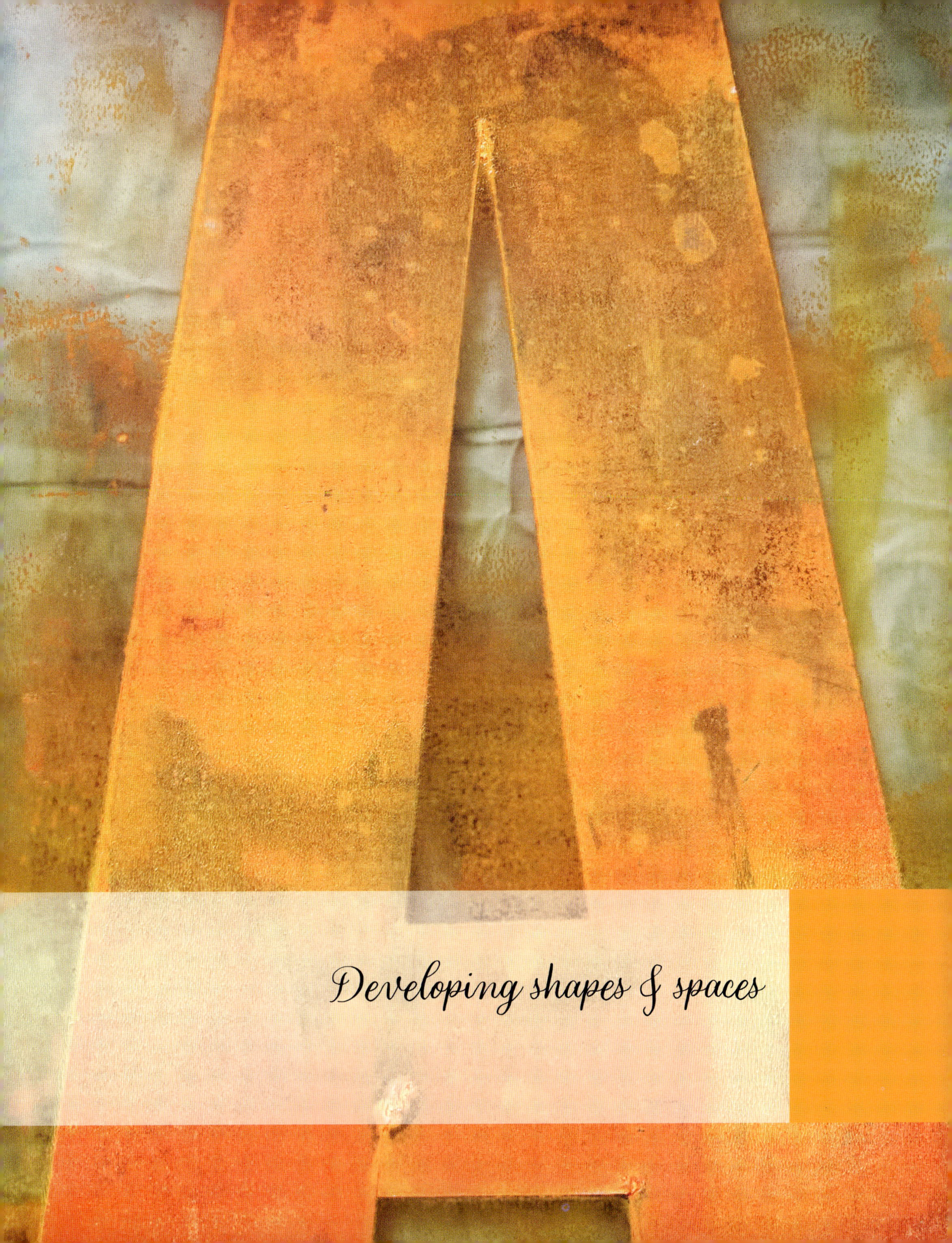

Developing shapes & spaces

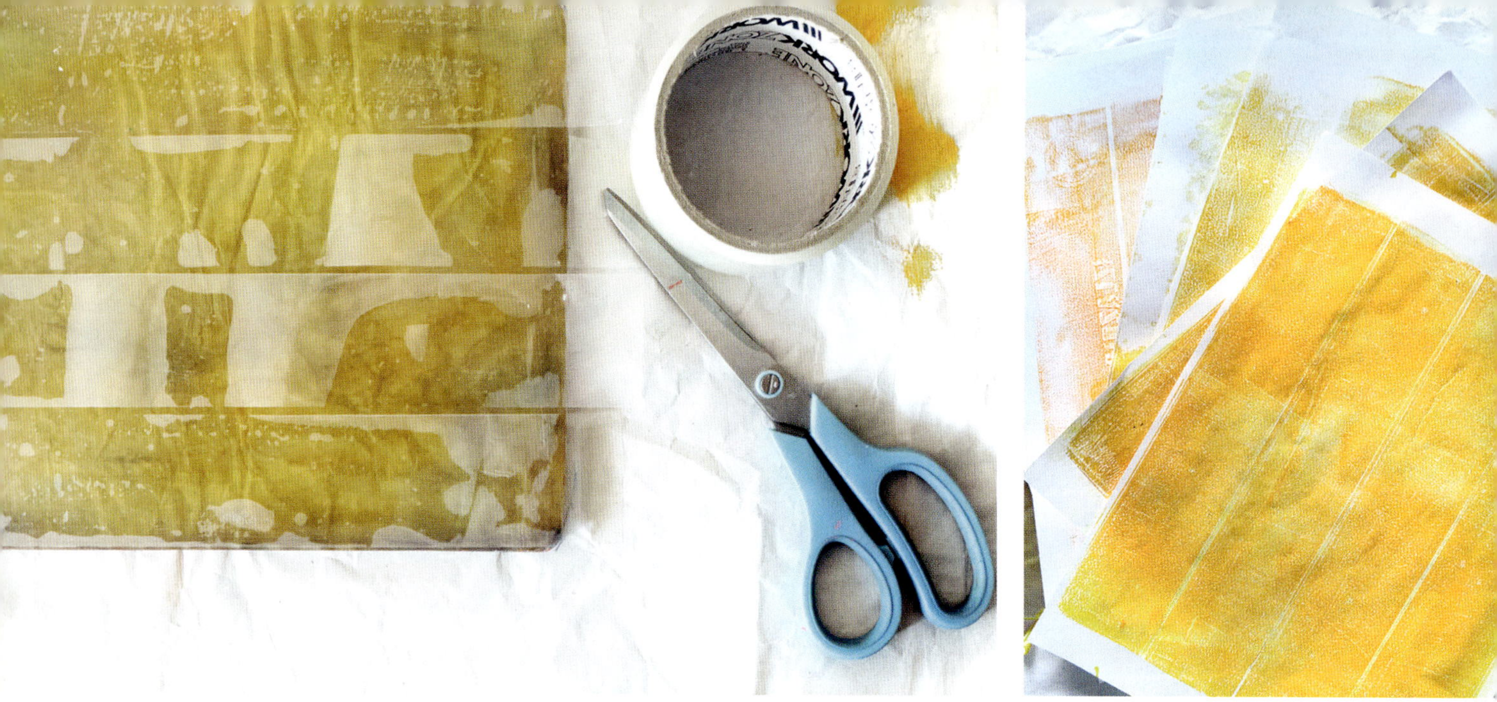

THE GRUNGE EFFECT

When printing, residue is often left on the gelli plate. You can clean the plate after each print, but you can also make use of the paint residues as an additional design element. A new layer of paint applied over the top will bond with the residue, reactivating it as the fresh paint and the old paint blend. They are then printed off together; this is known as the grunge effect, which results in areas with varied textures.

Using colours from the same colour family, such as various shades of yellow and orange in our case, produces vibrantly coloured spaces. The more contrast in the colours used, the more striking the effect will be.

Here, we combined the grunge effect with another technique. We can create lines using adhesive tape in various widths – wide, narrow, intersecting and so on. Additionally, using self-adhesive transparent film (commonly found in stationery shops, for instance protective film for textbooks), we can cut out shapes or letters to stick on to the surface. These smooth surfaces interact differently with the paint compared to the gelli plate, giving us a two-colour print from a single paint application. Paint residue also accumulates along the edges for the grunge effect.

If you remove the stencils before printing, a void area remains, through which the background can show (in the examples on the right, it is simply white paper).

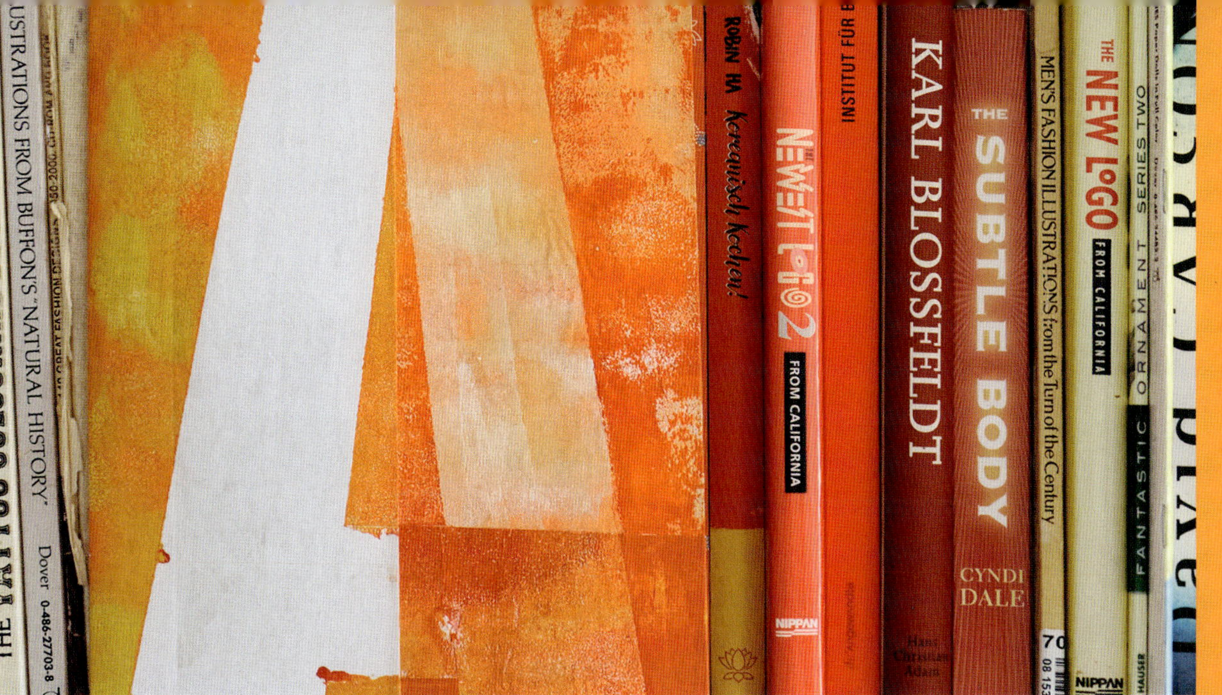

Printed once in orange: the colour gradations are the result of the different surface textures.

The less even the paint application, the starker the effect!

The stencil was removed before printing.

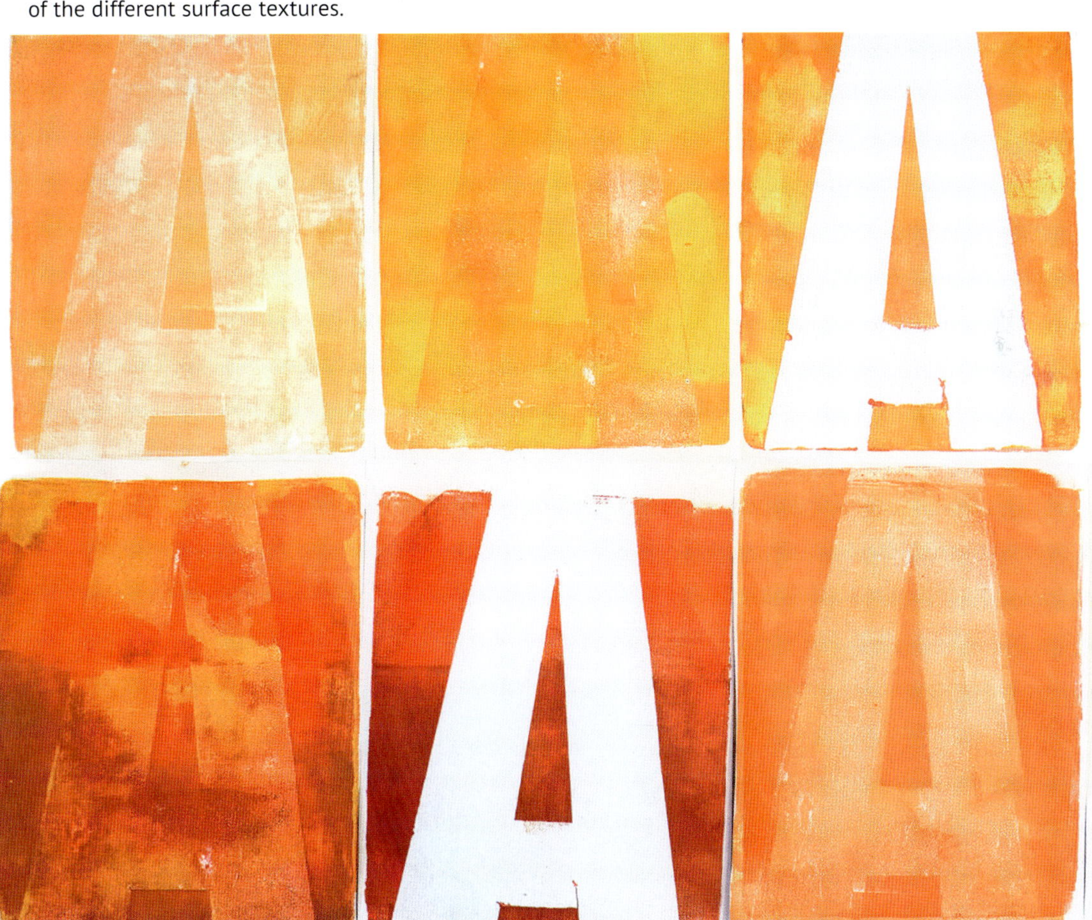

Two prints in similar colours, slightly shifted on top of each other.

The stencil was removed before printing.

First print in yellow–orange, then printed over in dark red.

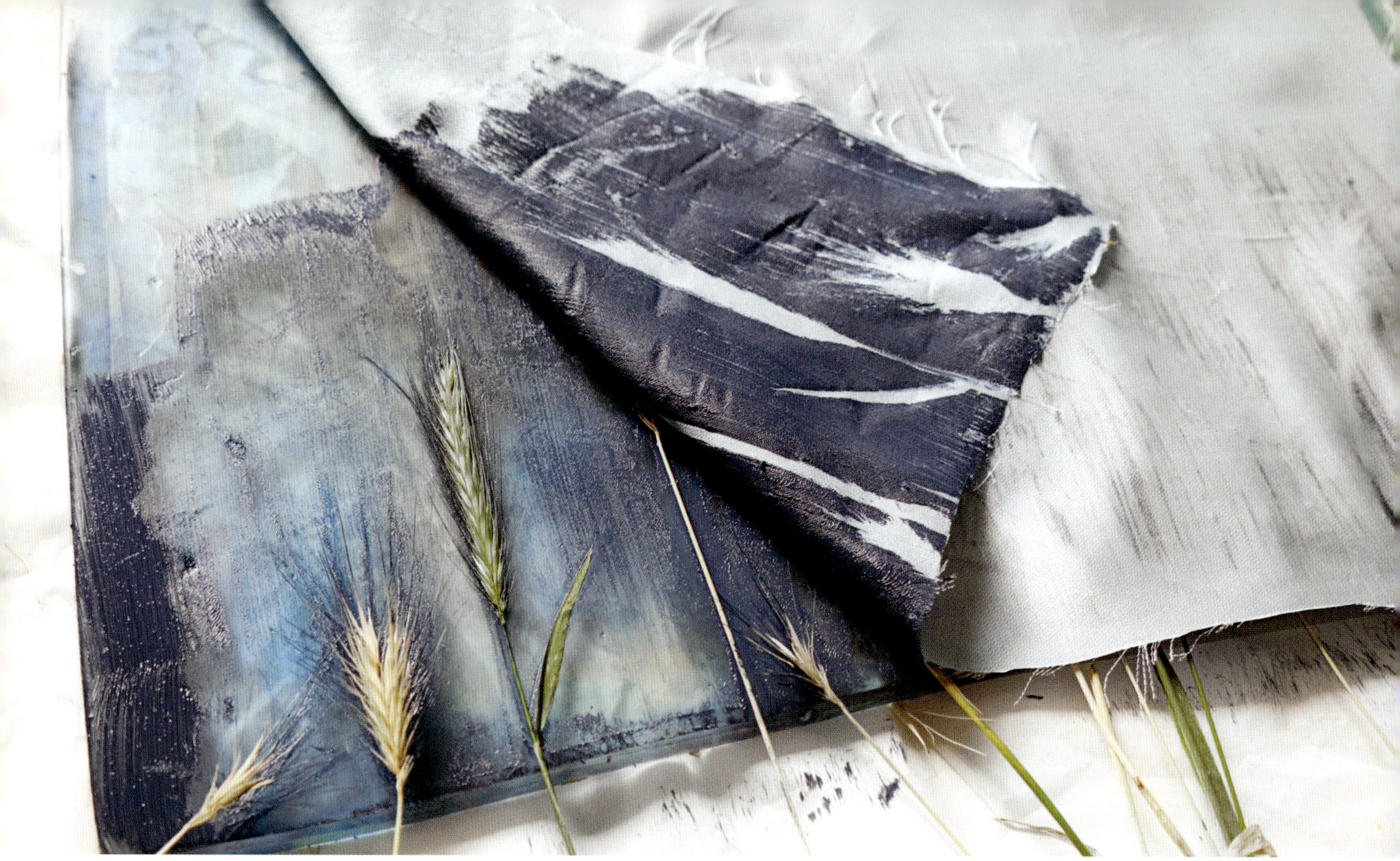

PLANT PRINTING

Printing with plants is a wonderful option for uncomplicated stencilling and produces truly magical results. The plants you use should be flat, to some extent, and should not disintegrate into individual pieces when you lift them back up from the gelli plate, otherwise you will be left with a lot of cleaning up after printing! These, however, are the only limitations.

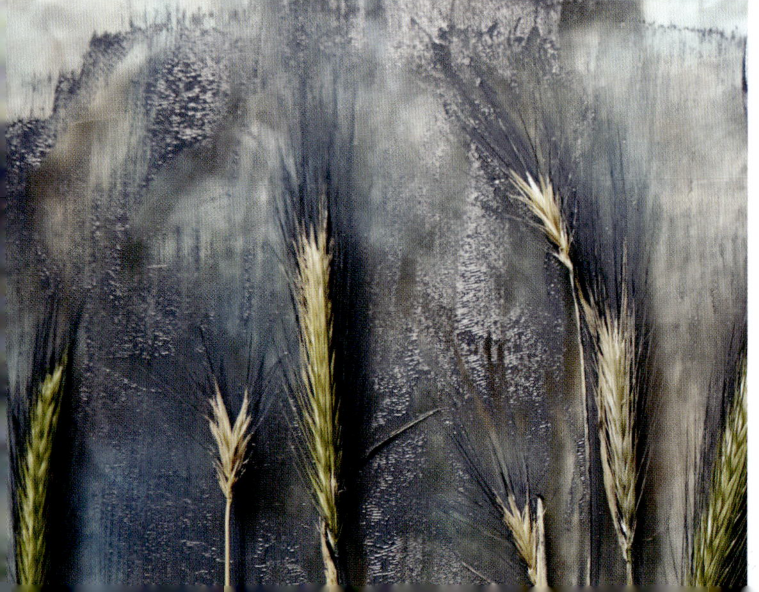

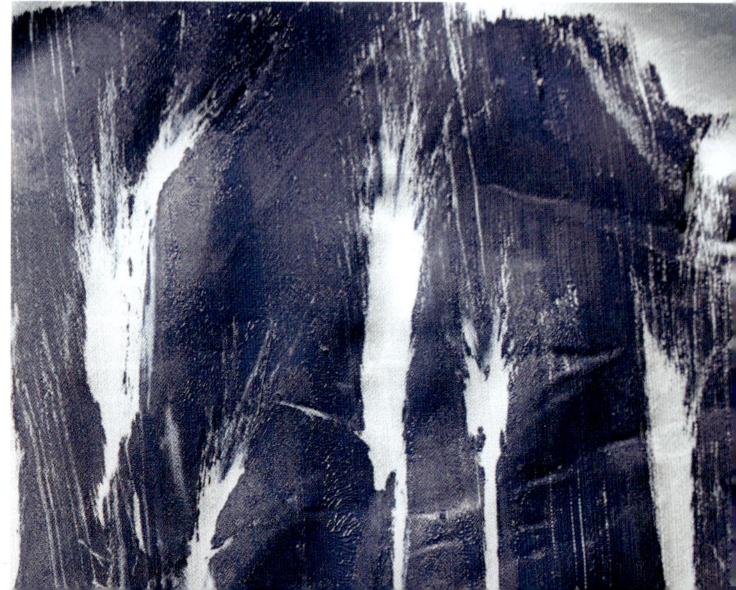

First, roll paint onto the gelli plate. The thicker the paint application, the starker the contrast to the white spaces.

Next, arrange the plant pieces on the plate appropriately. If we were to press them down and lift them again, we would be using them as stamps. However, for stencil printing, we leave them on the plate and place the material to be printed on top, then rub it well. Here, we've used grasses with long seed-heads, slightly raised. It's essential here to ensure that you rub well around the seed-heads. The paint should still be quite wet for this technique.

Then, lift off the material that you have printed on – most of the paint should now be gone from the gelli plate. Carefully remove the grasses (if you have left the stems hanging over the plate, just pull them upwards). What remains are traces of paint containing the imprint of the plants. If you work quickly, you can make another print, to create delicate, enchanting plant prints that combine beautifully with the stencil prints.

In the image at the bottom right, the lower section shows the stencil print (first print), while the upper section is the second print after removing the ears.

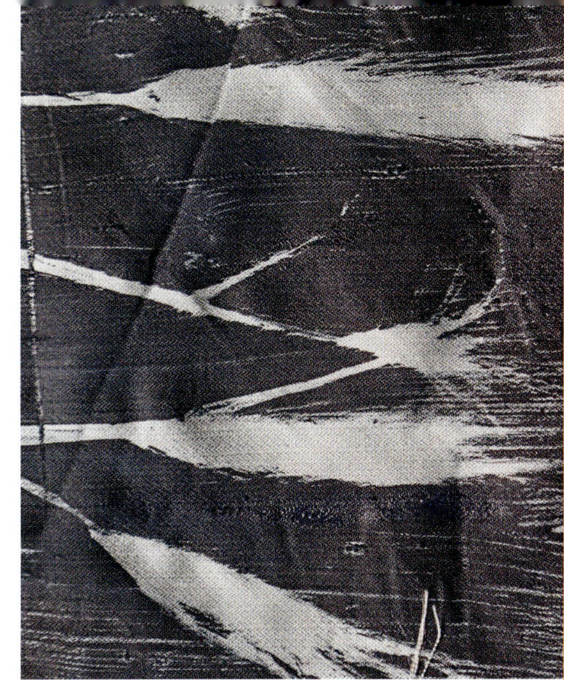

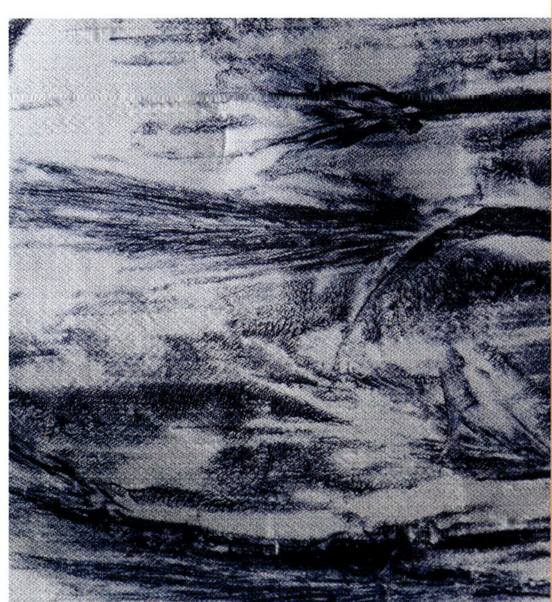

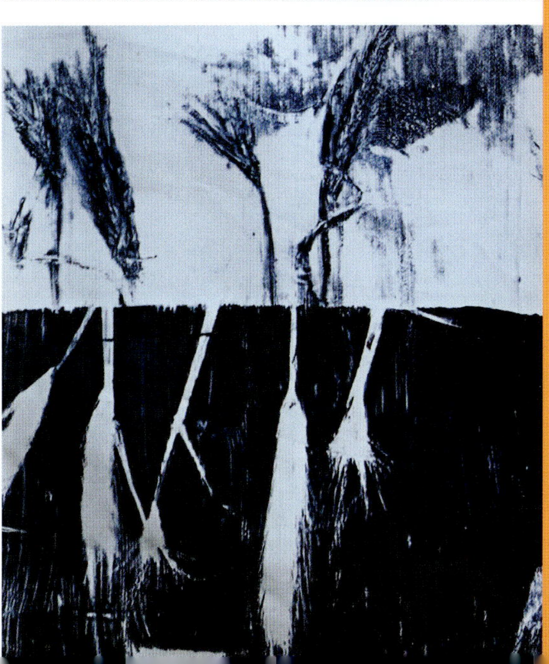

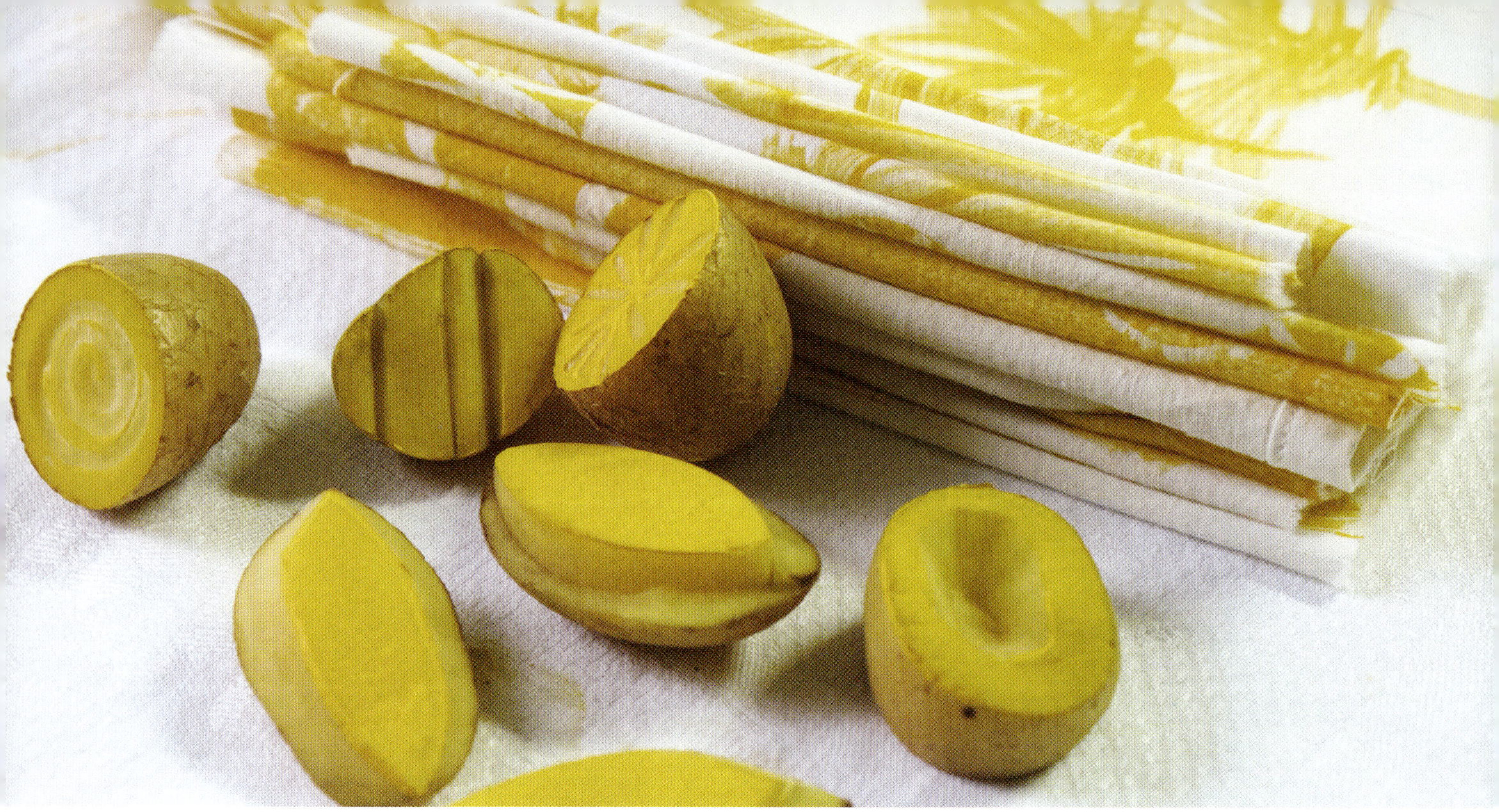

POTATO PRINTING

Potato printing may sound like child's play at first, but potato stamps are a wonderful way to quickly develop simple shapes and create your own fabric designs, as you can see on the bag on page 52.

For this type of printing, we are once again exploring the opportunity to print positively and negatively using the gelli plate. In this case, 'positive' is yellow on white (by transferring the paint from the gelli plate directly on to the fabric), and 'negative' is white on yellow (by removing paint with the potato stamp, so that areas in the print remain white).

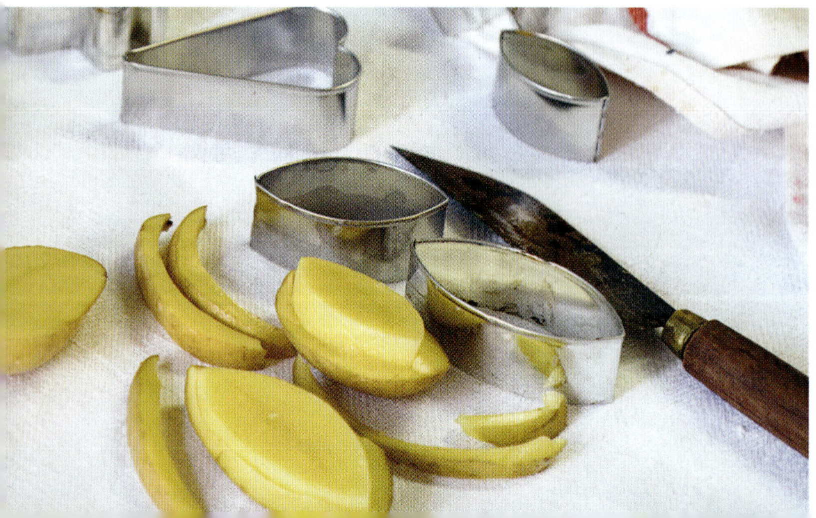

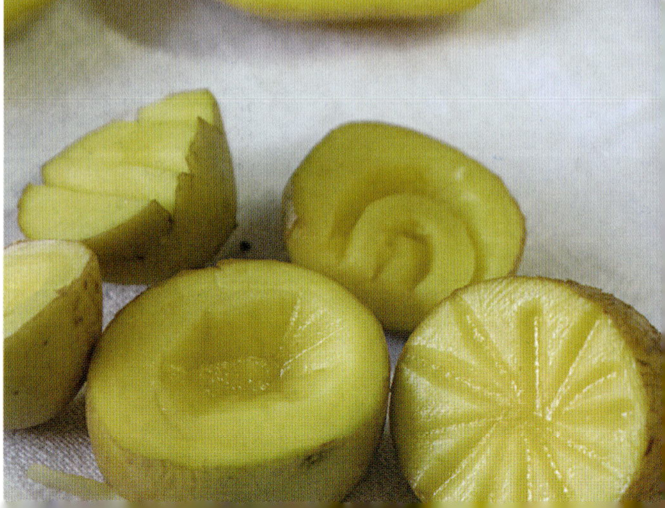

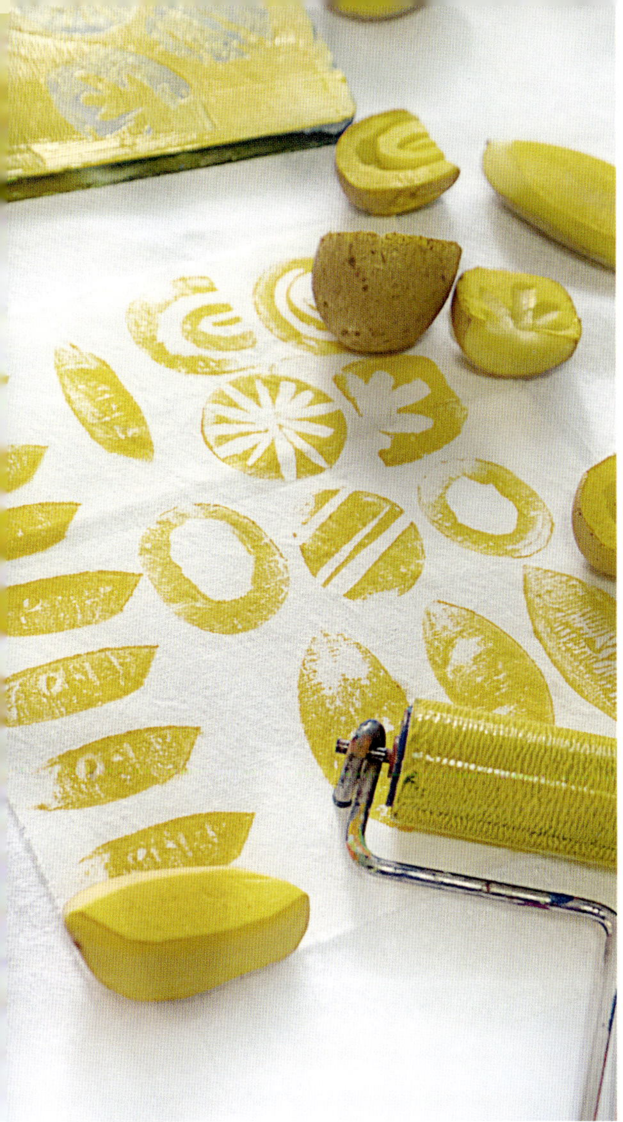

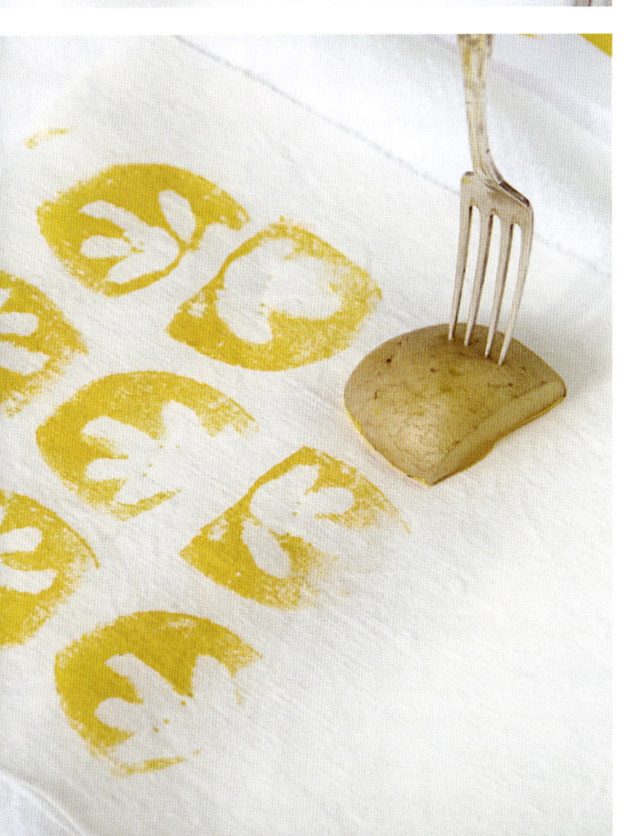

Potatoes come in various shapes but are more suitable for creating round or elongated stamps. You can cut shapes really quickly using cookie cutters, but the irregular forms that result from hand-cutting stamps can be more appealing. As well as kitchen knives, you can also use lino or wood-carving knives, for example.

Cut circles, spirals, rectangles, triangles, stars, flowers... Let the cut surfaces dry briefly before printing by placing them cut-side up on a kitchen towel.

Try it out:

- Choose your favourite stamp and print your first pattern.
- You can stamp patterns in equally spaced rows, randomly placed or offset at 45- or 90-degree angles.
- The shapes can be combined: you can make stars from elongated shapes, grids from stripes and so on.
- Test different spacings: circles or rings could touch or overlap; the pattern can be printed evenly over an area; or perhaps starting closely packed at one point and then more spread out over the rest of the area.

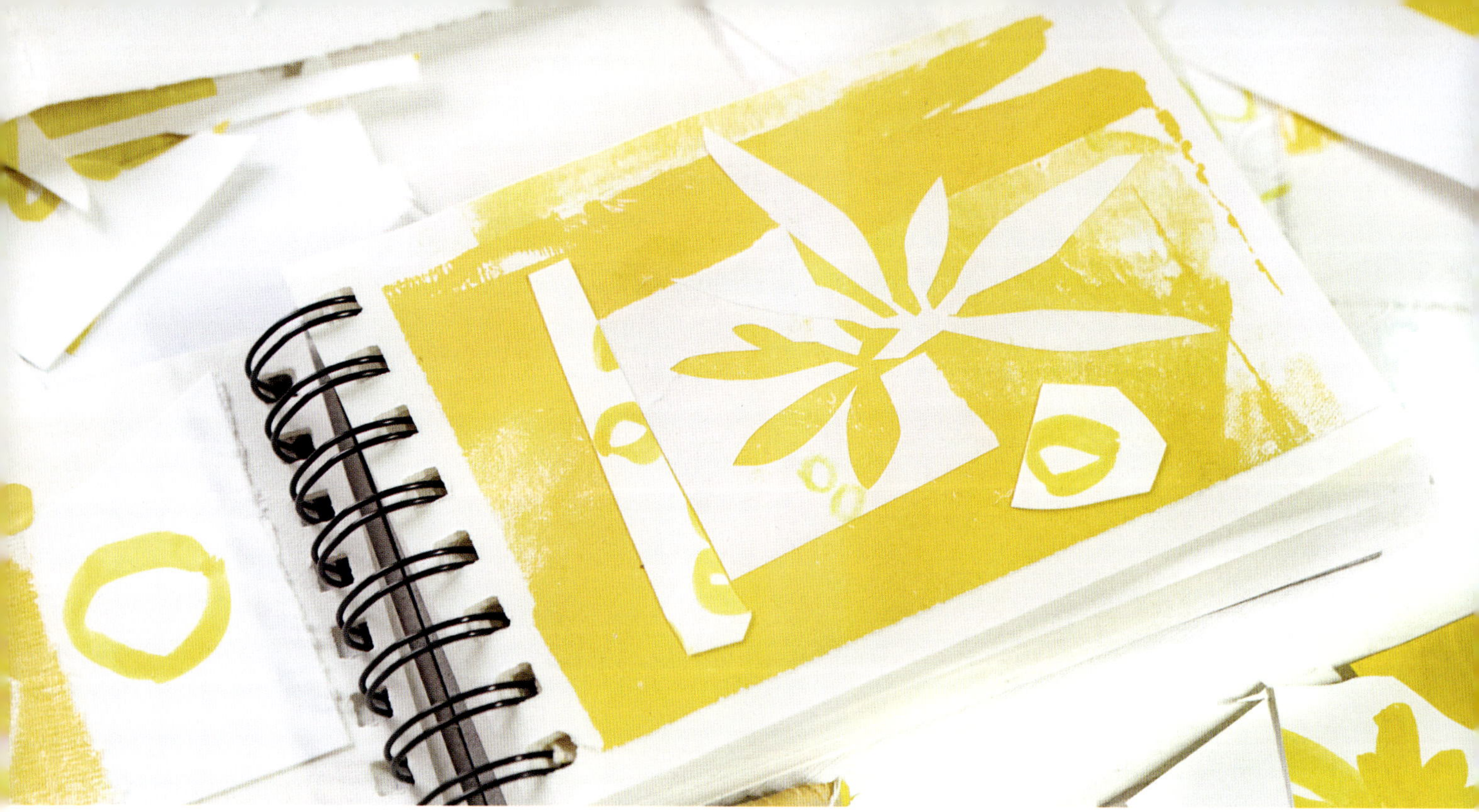

SKETCHBOOK WITH POTATO PRINTING

If you try potato printing, you will certainly produce many prints that you will want to keep and perhaps even frame. As always, the misprints that you are not completely satisfied with are well worth keeping for further use. Create a small sketchbook for your work in progress and fill it with leftover pieces or test prints.

Floral motifs are the obvious choice for potato printing, but you can also simply use stripes or patterns. Perhaps this will inspire you for your next project and lead you, for example, to plant-shaped foam rubber stamps – and thus to the next round of gelli printing.

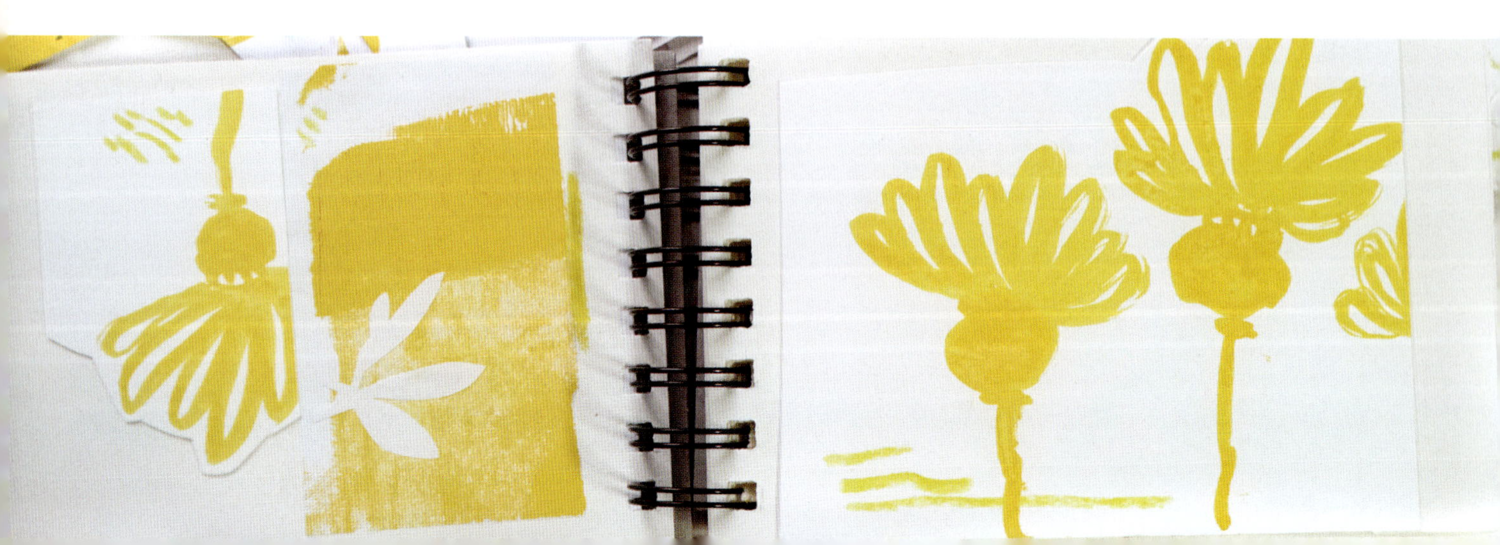

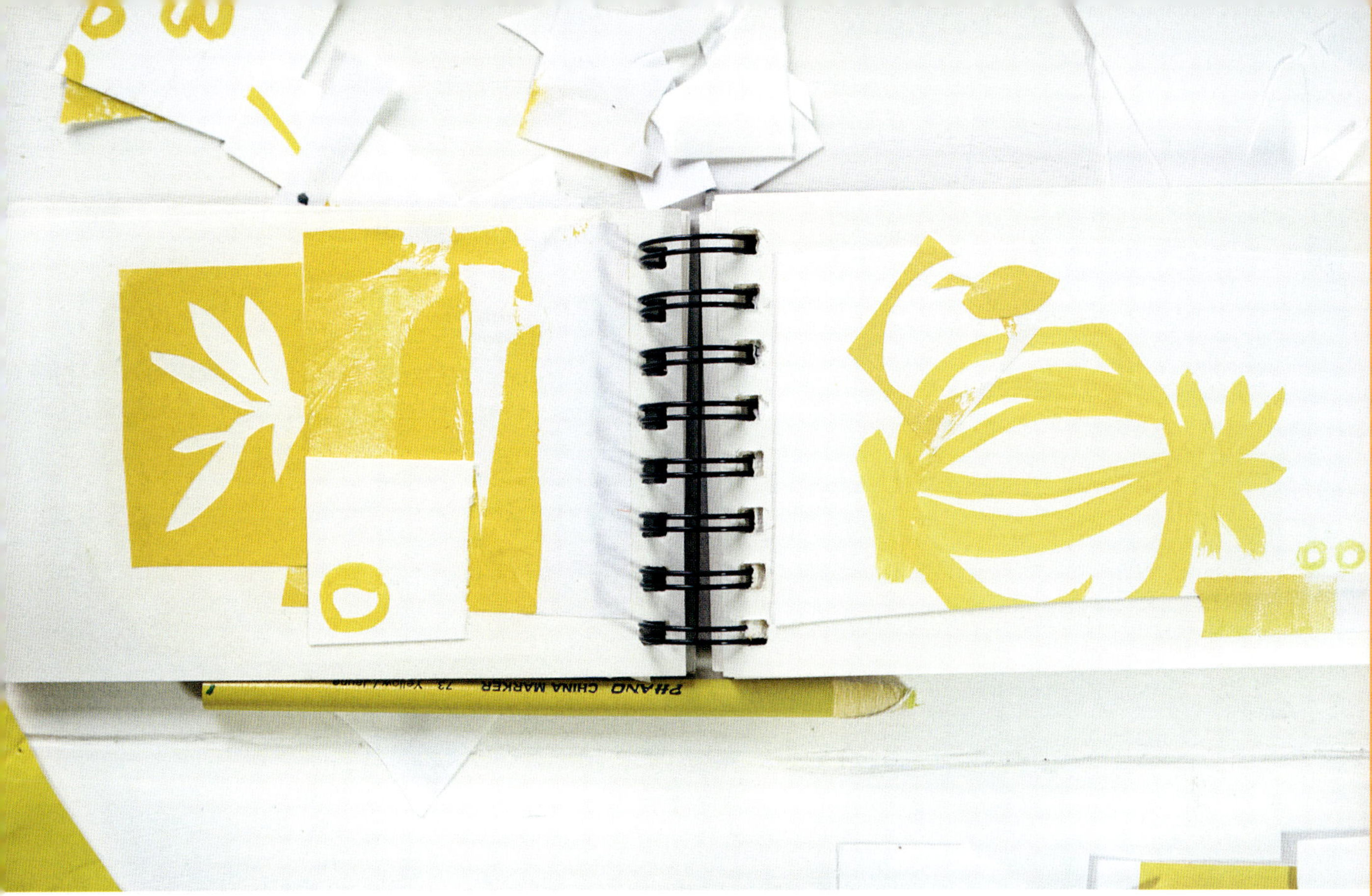

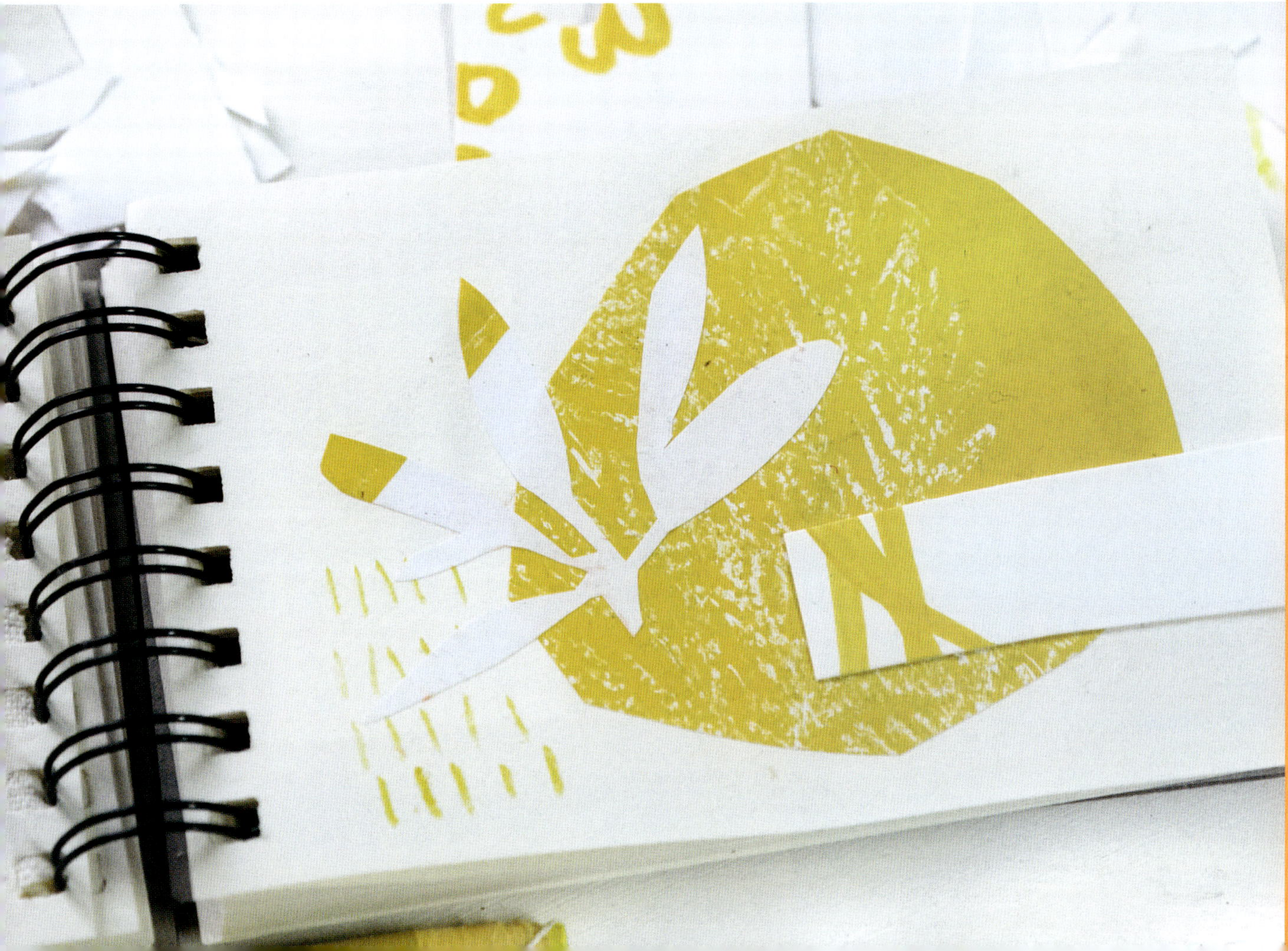

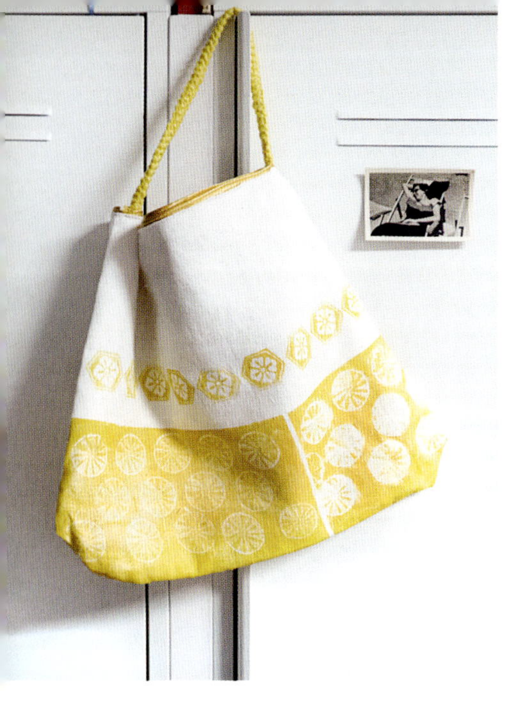

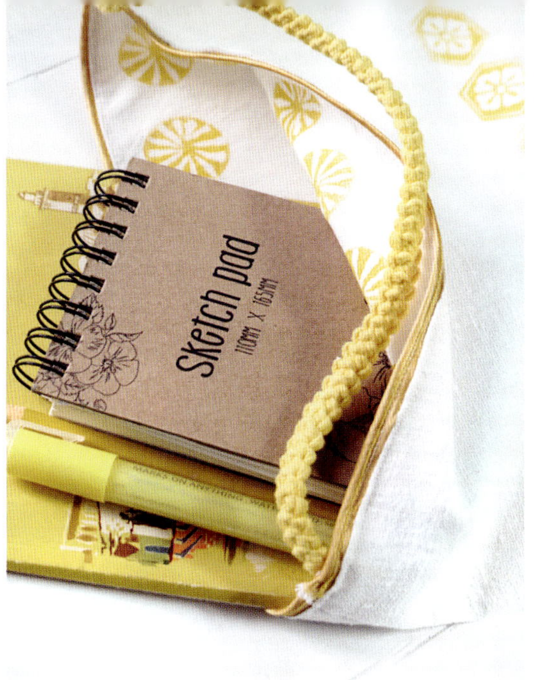

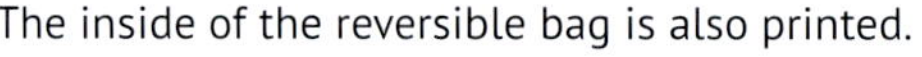

The inside of the reversible bag is also printed.

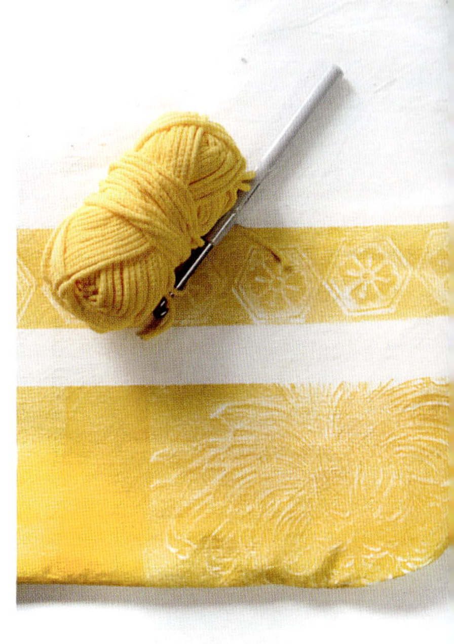

The reverse features a different design: white stripes (masked with tape before printing).

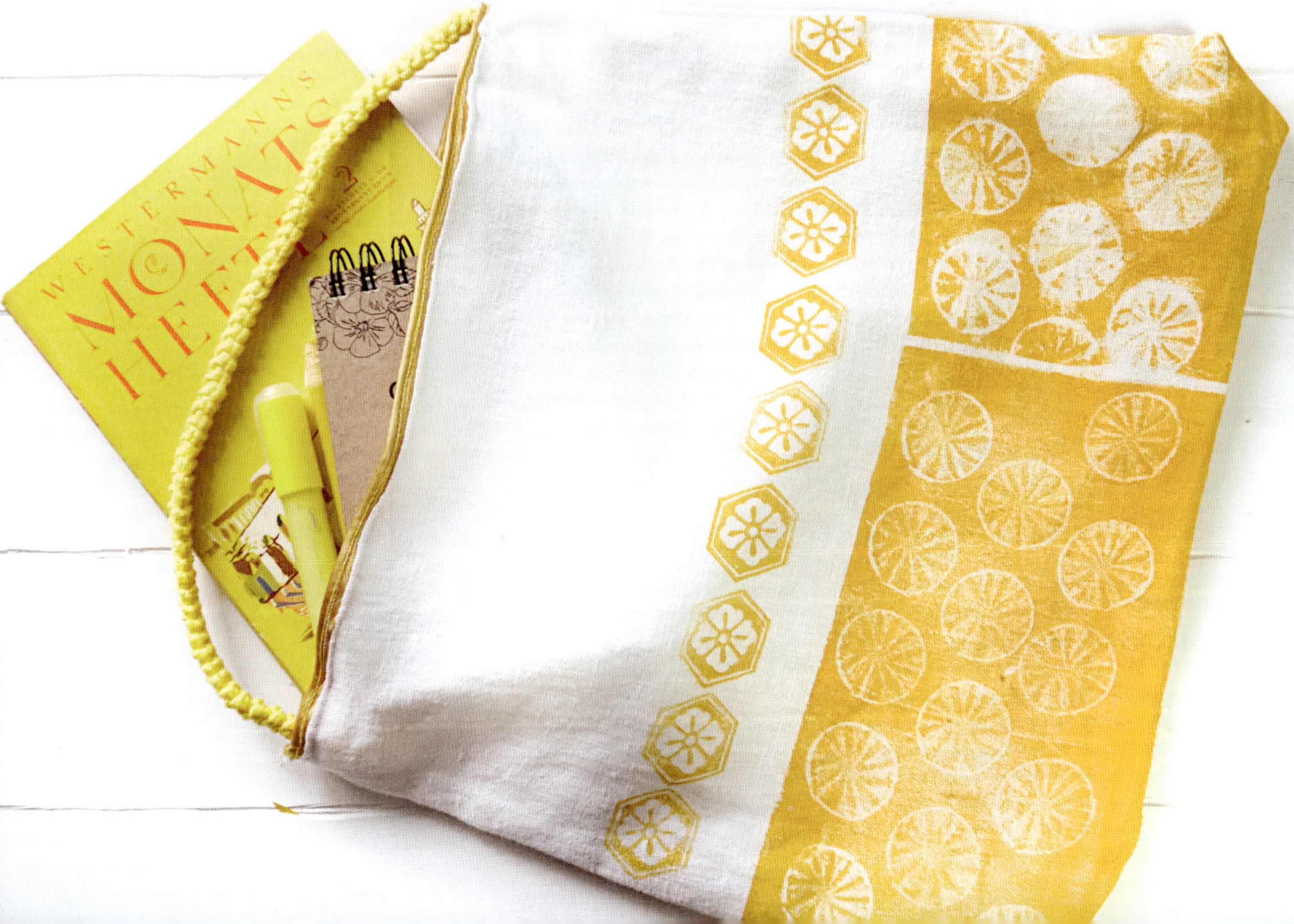

FABRIC COLLECTION AND YELLOW BAG

Even with a technique as simple as potato printing, you can create intricate designs thanks to gelli plate printing. You can use your favourite patterns to print small fabric collections and, once again, this demonstrates the unique possibilities of using gelli printing to achieve a variety of results in just a few steps using the negative and positive effect.

If you think one step further, you can print specific fabrics for an individually designed item. As an example, we have sewn a bag here. The fabric pieces were first cut to size and then printed to fit exactly. A colour-coordinated satin ribbon round the edge and a crocheted handle in the same shade of yellow complement the pattern design. See the shape of the bag in the illustration on page 137.

The bottom row of the print – the negative print – is stamped with potato print on the gelli plate. In the right-hand area, the paint was removed from the stamp before it was imprinted again; this makes the removed areas appear white. In the area on the left, the stamp was repeatedly pressed on to the gelli plate without being cleaned between presses. In this instance, the stamp does not take on much paint, and the impression on the gelli plate remains coloured, without strong white contrasts. The pattern row above it is printed with a lino stamp in positive print.

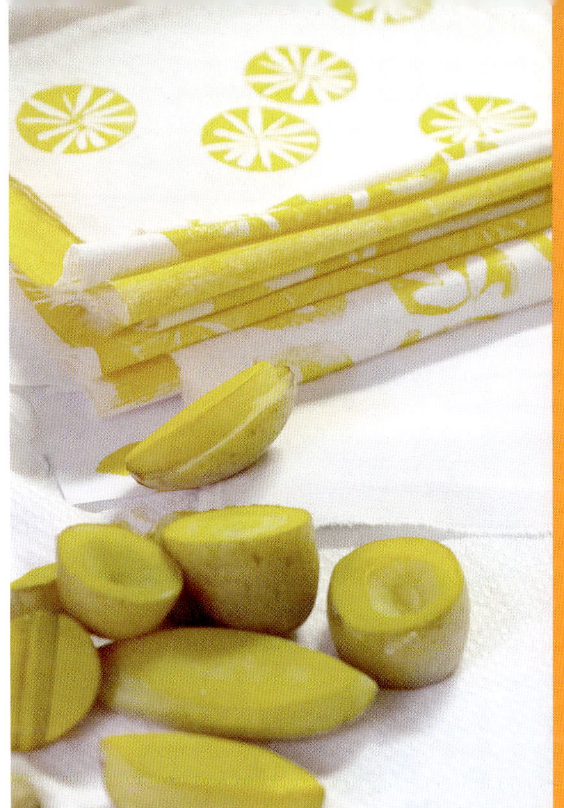

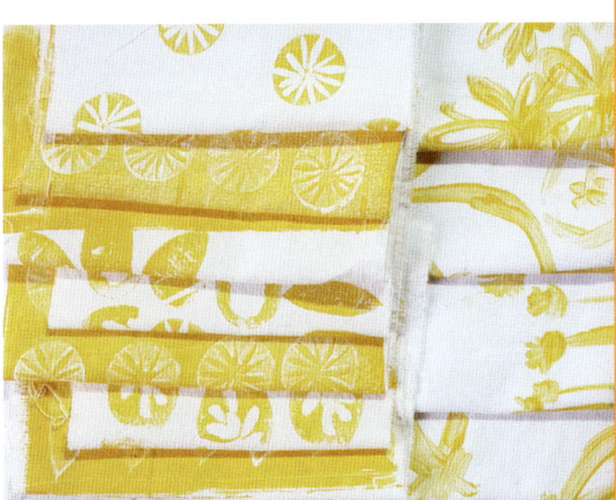

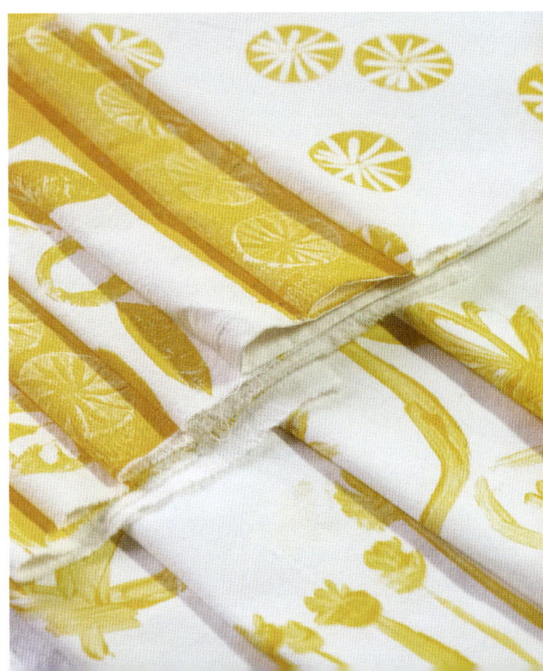

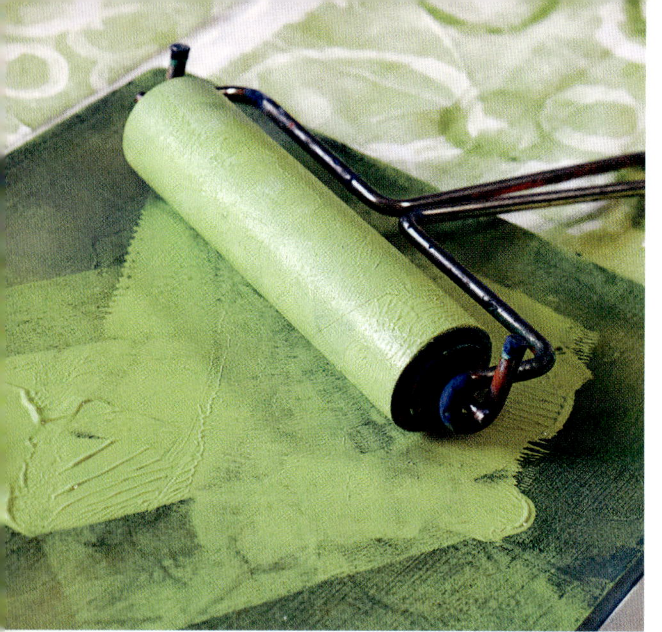

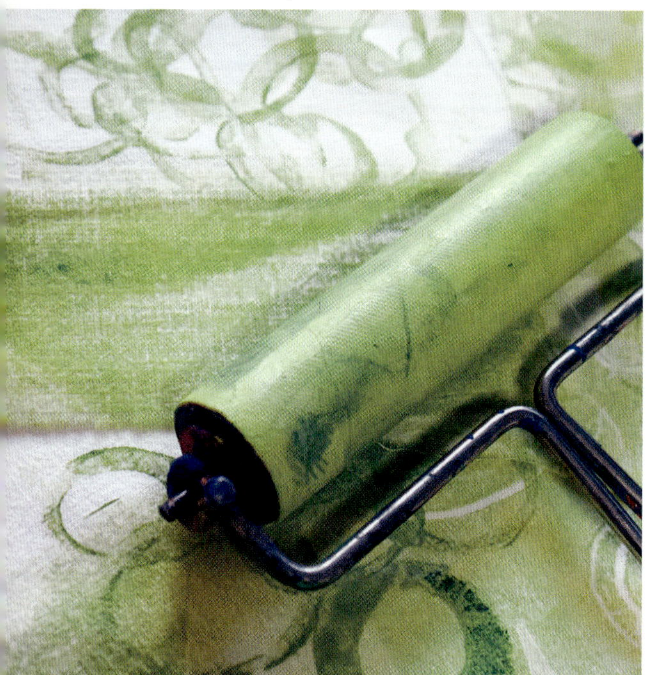

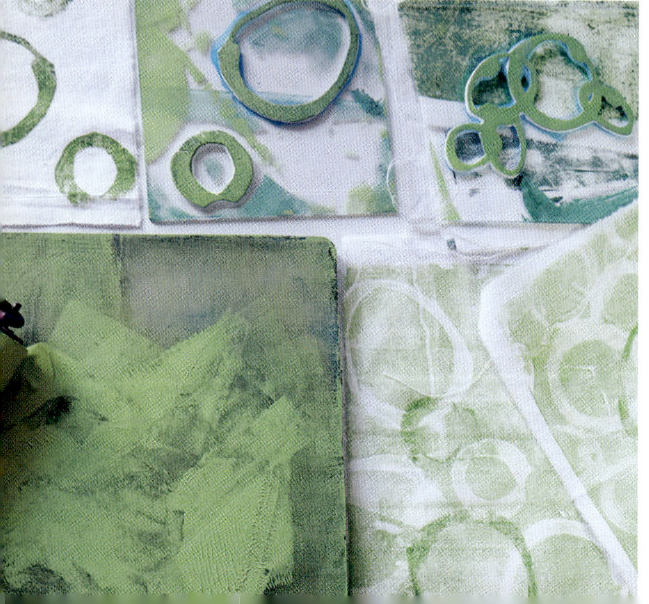

FOAM RUBBER STAMPS

Foam rubber is a material that can be used to make small and large stamps quickly and easily. If you glue foam on to a piece of cardboard or, as shown here, onto small acrylic plates, you can make stamps – or, even better, a whole stamp collection – with very little effort.

Foam rubber is available in different thicknesses: the thicker the material, the easier it is to print with. Foam rubber is almost as easy to cut as paper when using a cutter or scissors.

Foam rubber can be wonderfully 'engraved' with a ballpoint pen. If you trace a line two or three times firmly with a pen, the indentation will be so deep that these lines will appear as gaps in the print. On this stamp, only the outer edge has been cut out with scissors. All the other shapes were imprinted with a ballpoint pen.

Try it out:

Create your own flower stamp from foam rubber!

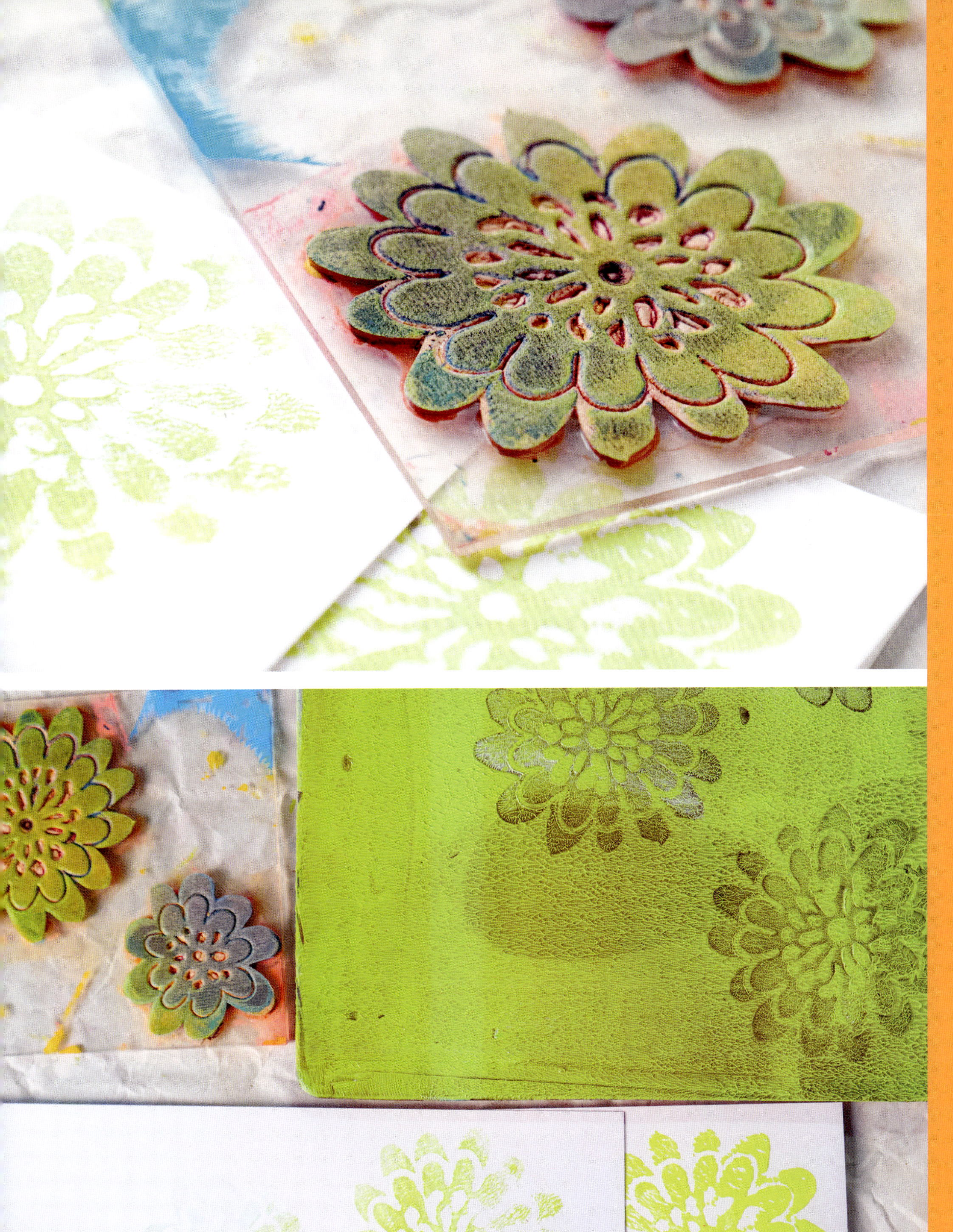

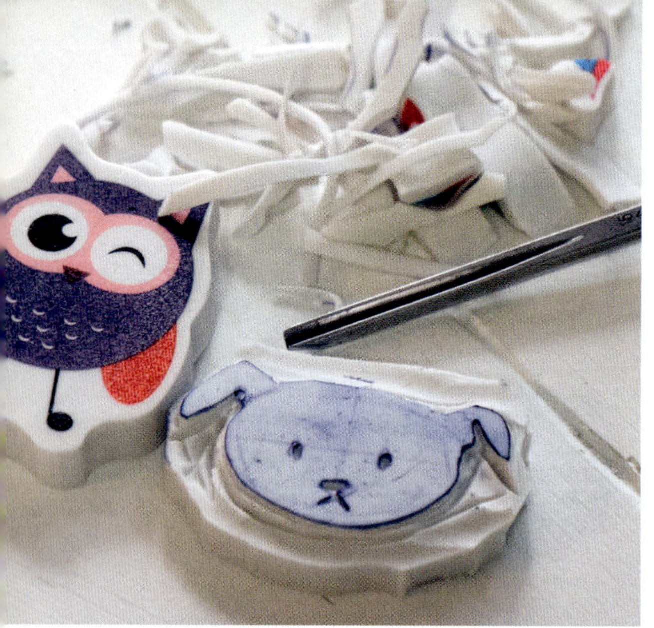

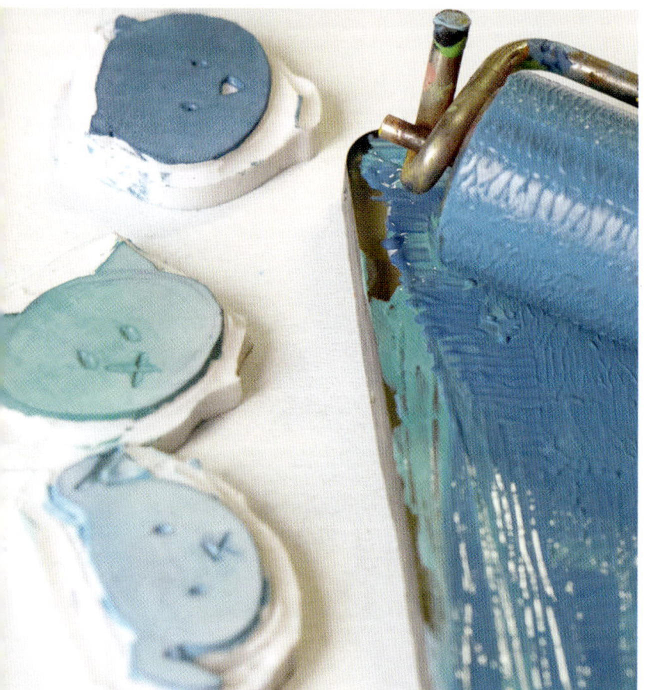

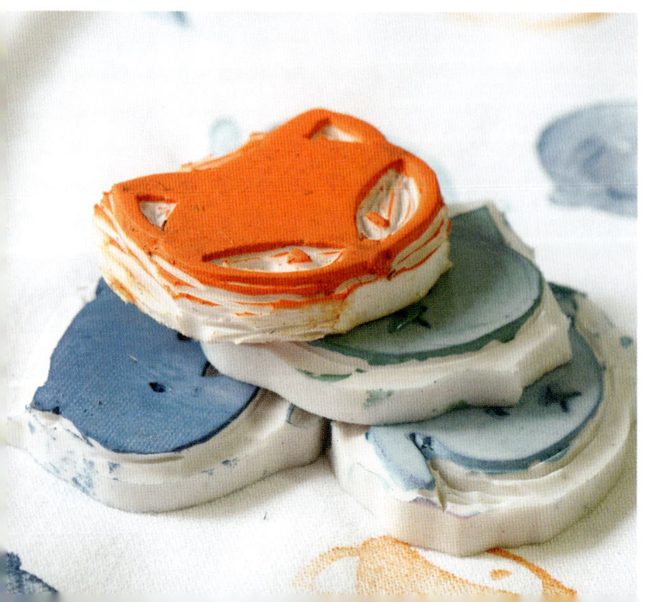

ERASER STAMPS

You can carve erasers just as easily as potatoes. The former have the advantage of lasting indefinitely. Use any solid eraser that does not crumble when used. In addition to the classic oblong erasers, you can also find more rounded erasers, often among the merchandise for popular animated films.

You can find templates for the stamps, which we have carved here with a simple linocut knife, on page 134. You could also use a sharp kitchen knife, pocket knife or a cutter.

The gelli plate also makes a wonderful mixing palette. Here, three colours in similar shades have been mixed by adding green and grey respectively. The whole thing becomes more vibrant if we then add a contrasting colour.

The gelli plate also served as a stamp pad: it was rolled, the stamp pressed into the colour and then on to the fabric.

By sewing two to four simple seams, you can quickly sew a lunch bag from the printed fabric, as you will see on the following pages – and it's not just for children.

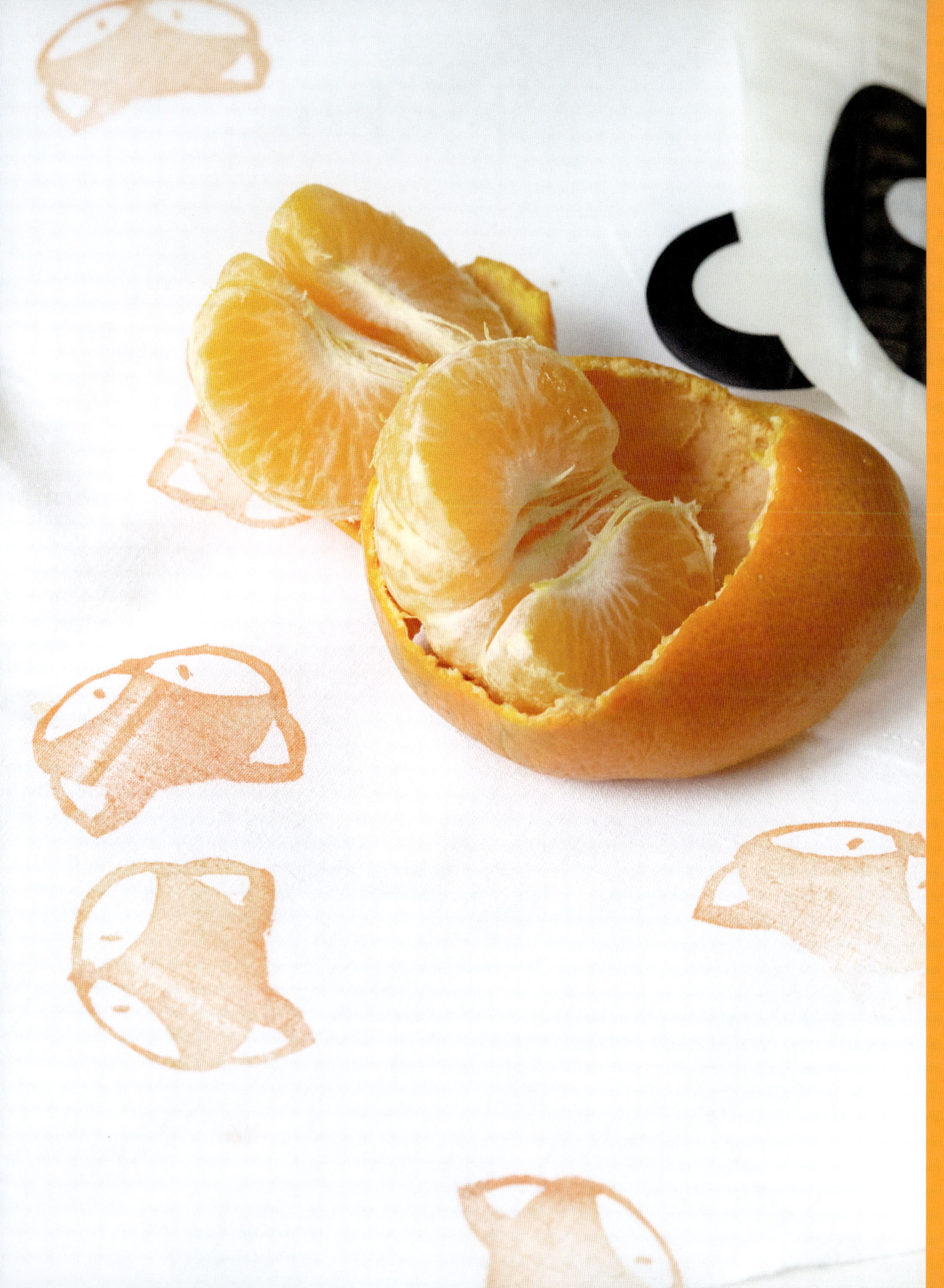

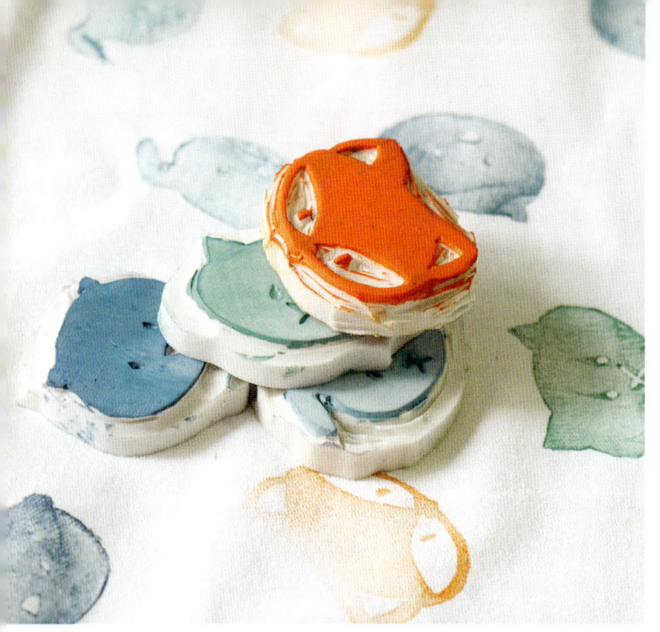

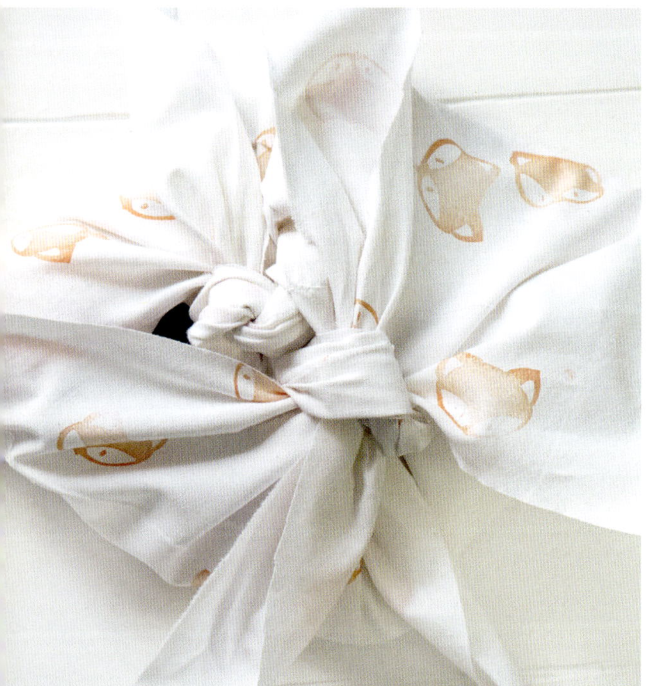

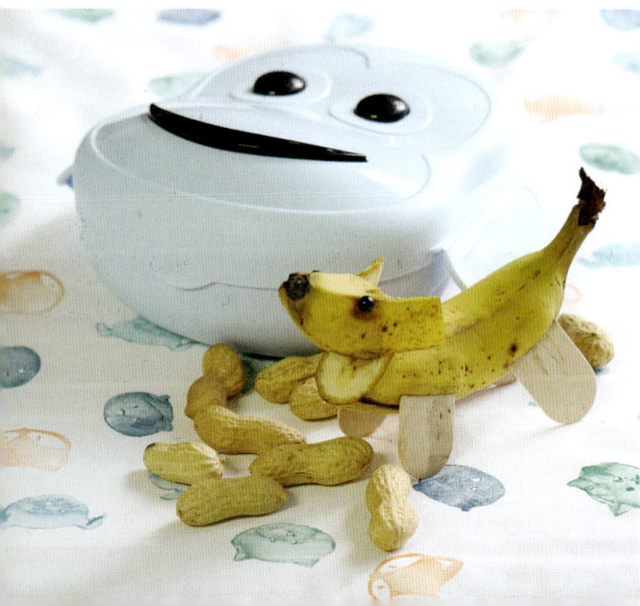

JAPANESE FABRIC BAGS

In Japan – the land of patterns and beautiful packaging – items are often wrapped in pretty patterned fabrics and knotted together to make small parcels or storage bags to keep food or yarn scraps, for example. You can also make a proper bag by tying the sides to a strap or old leather belt instead of knotting them together.

Following this tradition, we have printed simple lunch bags that can also be made as a bag in a slightly larger format. To make the bag, two triangular pieces of fabric are sewn together, as shown in the drawing on page 135. If you close the side seams, you get a bag. When not sewn together, the piece of fabric can be used as a mat or a pad, folded up smaller. Knot the ends to close. We can, of course, print on the fabric pieces using any gelli printing technique, and the result will always be beautiful.

If you have leftover pieces of fabric, no matter what shape or size, perhaps you could use fabric that you have printed yourself to wrap gifts for others. That means no more packaging going in the bin, and the wrapping fabric makes an additional gift.

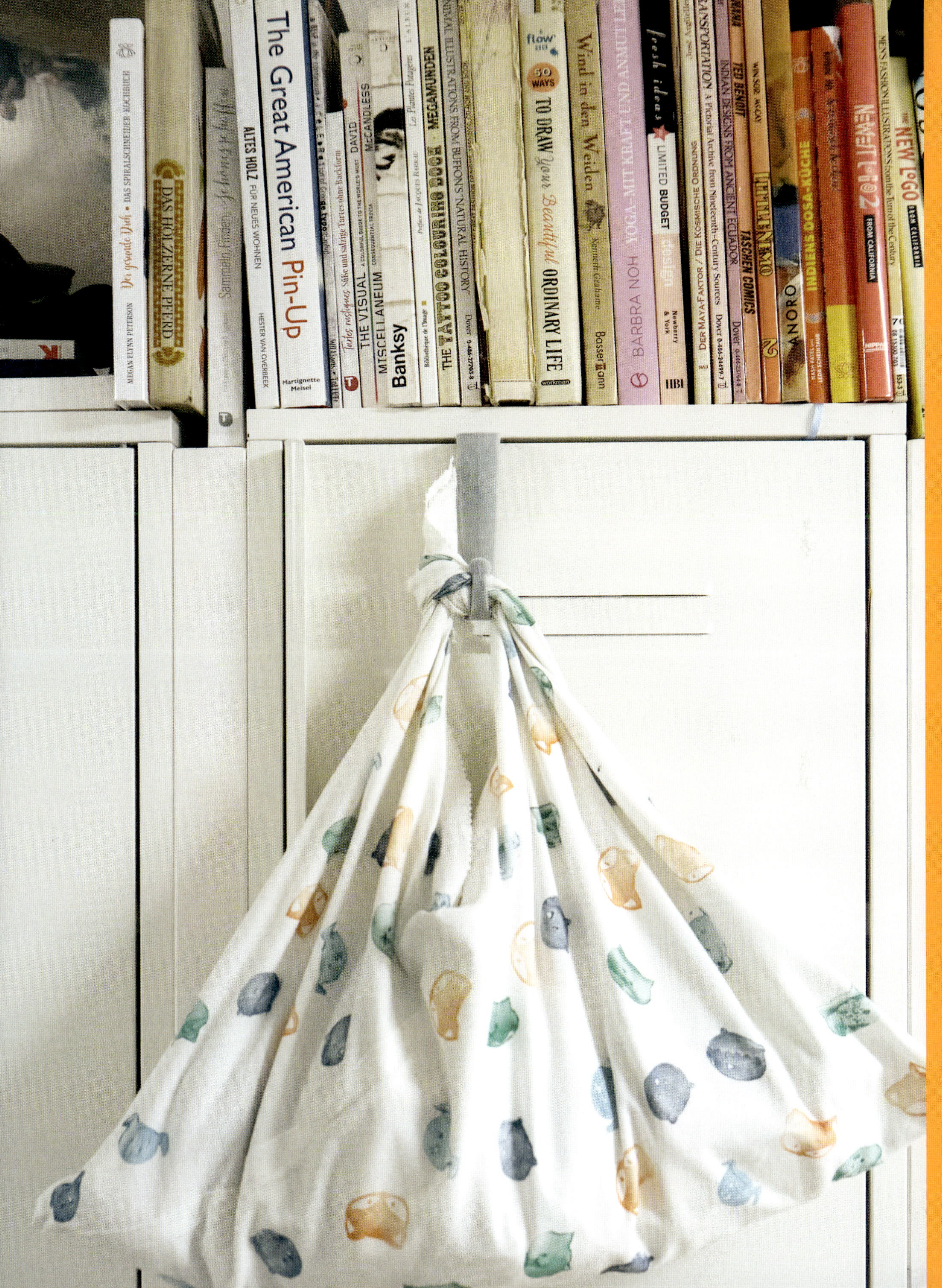
DAS HÖLZERNE PFERD
ALTES HOLZ FÜR NEUES WOHNEN
HESTER VAN OVERBEEK
The Great American Pin-Up
THE VISUAL MISCELLANEUM
Banksy
MEGAMUNDEN
THE TATTOO COLOURING BOOK
ANIMAL ILLUSTRATIONS FROM BUFFON'S NATURAL HISTORY
50 WAYS TO DRAW Your Beautiful ORDINARY LIFE
Wind in den Weiden
BARBRA NOH YOGA-MIT KRAFT UND ANMUT LEBEN
fresh ideas LIMITED BUDGET design
DER MAYA-FAKTOR / DIE KOSMISCHE ORDNUNG
INDIAN DESIGNS FROM ANCIENT ECUADOR
TASCHEN COMICS
ANORO
INDIENS DOSA-KÜCHE
NEWEST LOGO FROM CALIFORNIA
NEW LOGO FROM CALIFORNIA

Resist printing

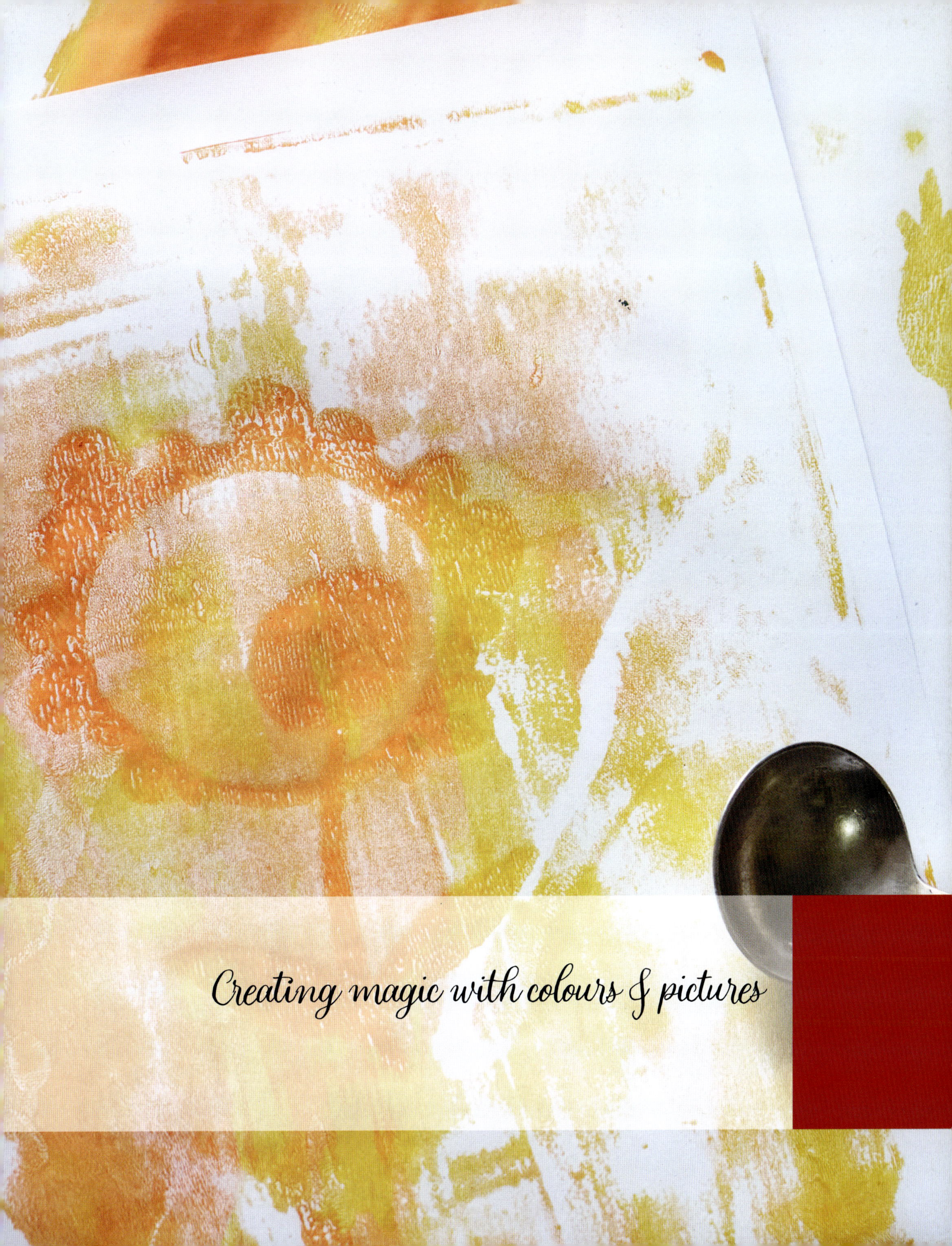

Creating magic with colours & pictures

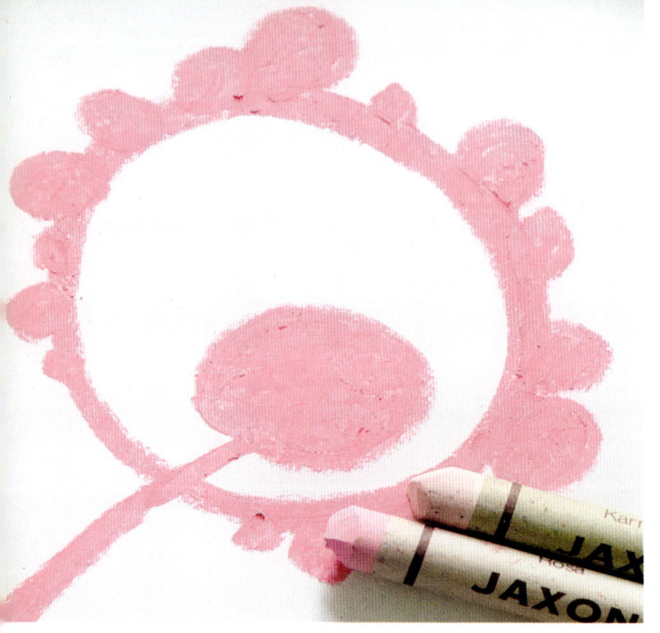

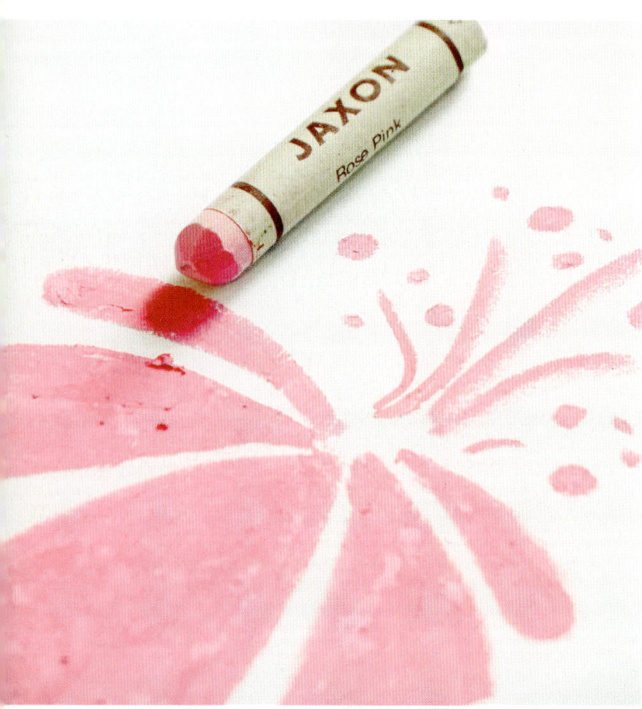

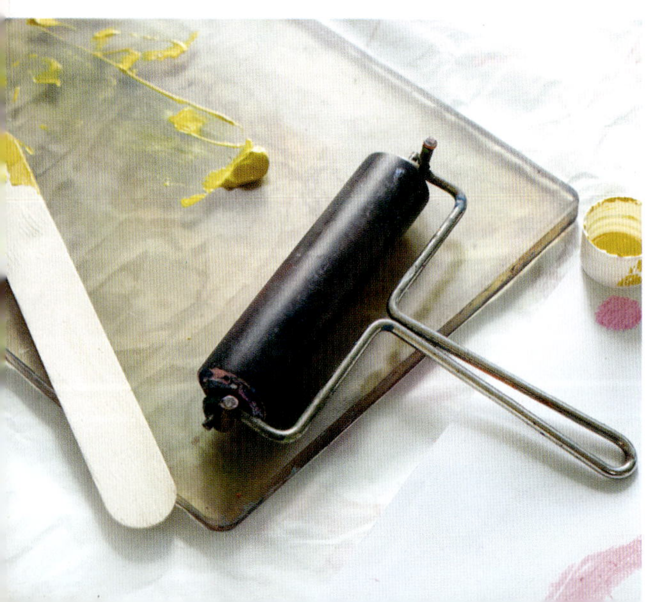

WAX CRAYON RESIST

Another gelli printing technique is resist printing. There are different variations of this – we will discover one here and on page 65.

We use materials that repel (resist) paints to achieve different paint applications in one print. We have already done something similar with the adhesive tape or adhesive film on page 44, and now we will use wax crayons. Please note that water-soluble wax crayons are available in art shops – these are only suitable for this technique to a very limited extent. The best results are achieved with normal wax crayons or oil pastels, and with a very thick application of paint.

First, draw your motifs on the paper using a crayon. The colour doesn't really matter, but if you choose colours that harmonize well at this point, all the prints will coordinate well with each other afterwards (the papers that you colour with wax crayons leave traces on the gelli plate, but are printed with the applied paint at the same time and can also be used). Perhaps you have developed new shapes in your sketchbook that you want to try out; but you can also draw thick circles, a large letter and so on. Simple shapes are better than complex ones.

Prepare at least five or six motifs, then apply paint to your gelli plate with a roller. Place one of the crayoned papers on top and carefully rub over it with your hand, a spoon or bone folder tool.

The more you rub, the less of the background paint will remain for the second printing.

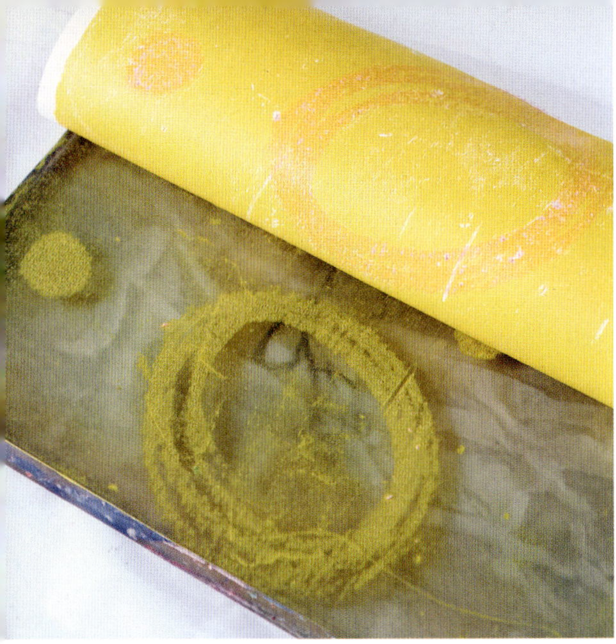

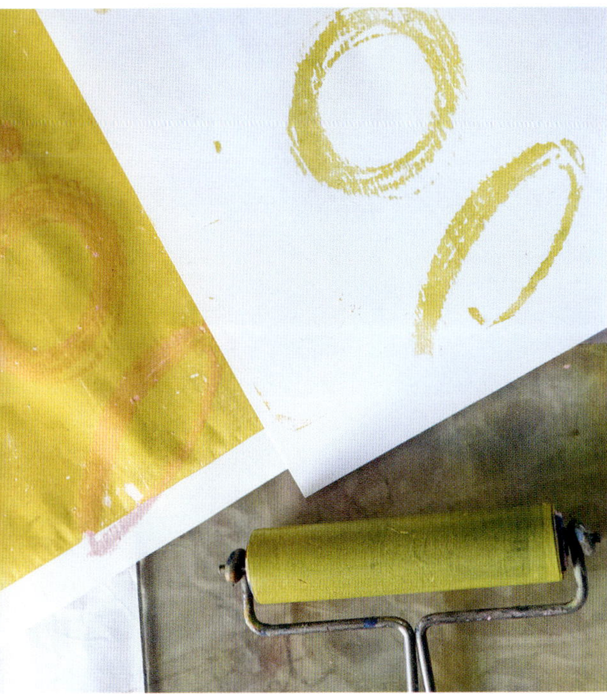

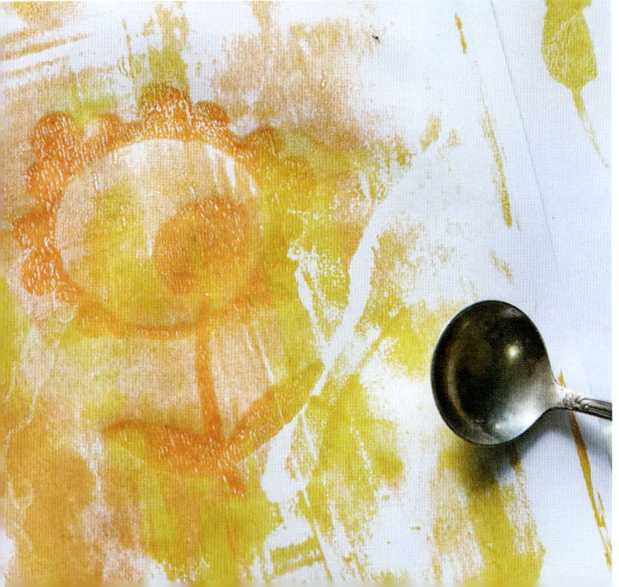

What happens now? Areas where you applied wax crayon to the paper will take on less paint; this means that there is more paint on the gelli plate. We can print this off with a second press – and so you either need to work quickly here, while the paint is still wet, or you leave it to dry completely and reactivate it with another layer of paint (either white or another contrasting colour). Both prints – the first print, where the wax colouration shows through the paint you have rubbed on, and the second print with the actual design – can be used later.

The resulting images retain the handmade texture that you get from using wax crayons. It means you can create interesting effects from very simple shapes.

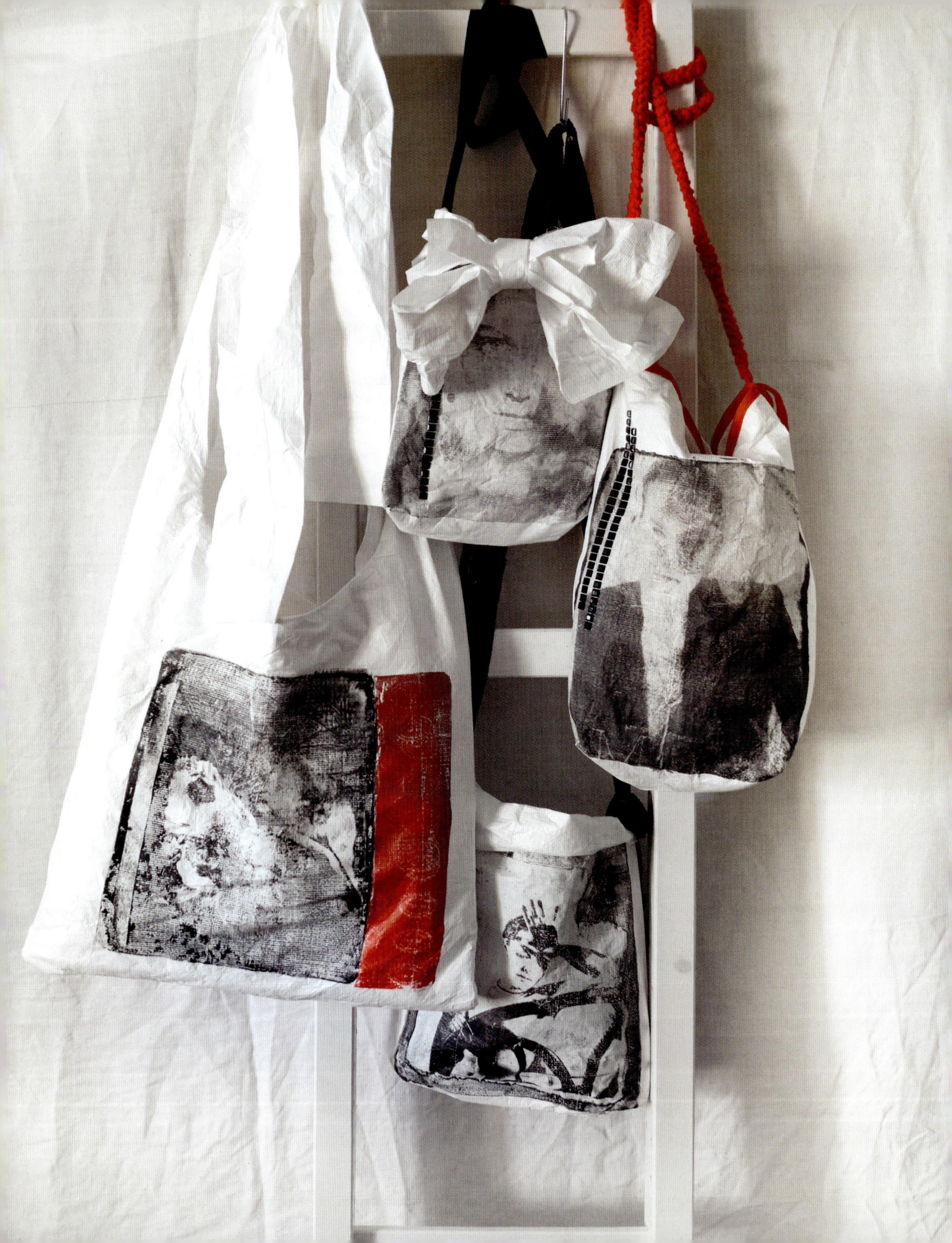

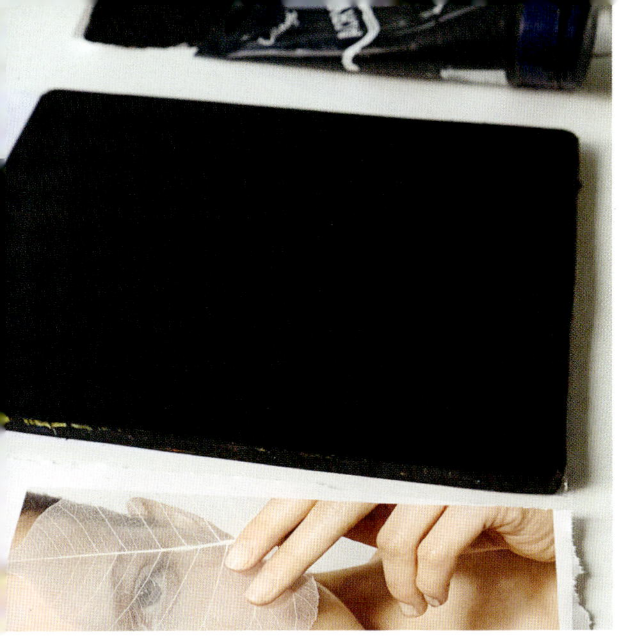

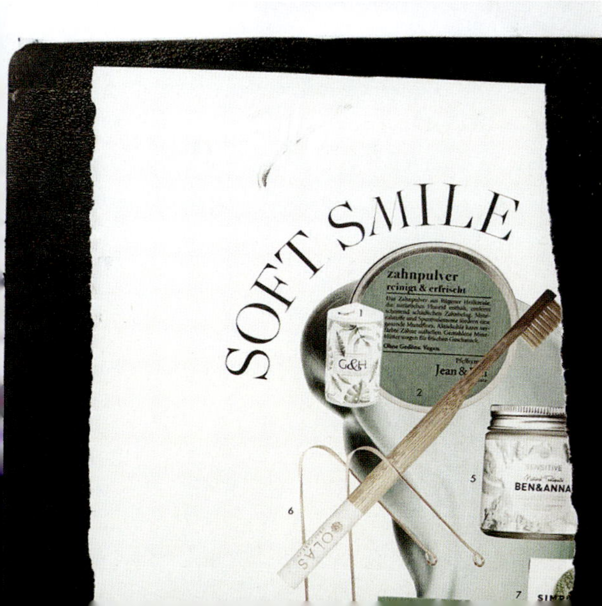

MAGAZINE RESIST

Sometimes, gelli plate printing has something of a magical quality. Each time that we lift a piece of paper or fabric from a gelli plate, the effects will be a surprise. Whether it is monochrome, multi-colour or in layers, there is always a random element which influences the print and thereby the result. That's why gelli printing is never dull!

However, the technique that we want to demonstrate now also looks magical in terms of the procedure. Complex images or smiling faces can be created on the gelli plate without much preparation. The technique is called magazine resist – just as on page 62, we are working with a resist technique.

The same principle – where wax crayon takes on and prints colour differently to the blank sheet of paper – can be applied to the pages of a magazine, without any prior processing. Here, too, different areas of the paper take on paint differently. The best thing is to try it out for yourself.

The procedure is actually very simple: apply paint to the gelli plate, transfer carefully on to the magazine page, allow the gelli plate to dry, apply the contrasting colour, and print. As the small details are important for this technique, the following pages give you a few tips on how to achieve good results (more) quickly.

We have used a special material for this technique: Tyvek® (see page 108), but the technique also works with paper or fabric that is not too coarse.

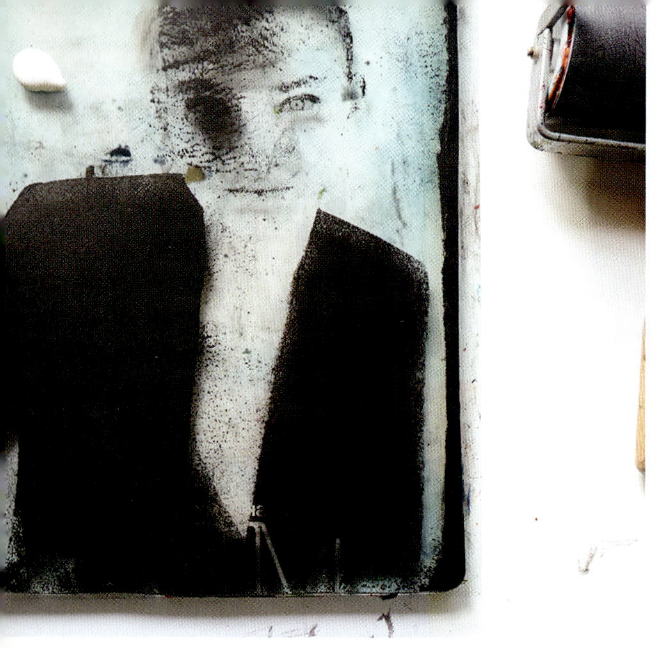

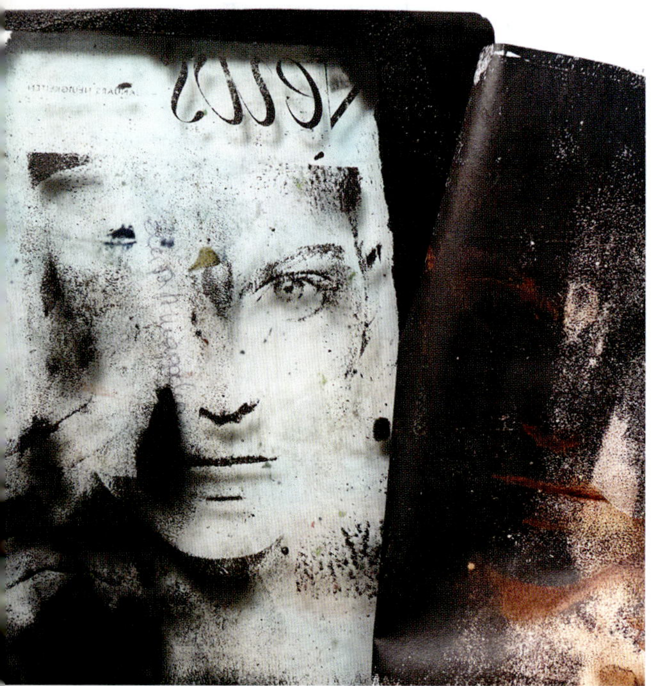

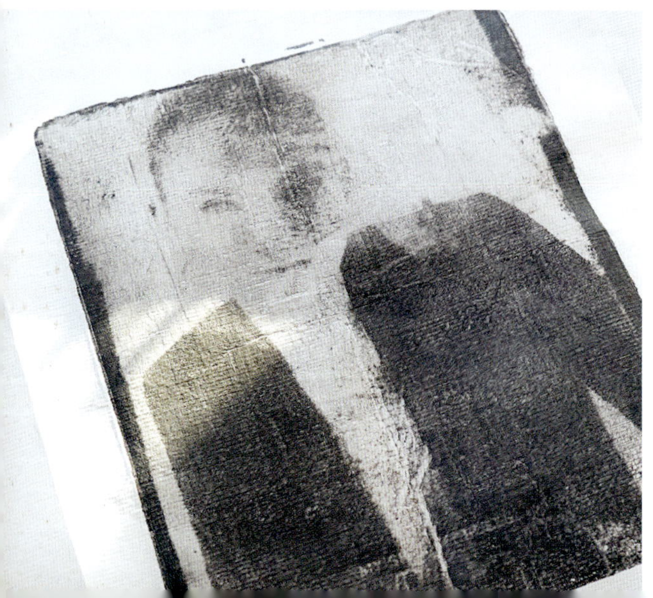

1. Prepare all the materials you want to use for printing. This technique must be carried out quickly.

   The results depend partly on the magazine pages used. Glossy magazines, such as fashion magazines, usually achieve good results, but we have also achieved good prints with interior design magazines or even magazines from a pharmacy. You may want to carry out a few tests before you find the right medium, the right colours and the right speed – keep at it and keep trying.

2. The choice of motif. Images with strong contrasts and simpler shapes are more suitable. Perfume adverts or advertisements for beauty products which only show a face in close-up, for example, are easier to make out than a landscape or a small-scale photograph in print.
   Fonts of all kinds are ideal for printing, so collect headlines, quotes or beautifully laid-out numbers.

3. Apply the acrylic paint evenly and fairly thinly to the gelli plate using a lino roller. Thick and highly pigmented paint (i.e. the more expensive artist's acrylic paint rather than the cheap tubes from the craft shop) definitely delivers better results here. You should use a fairly dark colour for the first layer of paint and a light contrasting colour for the second, otherwise your print will look like an old photograph negative.

4. As soon as the paint has been rolled on, place one of the prepared magazine pages on top and rub lightly over it.

   Laying it on for longer or rubbing harder will take paint away instead of adding it! The magic only takes about three seconds.

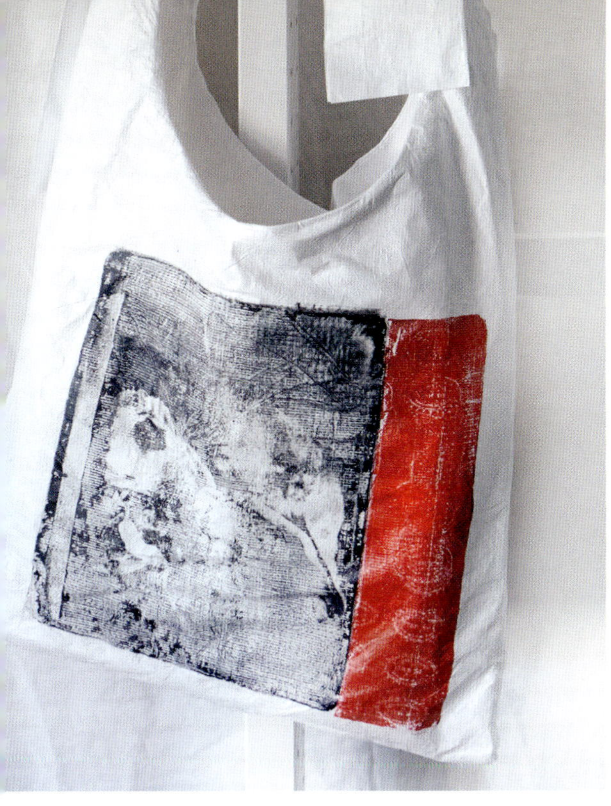

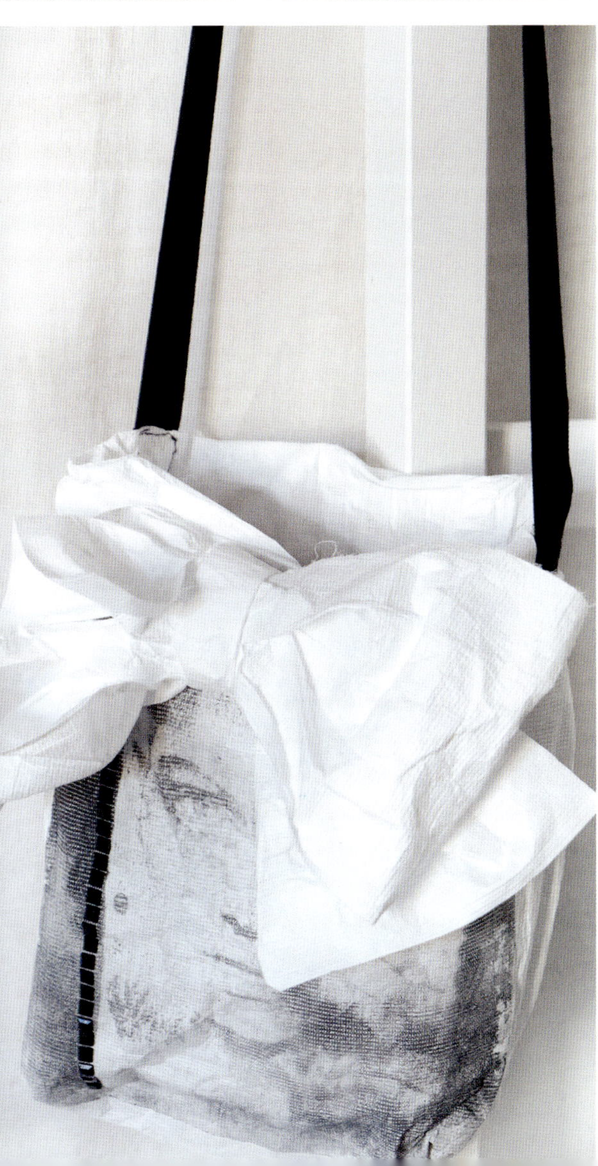

5. You can rub off the background completely or leave parts of it. This will result in less or more paint being applied to the individual areas.

6. Once you have carefully removed the magazine page, you should be able to see the image design on your gelli plate in simplified form.

7. Allow the paint to dry, as this time we are working with several layers of paint. It should dry quite quickly as we are using a thin layer of paint for this printing technique. We know from the grunge technique (see page 44) that dried paint residue on the gelli plate can be reactivated when fresh, wet paint is applied over it. This can be used in gelli printing specifically for multi-coloured prints – and that is what we are going to do here.

   Once the first layer of ink with the magazine print is completely dry, roll another thin layer of paint over it. The following should be observed:

   a. Use a contrasting colour. In other words, use a light colour if you have previously printed in a dark colour, or a colour in complementary contrast. You want the image from your magazine to be the main feature of the print, so emphasize it as much as possible.
   b. Normally you can apply paint directly to the gelli plate, and then roll it out with the brayer until the application is even. However, this is dangerous when using this technique in that the bottom layer of paint can dissolve or detach. It is therefore much better to properly roll out the second colour on a small glass plate or a plastic bag rather than the gelli plate (but don't use absorbent material like paper as it will absorb too much paint). When the paint is evenly distributed on the brayer, apply it quickly to the gelli plate. If you want it to be more colourful, you can mix additional colours in at this point, as long as the application follows quickly enough.

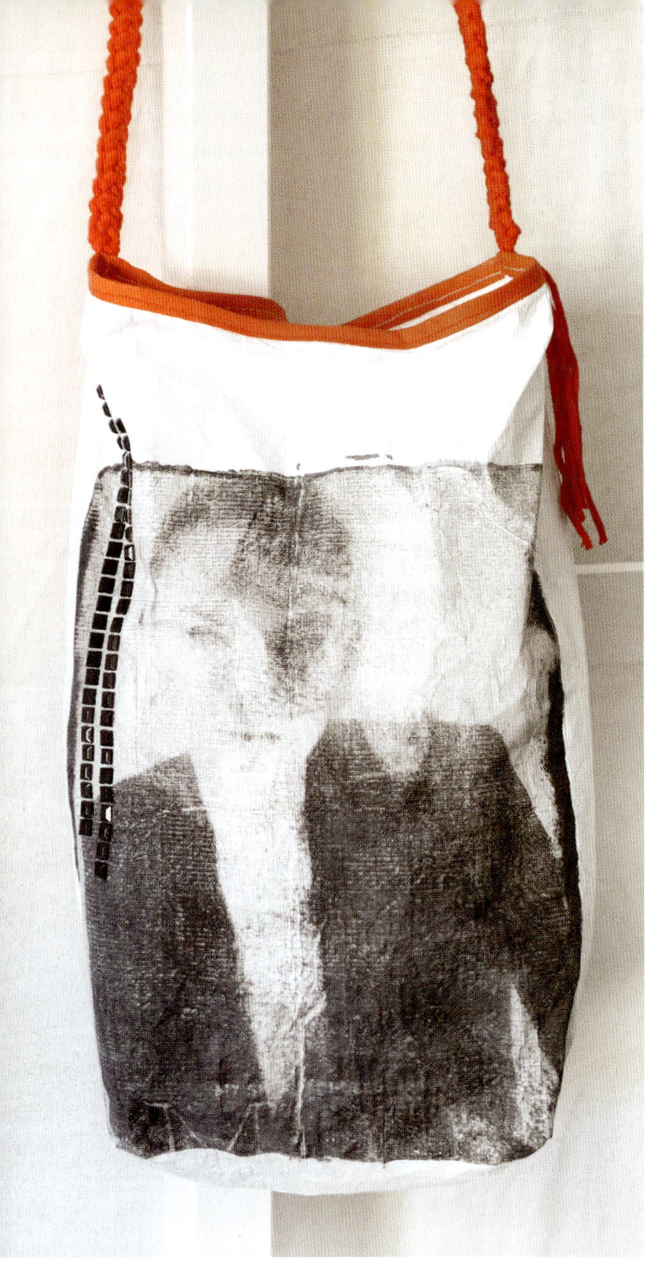

8. Now make the actual print by placing a sheet of paper on top and then rubbing firmly, for instance with a spoon.

The whole process is easier than it sounds. Once you get the hang of it, this technique can become almost addictive. As mentioned, a lot depends on the magazine page and on the paint, so you may get better results with your materials using other approaches. Just try it out and don't get discouraged!

One final tip to finish. If you roll out the paint very thinly on the first application, it may appear translucent in the print. For more contrast and opaque prints of the magazine pages, here's a trick: roll over the whole gelli plate with a thin layer of paint and let it dry. Don't place a magazine page over it yet! Then, roll on another thin coat in the same colour and proceed as previously described. This second paint application activates the first but does not alter the printing properties (as a single, thick paint application would). This way, you print two thin layers overlapping each other with an almost opaque coverage.

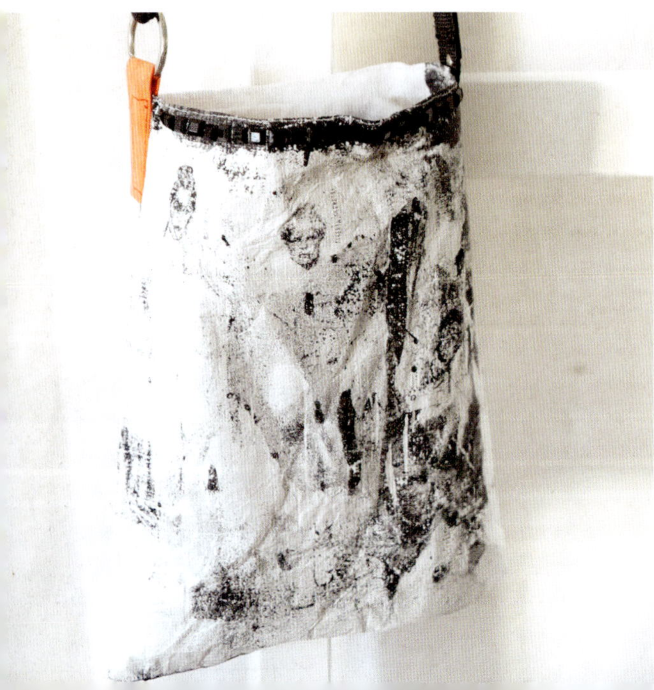

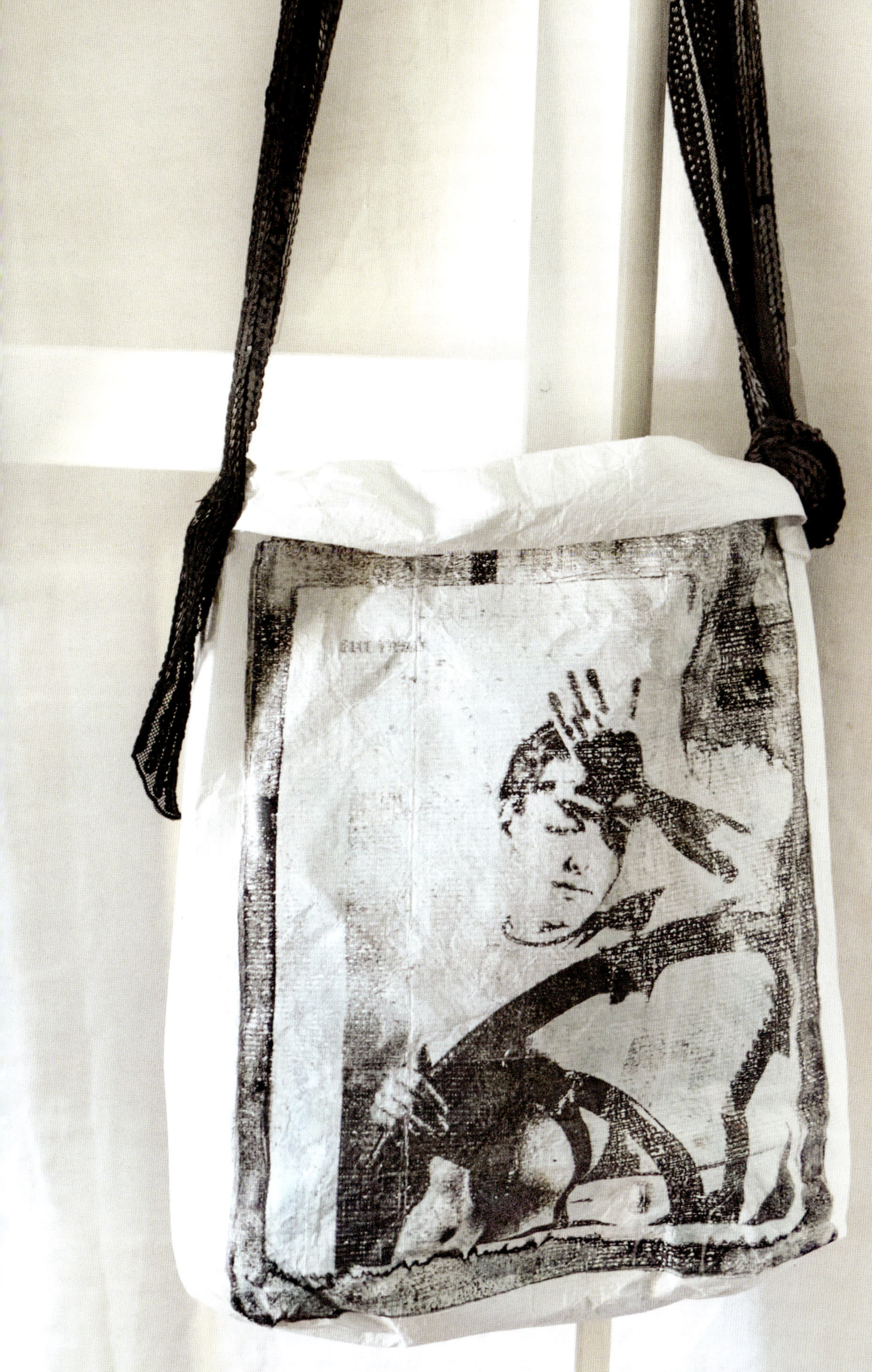

Watercolours

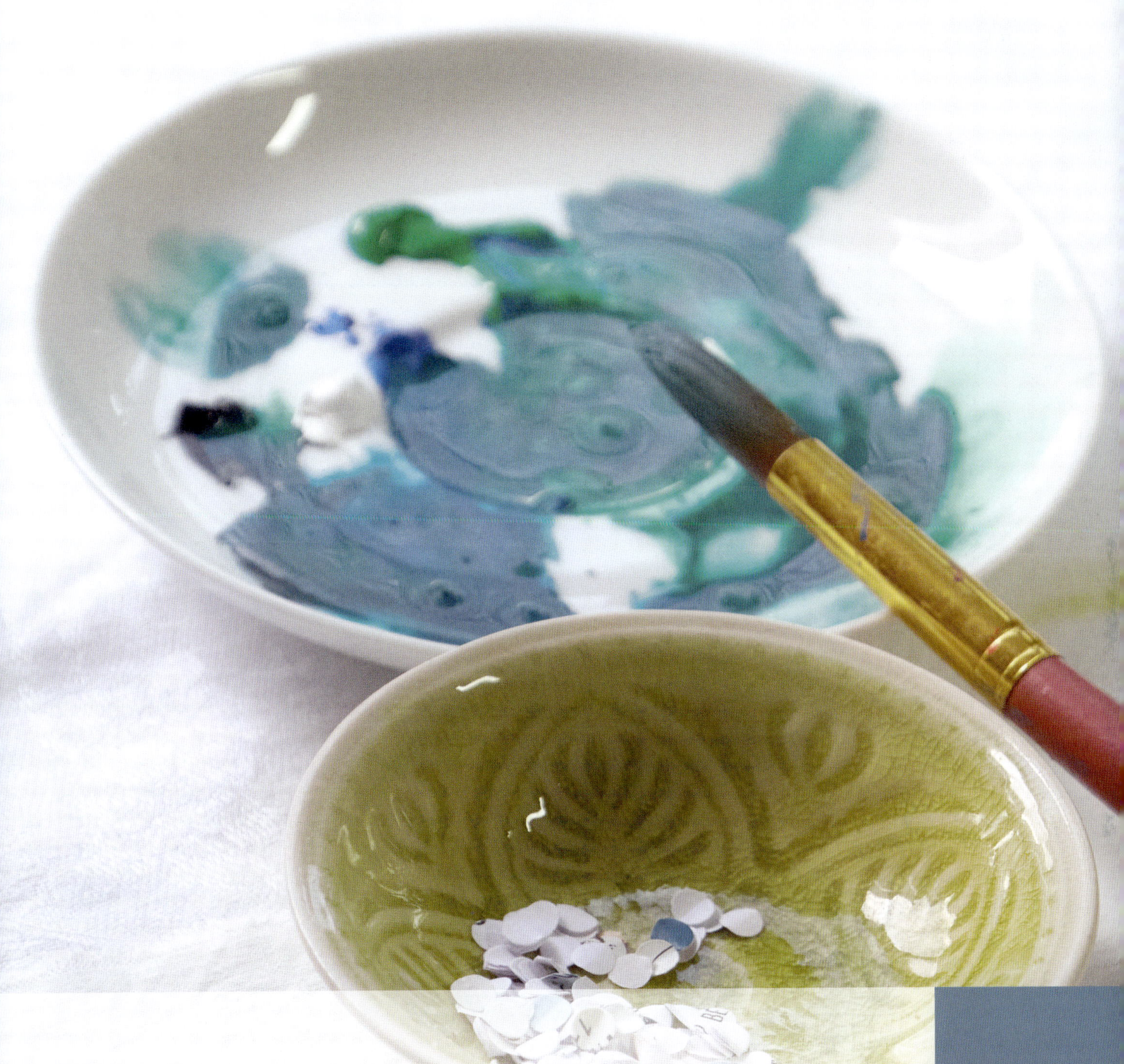

Experimenting with paints

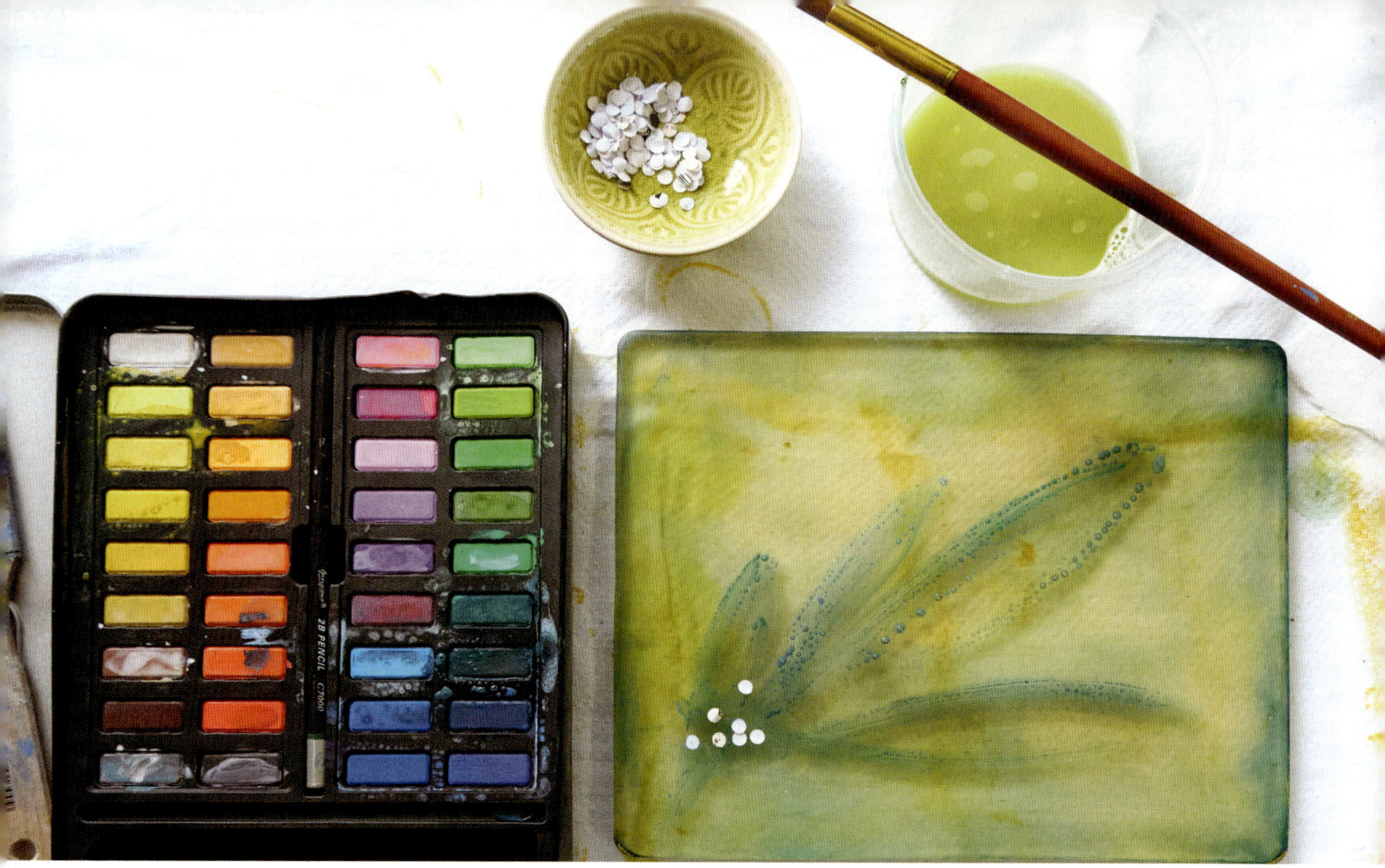

USING WATERCOLOURS

You can use virtually any kind of paint on a gelli plate, from ink pads and acrylic markers to any type of paint in tubes or bottles. Try it out at least once and be amazed at the results. With most paints, it makes sense to let them dry once and then paint over them with a second layer, this time preferably with acrylic paint.

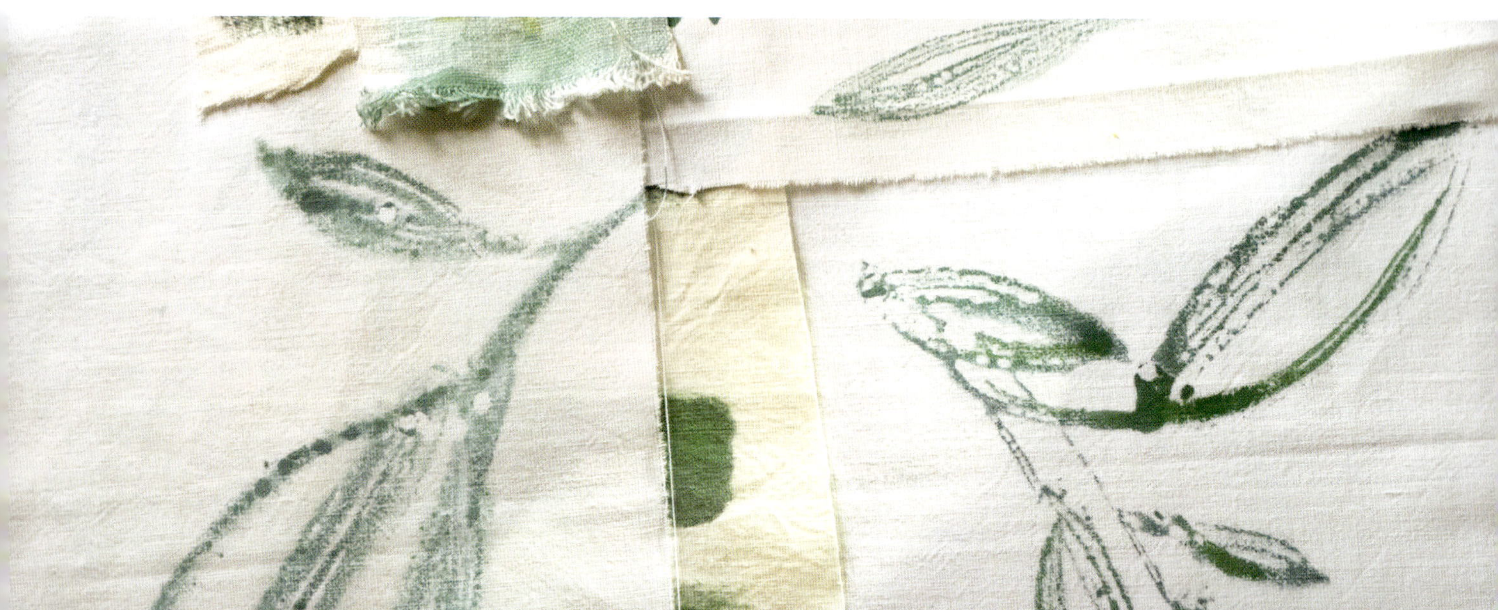

One special case is watercolour. As already mentioned, gelli plates are slightly water-repellent. You apply the paint, and it begins to bead up and shrink into areas that change the original paint application. This also happens with over-diluted acrylic paint, but more often with water-based paints. Nevertheless, it is worth a try because you can create interesting effects that you might like to use for mixed-media projects.

There are really only two tips for working with watercolours: stir a lot of pigment or paint into the water and work quickly! A tiny amount of washing-up liquid may help to reduce beading.

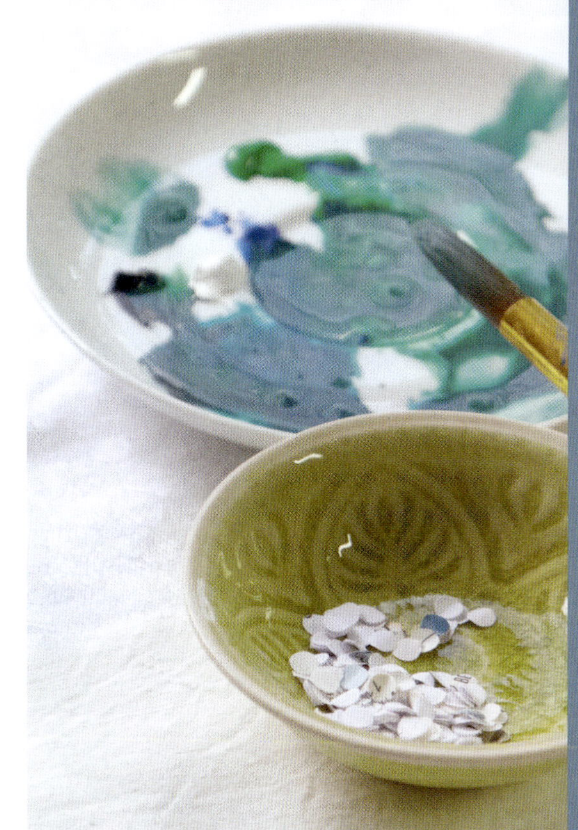

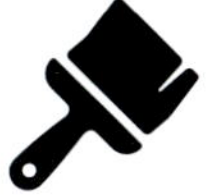

Try it out:

Watercolours cannot be fixed to fabric, so the printed item will not be able to be washed afterwards; and too much water on paper can make it curl up. However, watercolour works wonderfully for sketchbooks or journals. As an additional effect, we have used small paper circles from a hole punch to depict flowers or seeds – simply place them on the gelli plate before printing and you will get lovely white cut-outs as shown in the picture on the right. White accents always make the surrounding colours glow!

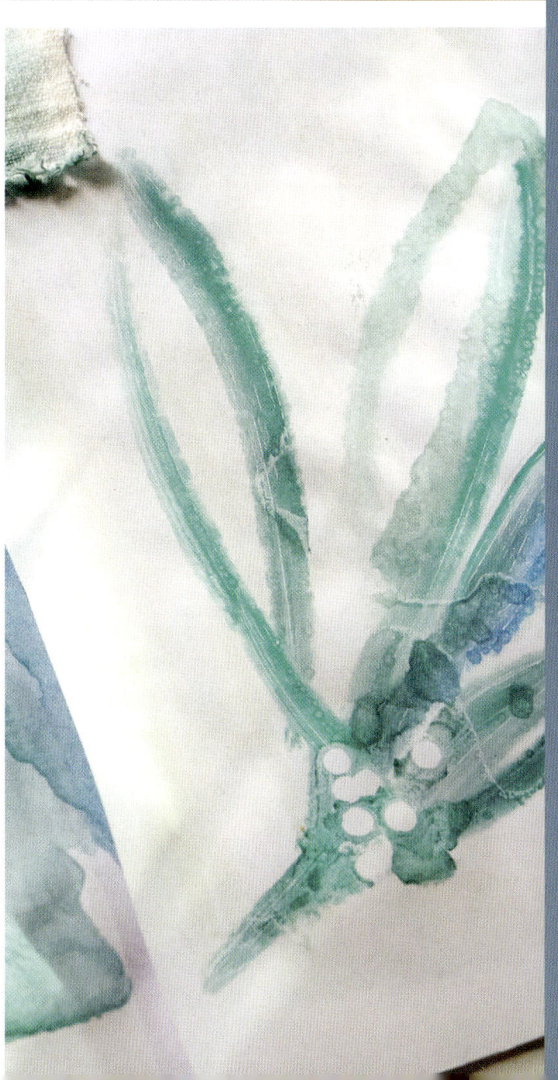

Freestyle

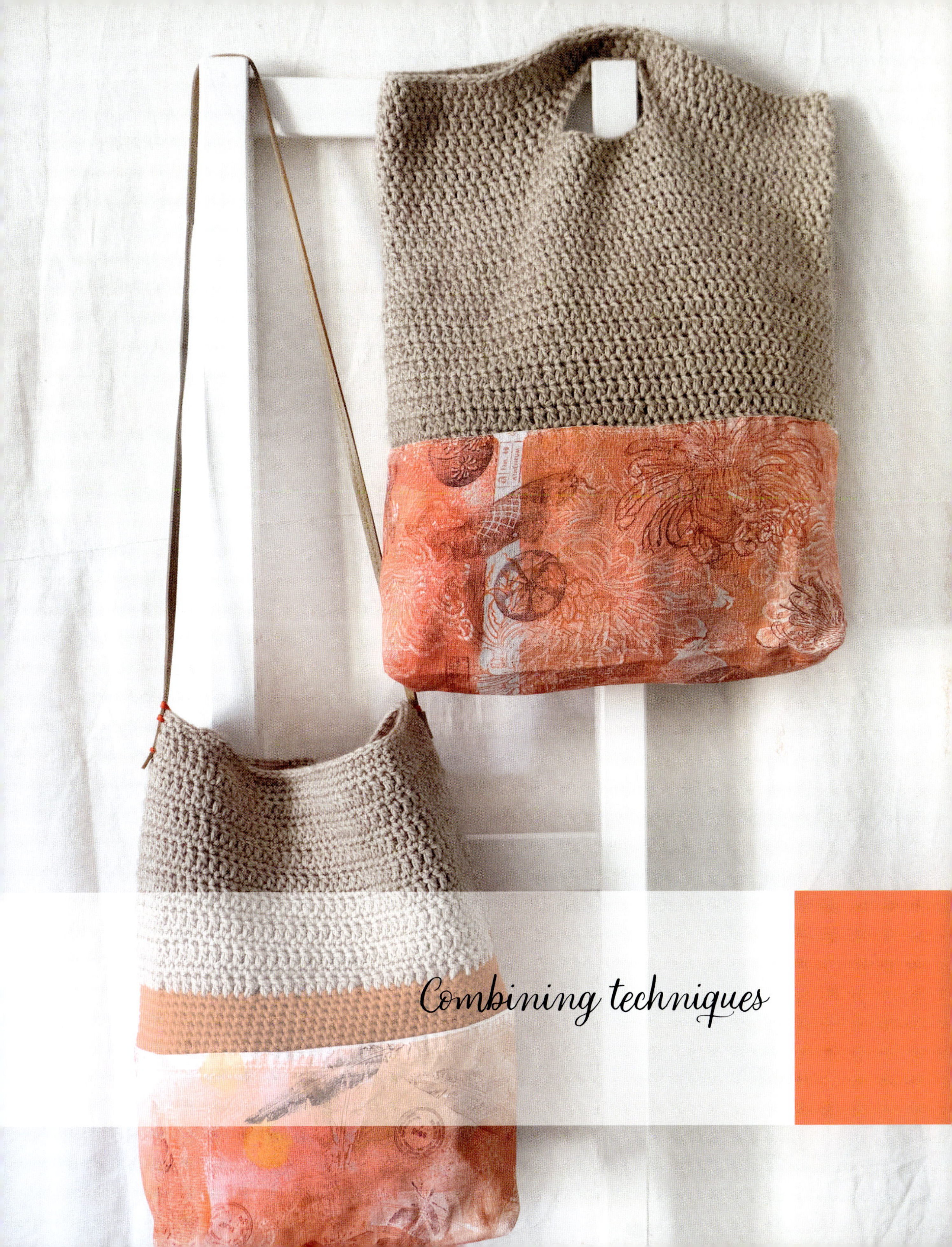

Combining techniques

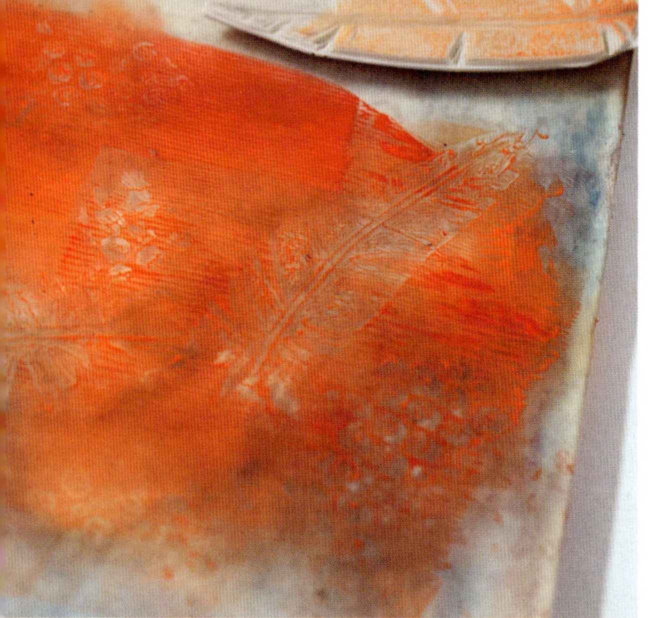

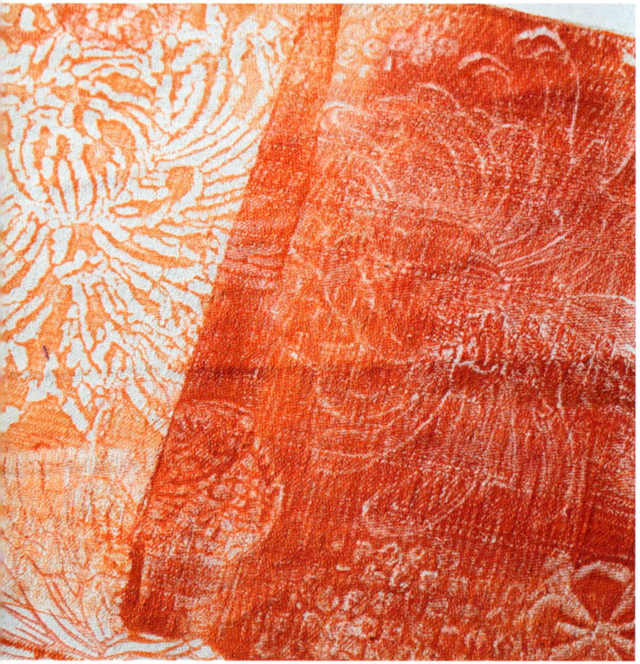

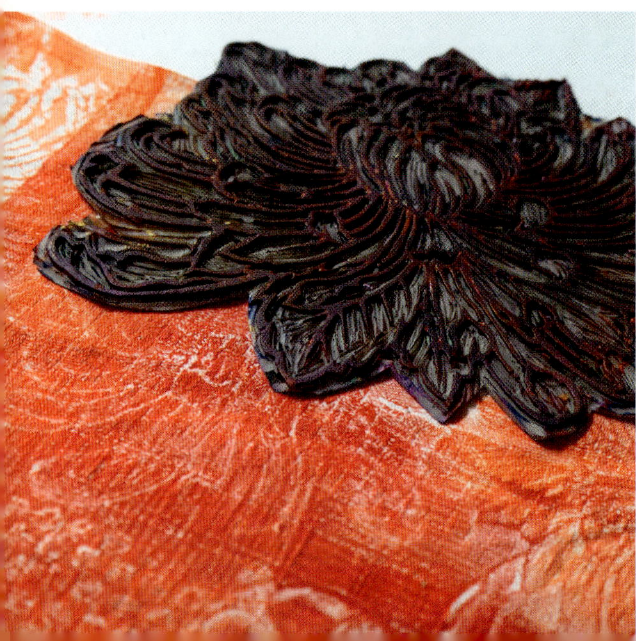

PRINTING FREESTYLE PATTERNS

This pattern looks elaborate, but is easy to make using a combination of techniques we already know.

1. First, choose your colour combination: a lighter colour (in our case, cherry red) and a contrasting colour from the same palette (here, dark red).

   All other colour shades are created by printing with a slight transparency. This results partly from the paint application on the gelli plate: the thinner, the more transparent the paint. At the same time, we have printed on a coarser fabric, which does not absorb the paint as evenly as thinner fabric or paper. Additional effects can be created if you press more or less firmly in some places during printing.

2. As can be seen in the picture above left, with this printing technique the paint is not distributed over the entire gelli plate. If we let it run out at the sides, the print will not have defined edges. However, we can work just as well with clear edges and, for example, leave white spaces in between. Try out what you like best.

3. Now we stamp! If we press the stamp firmly onto the gelli plate, we remove all the paint we already applied there; the motif will appear white afterwards. If you want to use the same motif several times, print it on a piece of paper between uses so that you are always working with a paint-free stamp. Only then will you get really white spaces and textures. If you take a stamp and press it repeatedly onto the gelli plate without cleaning it in between, you will get less sharply defined patterns. This is because as long as paint is still adhering to the stamp, it can only take up a small amount of new paint. The result is more of a tone-on-tone print

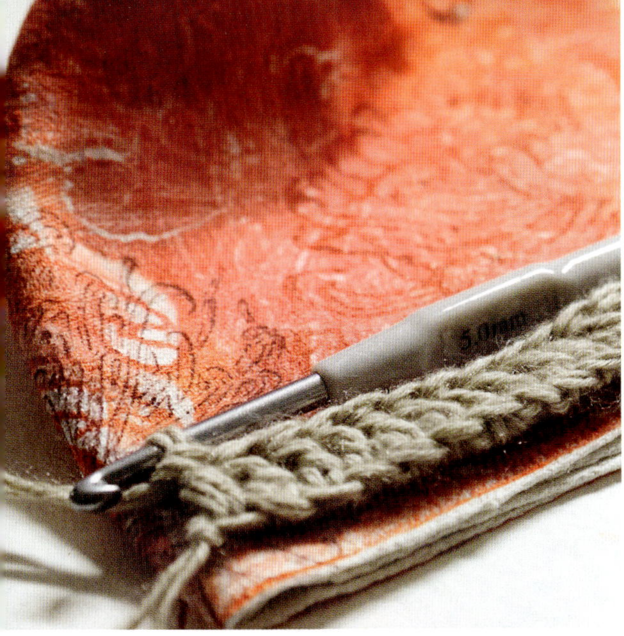

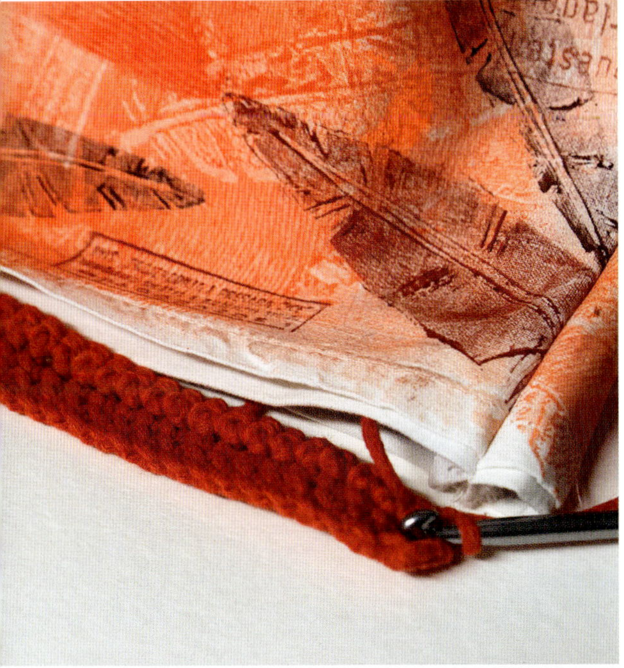

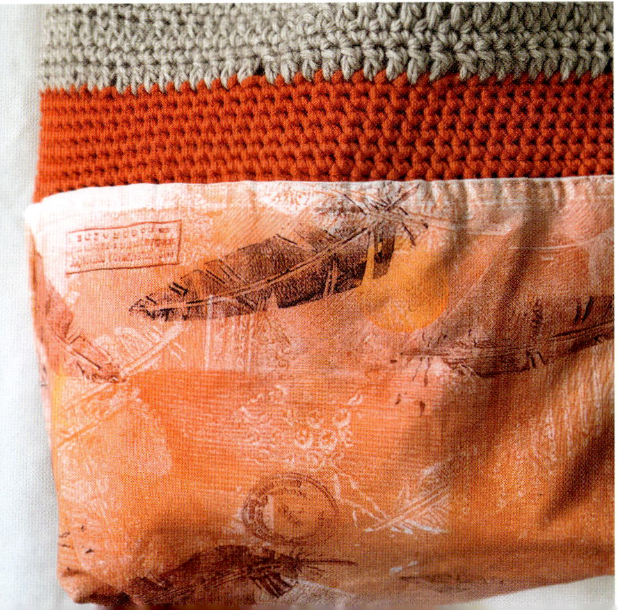

with a few white flashes (these can be deliberately created or intensified, not only by placing the stamp on the plate, but also by slightly dragging or smudging it). We have done this here with the background patterns to create a variety of colour and shape gradation.

4. In this way – with overlapping areas – we print the entire surface that we want to fill. You can decide how dense you want the colour and pattern by printing single or multiple layers. You can try to achieve a more even application of paint, or you can print in a colourful, high-contrast mix. See what works and what you like best.

5. To crown it all, use the dark colour to create accents. When doing this, stamp your motifs as opaquely as possible – for example with a saturated colour application. The greater the contrast between light and dark, the more the motifs will stand out. The weaker the contrast, the more uniform the finished print.

So, in short: print the surface slightly transparently with the lighter colour. Motifs that are not printed and remain white stand out more. Shape the area by printing on top of it until you achieve the desired effect. Finally, create accents with the darker contrasting colour.

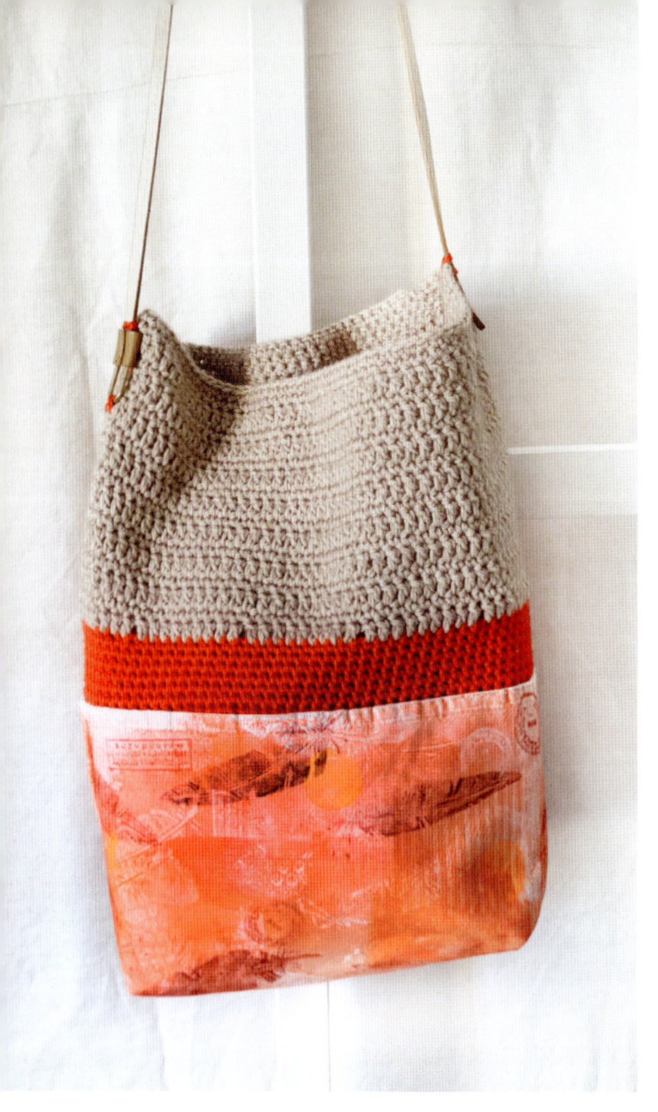

COMBINING WITH OTHER MATERIALS

In the frenzy of the endless variations of colours, shapes and textures that gelli printing makes possible, it is easy to forget another option: combining it with other materials.

You can print and stick on book pages or printed paper (see also the projects on pages 113 and 124). If you work with fabric, you can combine your own printed fabrics with shop-bought ones, spice them up with coloured ribbons and leather – old belts make wonderful straps for bags – or you can add crocheted or knitted pieces, as shown in the pictures here. Instructions for almost all the techniques are available online. Perhaps you will also discover another new hobby along the way – or rediscover skills that you had almost forgotten.

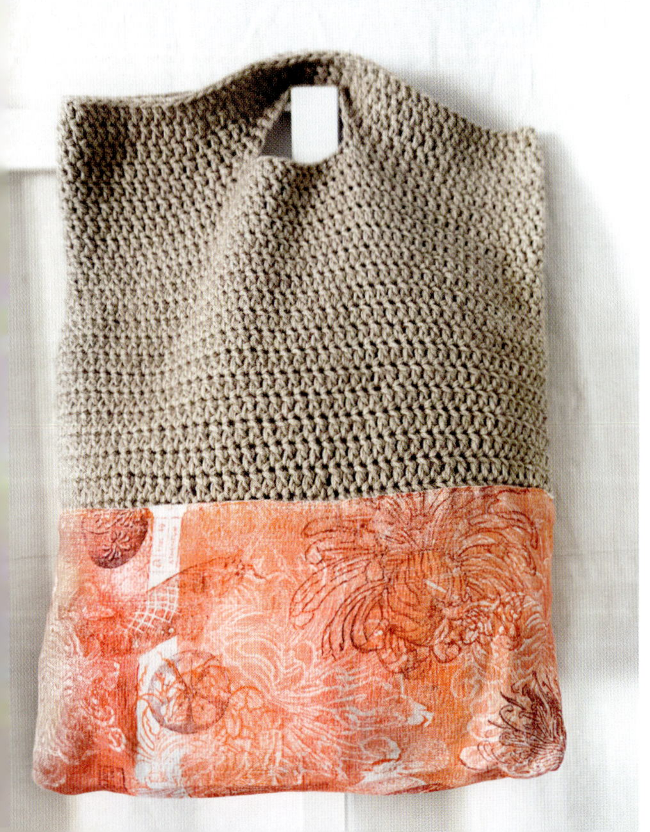

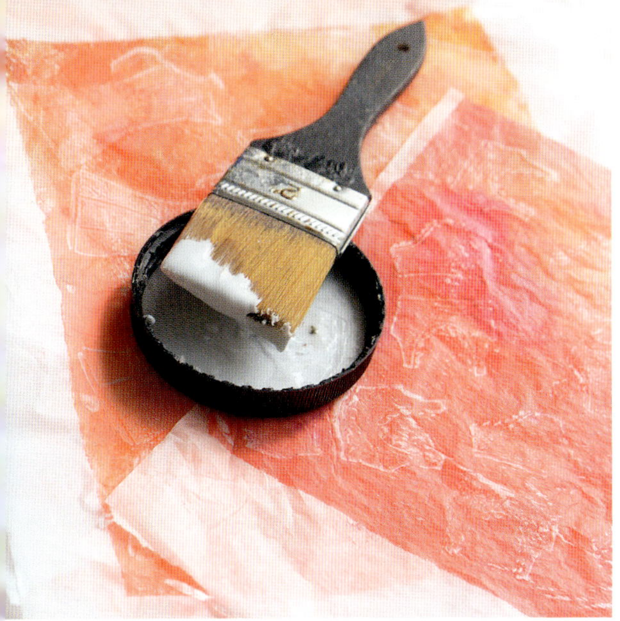

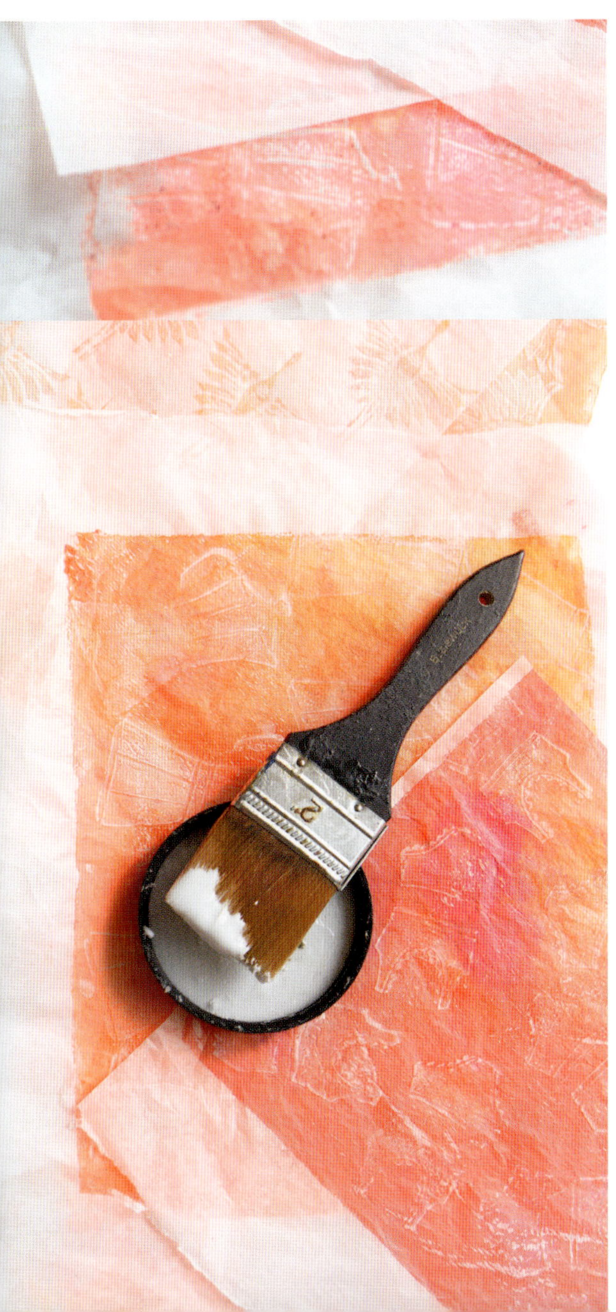

PRINTING ON TISSUE PAPER

If you've already gained some practice and experience with your gelli plate and are perhaps looking for a little challenge: try printing on tissue paper!

As tissue paper is very thin and tears easily, printing on it therefore requires a little finesse. Don't apply the paint too thickly, and the paper should only be pressed on briefly and then quickly (and carefully) peeled off.

While it is difficult to print on, working with tissue paper can have great advantages: as the tissue paper is so thin, it is very easy to cover objects with it. It is not bulky and can even be stuck over slightly curved shapes. It is best to coat the object with a little diluted wallpaper paste, bookbinding glue or craft glue, and then press the tissue paper onto it. If necessary, cover with another layer of glue or a clear varnish to finish. You will find more instructions for working with tissue paper on page 117.

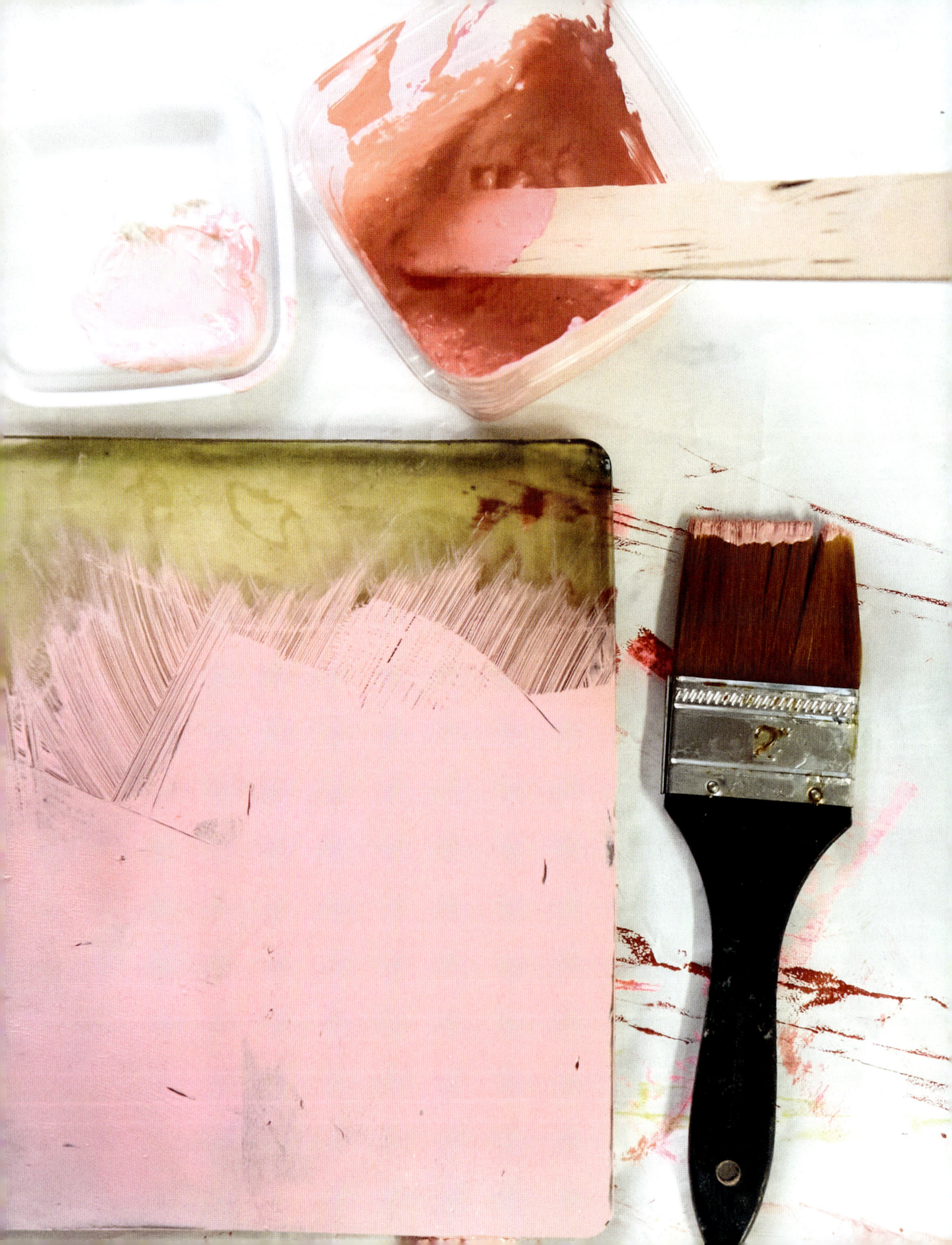
2"

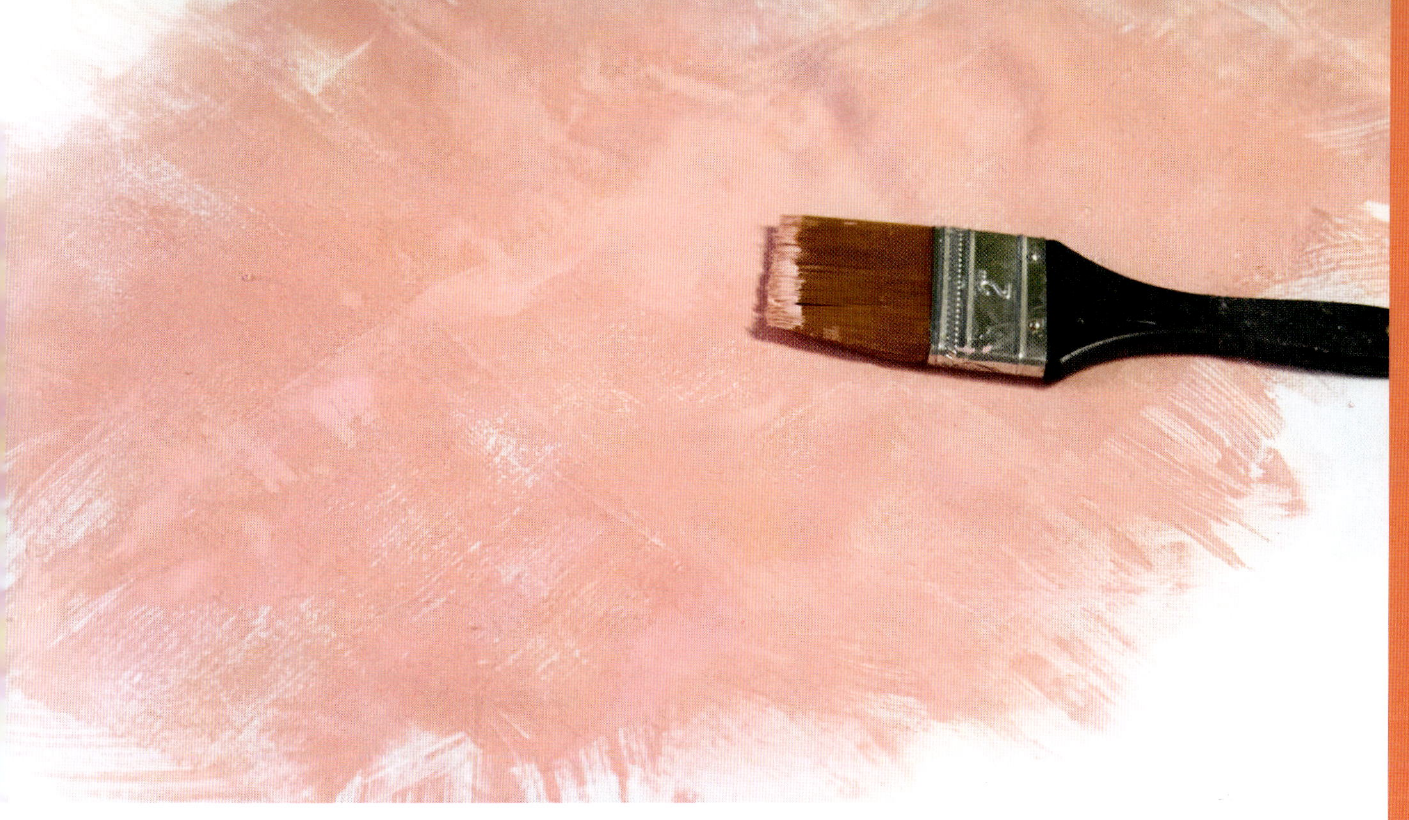

LARGE AND SPLIT PRINTS

Gelli plates have one limitation: their size. People tend to scale their projects accordingly, but let's think a little more broadly and on a larger scale here. We can, of course, make split designs – by joining several prints next to each other – which together results in a larger print.

We are now printing four areas next to each other, roughly the size of four gelli plates. Of course, this can be extended to six or nine or more plates. For this technique, it is better to use the gelli plate as a large stamp – so we do not place the paper or fabric onto the gelli plate as usual, but the gelli plate onto the fabric. As it is transparent, you can see the edge exactly and position the prints accurately.

If you are working with fabric, you can carefully fold it around the gelli plate, turn the gelli plate over, and spread the fabric out again. Rub it down as usual with your hands, a spoon or a bone folder. Paper sticks more easily to the paint, so you don't need to wrap it or fix it, just be quick when turning it over.

There are various ways to split designs for printing, as demonstrated in the following two projects.

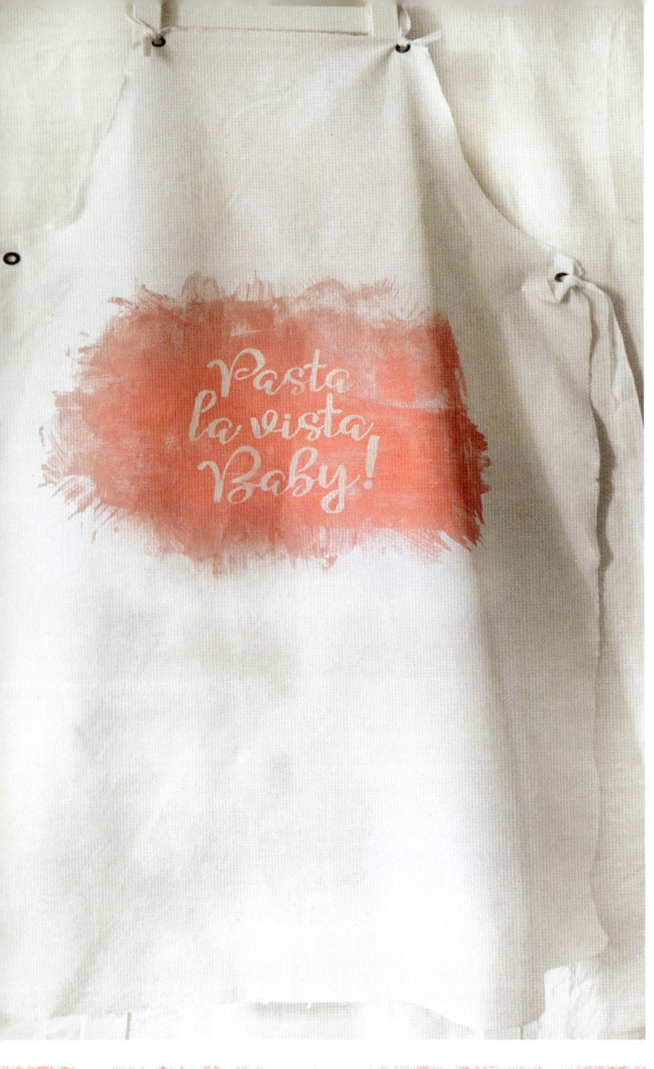

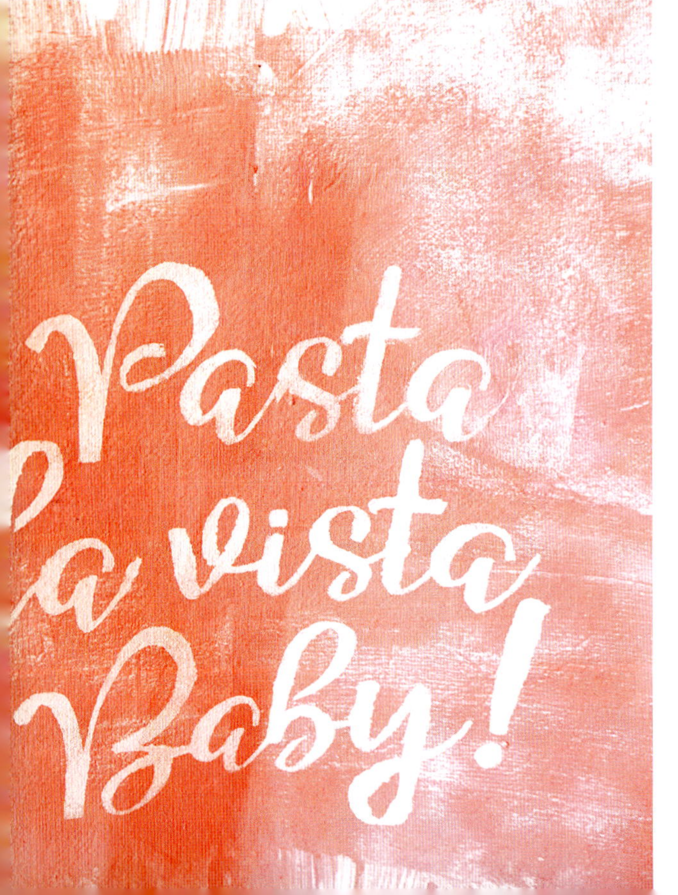

PRINTED APRONS

For our pink apron, we kept the background design simple; the brushstrokes create a lively surface for the text. You can find the text as a template on page 143.

We cut out this template by hand. If you have a plotter, it is even easier to make stencils. It is worth the effort to cut the lettering from foil, because this apron is so easy to make that you will surely be making more than one!

1. Cut a piece of fabric slightly larger than the template on page 137. Roughly measure the desired shoulder width and length of the apron, and transfer the outline freehand to your fabric piece folded lengthways in the centre. If you wish to finish the seams of the apron, you should cut them with a seam allowance. You can, however, make an apron yourself without sewing: if you cut the fabric with pinking shears, you will prevent fraying even without hemming.

   You can attach the ribbons for the neck and for tying the apron by punching eyelets and knotting the ribbons on. Alternatively, you can sew them on with a few stitches (for example, stitching back and forth a few times) by hand or on a sewing machine. The whole apron can look a little handmade and simple. You can also buy ready-made aprons in craft shops to print onto.

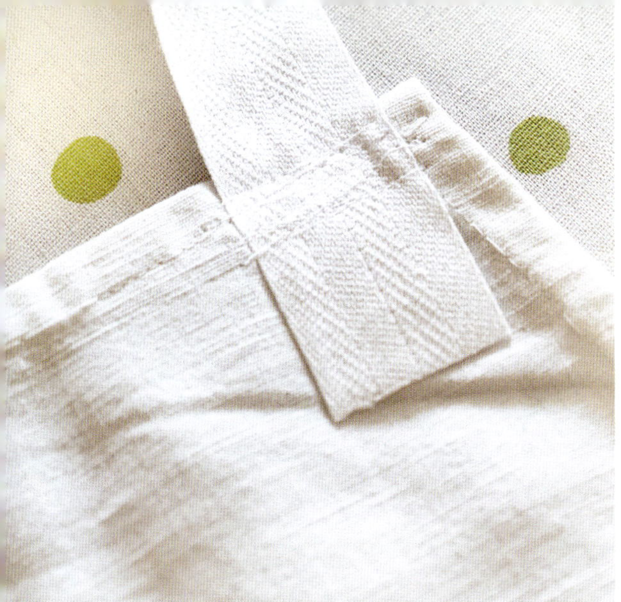

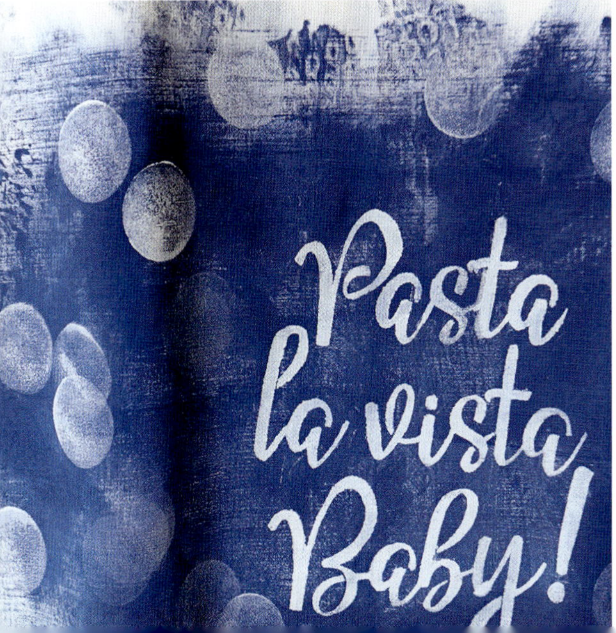

2. For our blue apron, we split the prints exactly as described on page 81. However, we added texture to the edges of the coloured surface: we used bubble wrap and a round piece of foam (packing material) to remove paint at the edges and soften the transition into the white.

3. To create a more airy transition to the white background, we then used slightly thinned fabric paint and a piece of foam to imprint some large, transparent white dots. However, nobody says that the joins have to be invisible! Gelli printing thrives on spontaneity and experimentation.

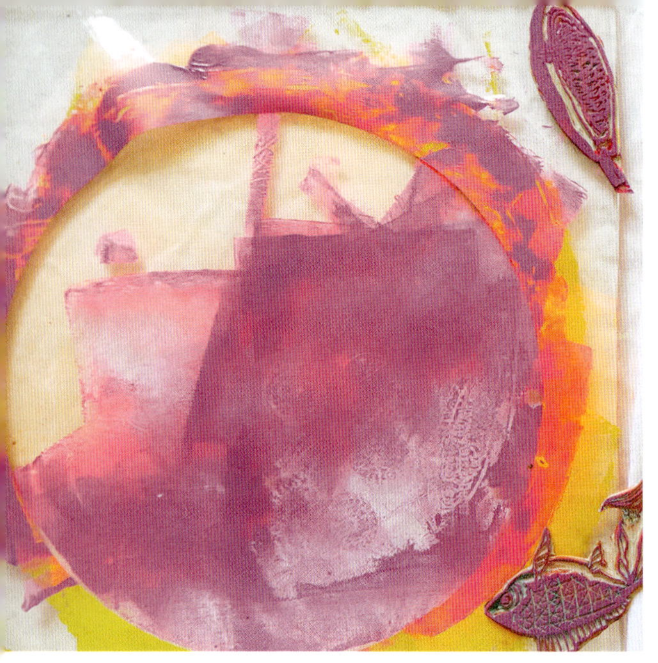

PRINTING MANDALAS

When you think of gelli plates, you automatically think of them as rectangular, even though they are now available in other shapes. Let's print some mandalas using round gelli plates! There are different variations, but ultimately, they are all based on printing a circle on a rectangular gelli plate using stencils.

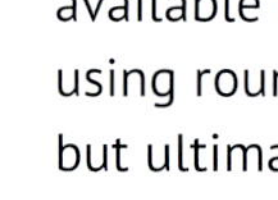

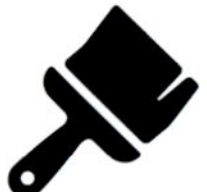

Try it out:

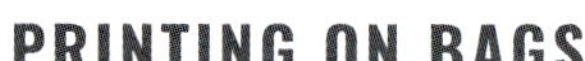

PRINTING ON BAGS

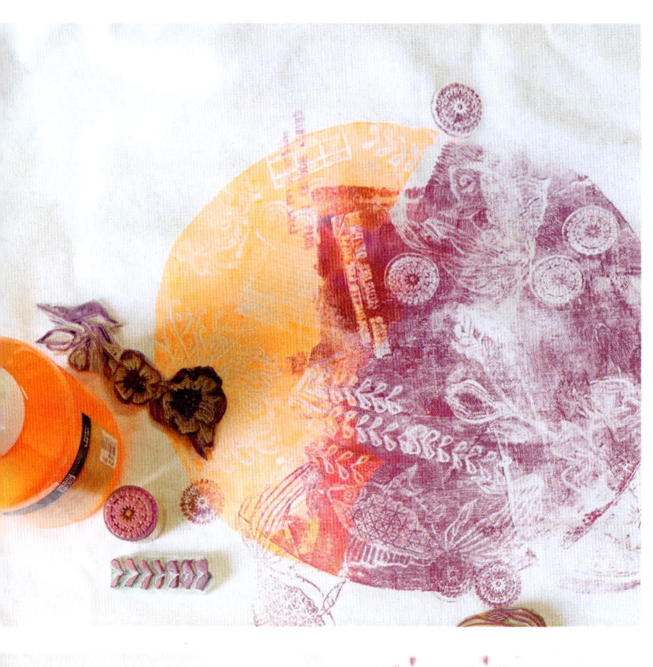

The simplest option is using a stencil. Round stencils are easy to make by running a cutter or sharp knife around a plate or other round object of the right size. You can cut the stencil out of paper or thin card. Printing mandalas is so much fun that it's worth having a sheet of them, which can be used again and again. This could be made from packaging material or a spare piece of card.

Cut the template to the exact size of the gelli plate to make it easier to print several colours.

We have used two complementary colours for the bag: a bright neon orange and a darker purple. The border between the two colours can either be designed as a clean line or a smoother transition. To break up the motif, we have also allowed individual stamp shapes to protrude over the edge.

If you start with a more or less round motif in the centre and then work repetitions outwards, you will always end up with a kind of mandala shape. We have designed it very freely in this version.

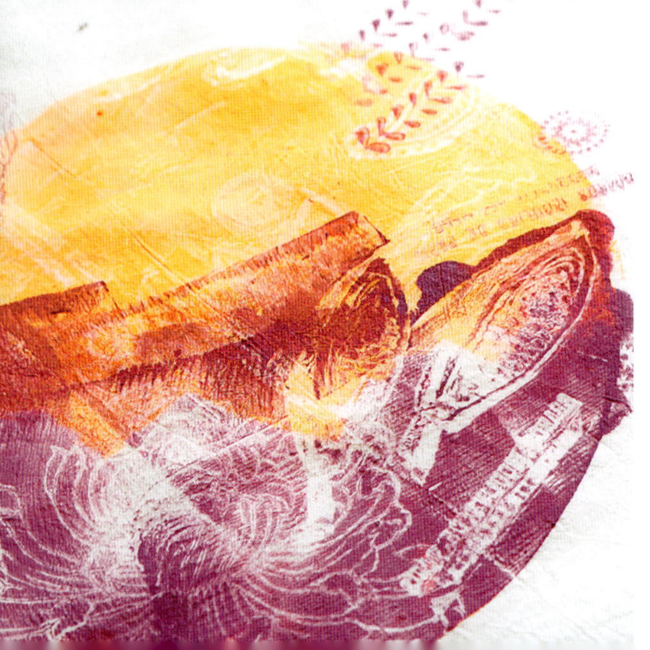

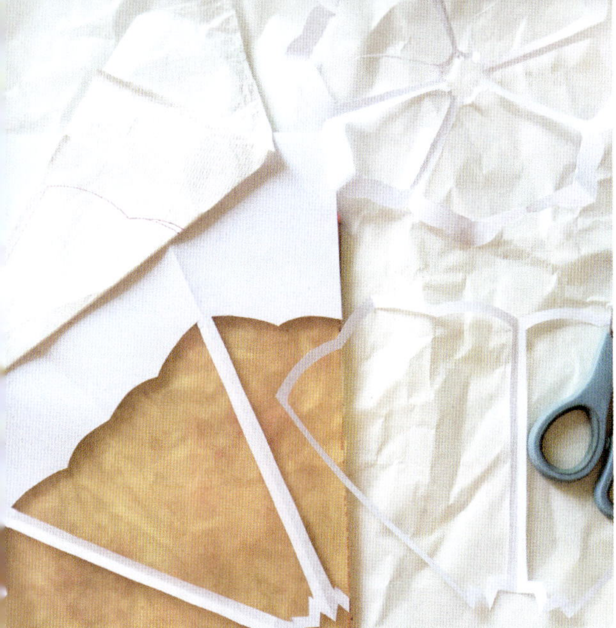

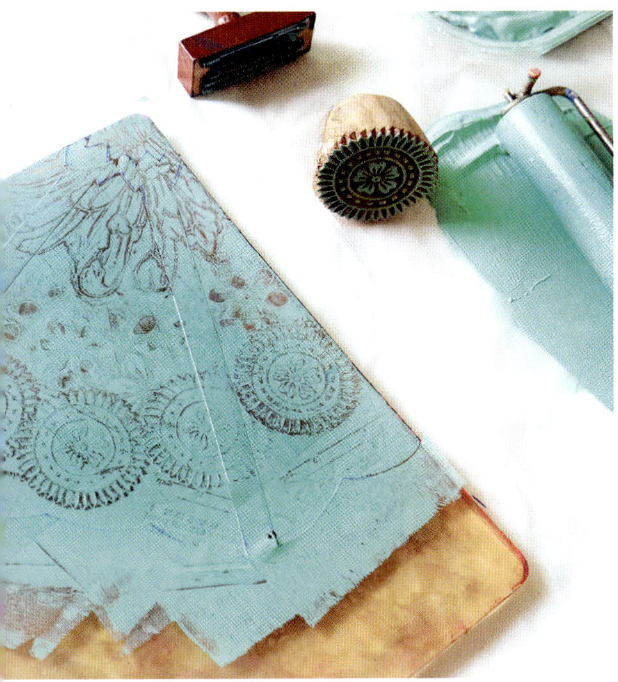

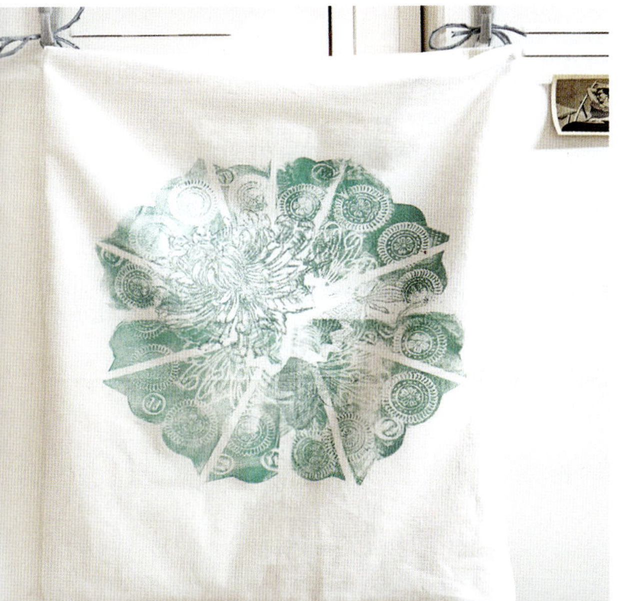

LAUNDRY BAG

If you want to print clearly defined mandala-like shapes, cut out a slightly more complex stencil. We have cut the round stencil into quarters. This reduces the cutting required, and we can print a motif four times as large. You just have to be a little more careful when printing.

Do you remember paper stars? You probably cut them out as a child. You can use the same principle to create a paper template. A square piece of paper is folded in half, and half again, and then diagonally towards the centre. For a very intricate template, you can fold it once more, but for this the paper needs to be very thin. We don't cut out a whole star, but only a quarter, as shown in the picture at the top left.

1. Depending on which of the folded sides you cut from, you will get different results: one with bars on the outer edge of the template and one without. Try it out – it only takes a few minutes each time. We need the version without bars on the edge, as we are putting the four prints together here.

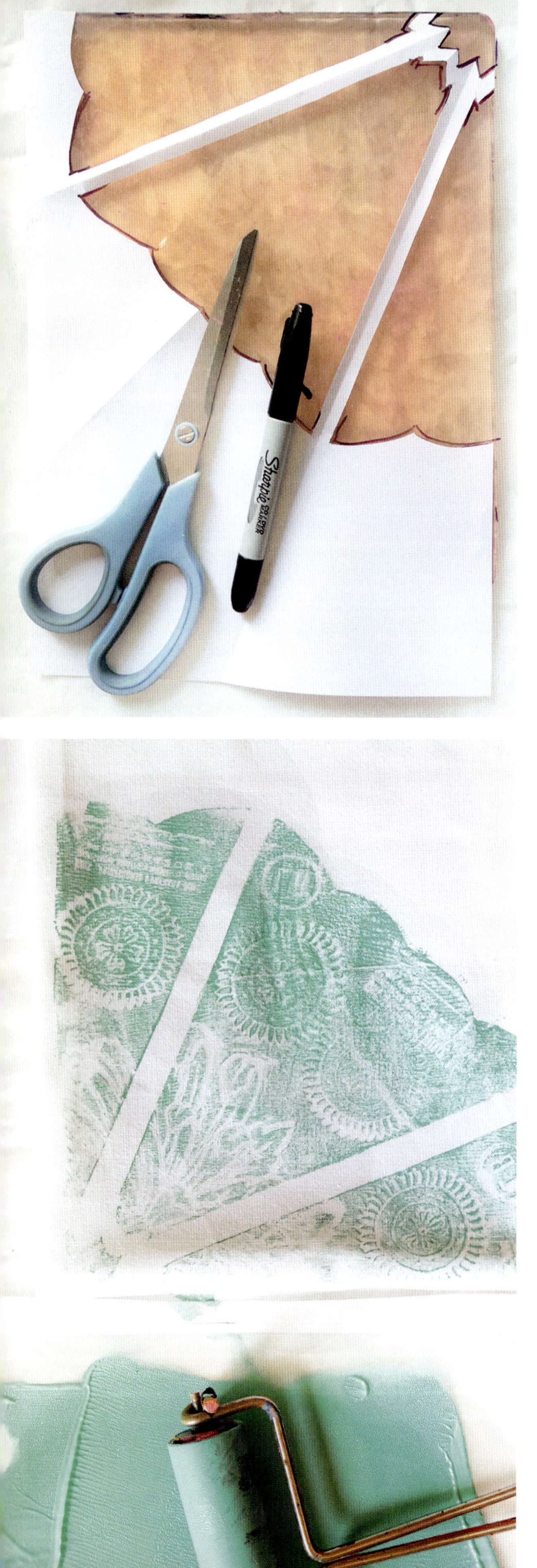

2. Because we want to print four times, we either have to cut four identical paper stencils or transfer our paper stencil on to a film. We can do this easily by marking the lines with a pencil and then tracing the outlines with a ruler and cutting them out (see picture on the left).

We print four times with this film. Place the film on the gelli plate, roll on the paint, and the pattern is pressed in. Remove the film just before you print the paint onto the fabric; if you remove it before imprinting the pattern, you may smudge the edge. If paint ends up in the areas that will later be white, you can carefully remove it with a cotton bud.

As we do not have any bars on the edge of the stencil, we do not have to work as precisely. The bars between sections are created by leaving a small gap on the fabric.

The easiest way to print is to fold and lay out the fabric before you start applying the paint. Hold the fabric over your gelli plate and check how you need to position the joins.

This all sounds more complicated than it is. Essentially, you have a stencil that you print four times, always turning the fabric at 90-degree angles.

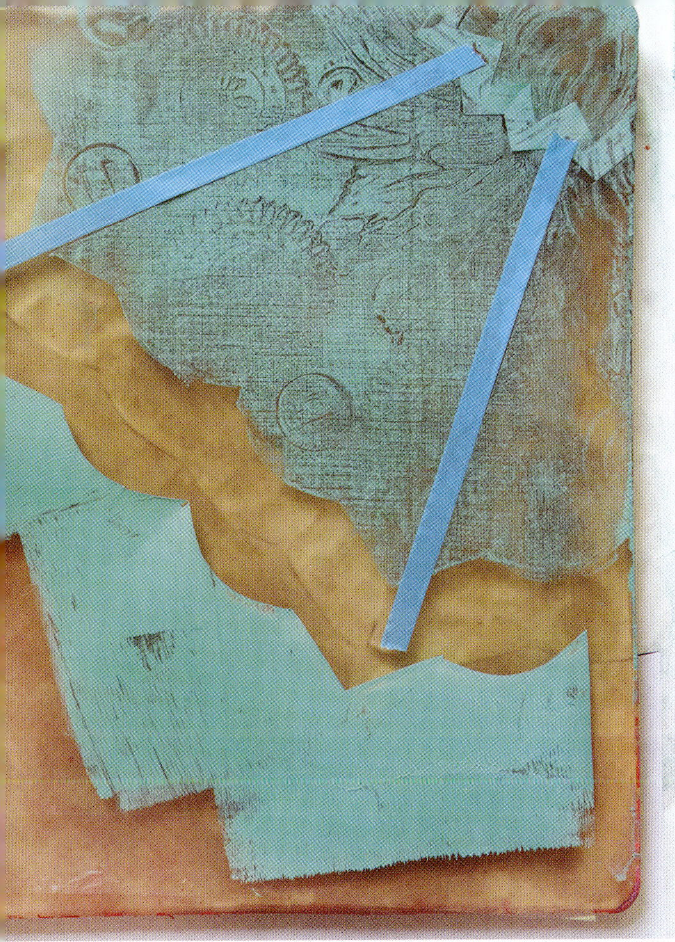

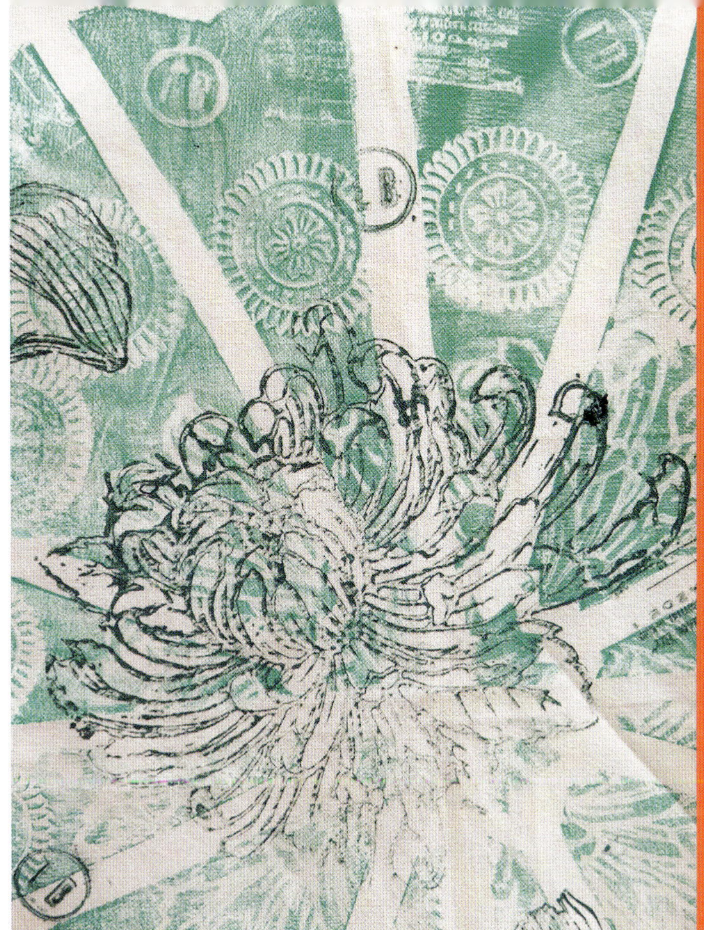

VARIATION

Another way to create a stencil is to cover the areas with narrow washi tape or adhesive tape. Then you only need the inner part of the 'star stencil' and an outer edge, as can be seen in the picture above left. Alternatively, you can also use the same circle template you made for the bag project on page 84.

For the laundry bag, we printed the actual mandala in a lighter mint green and then printed individual motifs over it using a darker green (black added to the original colour).

The laundry bag itself is basically sewn like a large pillowcase (which means you can also repurpose old pillowcases). Attach two ribbons to the top edge and knot.

A sketch of the laundry bag can be found bottom left on page 134.

2

From print to design

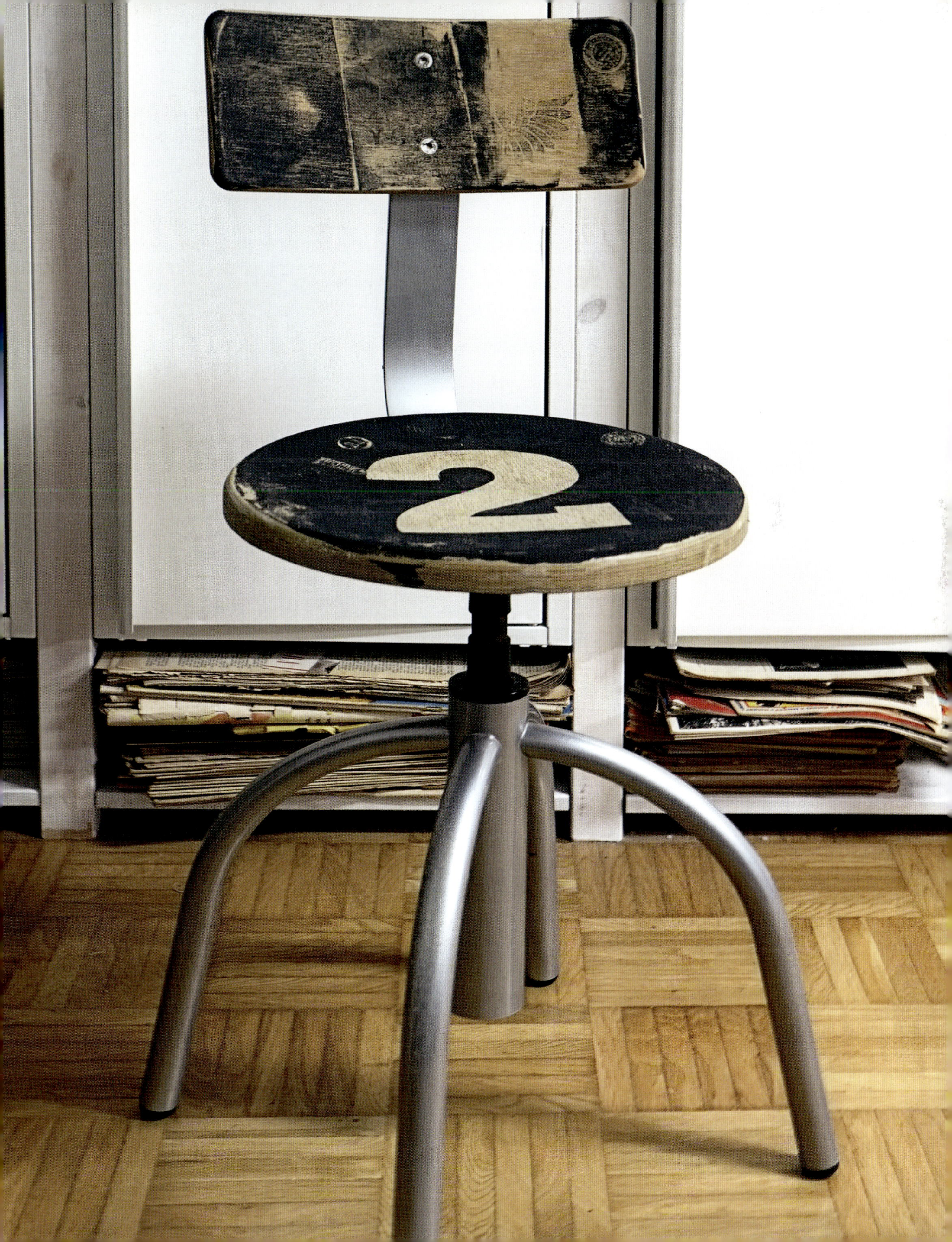

A WHOLE NEW WORLD OF GELLI PRINTING

The great strength and fascination of gelli printing lies in its experimental approach and in the fact that you could print for days with little preparation and material. If you search online for 'gelli print', you will find countless videos showing exactly that: stacks and stacks of printed, colourful paper. We have entered into a kind of 'printing frenzy' ourselves often enough; we know this effect from our own experience.

At some point, we asked ourselves what else might be possible, and we discovered a whole new world! Gelli printing enables professional printing with professional colours on paper, fabric and a variety of other surfaces. Anything small can be printed off the gelli plate – we even tried it with Easter eggs (although less curved surfaces are easier to print on). For larger objects, you can use gelli plates like giant stamps and press them on; as they are transparent, positioning is no problem.

We have developed projects for this book that go beyond the experimental approach. There's nothing wrong with experimental printing, it's great fun – and we still do it today – but we also plan and create specifically. This is where design begins: developing the concept for a gelli print and then bringing it to life.

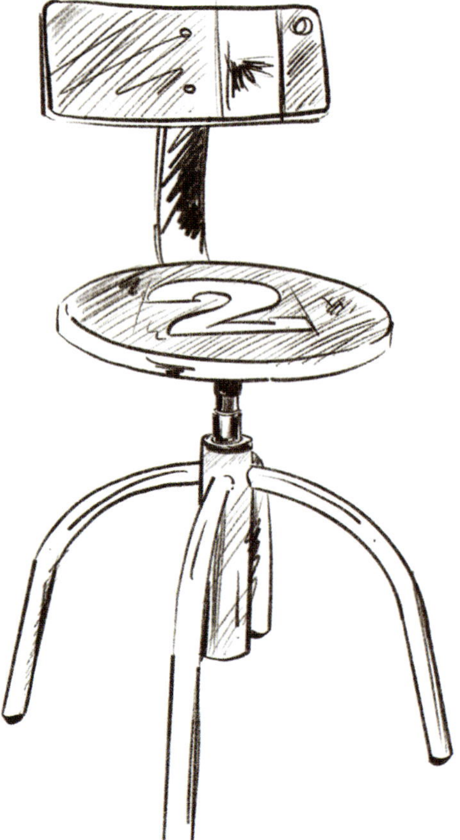

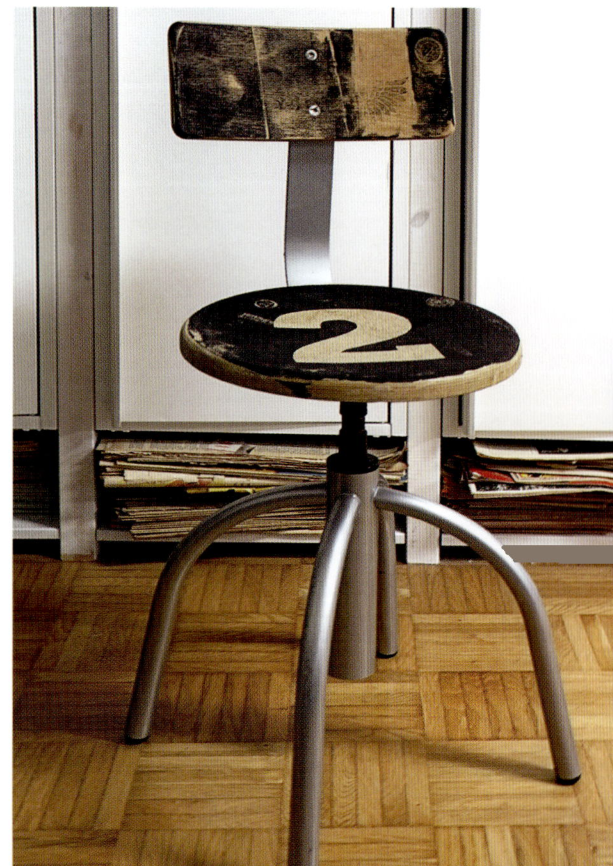

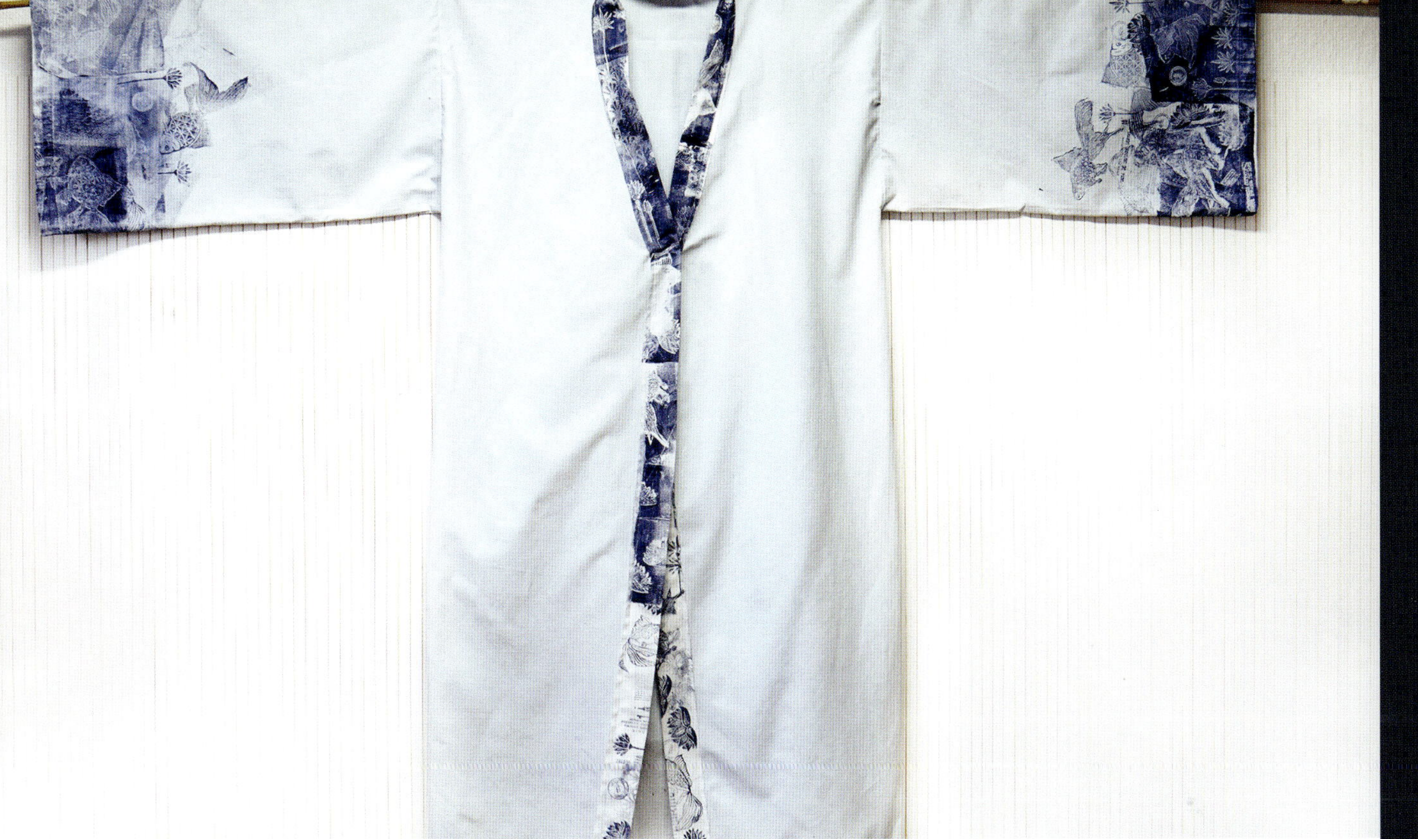

A good example is this workshop chair (pictured opposite). The backrest was printed experimentally: we only wanted to create contrasts and leave part of the wooden surface unprinted. For the seat, however, we thought carefully and made a sketch in order to achieve a final result that would make us happy.

Your projects don't have to be ambitious. We started off experimenting with the potato stamps, but then developed a small fabric collection from them (see page 53) and a bag design that combines the best print results. Or, as in the picture above, we sewed a kimono from an old bed sheet. The sleeves and the panel on the front are printed using the freestyle technique (see page 76). On the back of the kimono we printed a picture based on a famous Hokusai woodcut. A simplified version of the wave (see page 140) was used as a template and the design was also partly created using household items and stencils (you will find detailed project instructions on page 126).

As we've said: anything goes, everything is allowed! Our project section is intended to show that so much is possible beyond unplanned, experimental printing.

Thinking 'from print to design' means that we can design objects in our environment ourselves – in our favourite colours and with our favourite motifs. Do you need a cushion for your new sofa or a splash of colour in your favourite shade? With gelli printing you can design everything according to your own wishes.

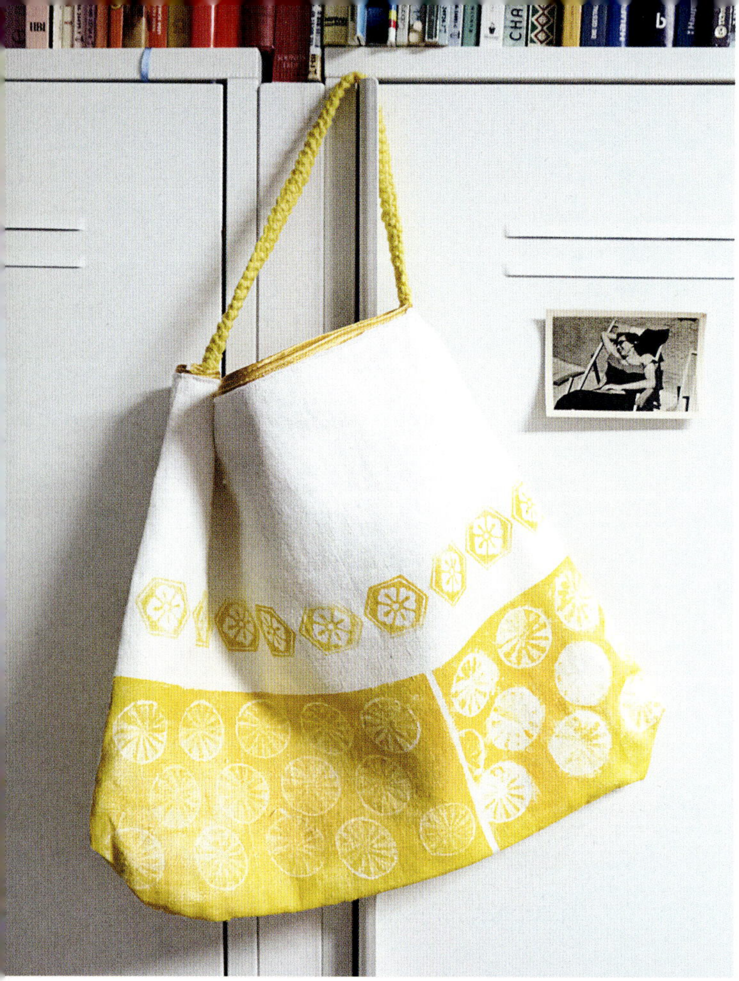

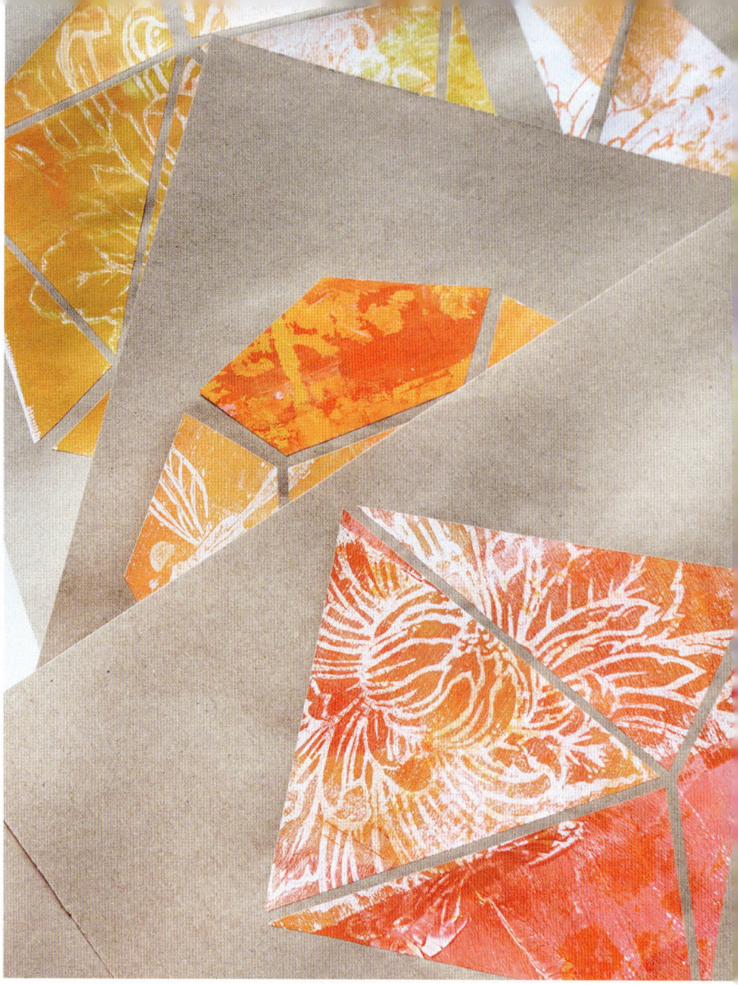

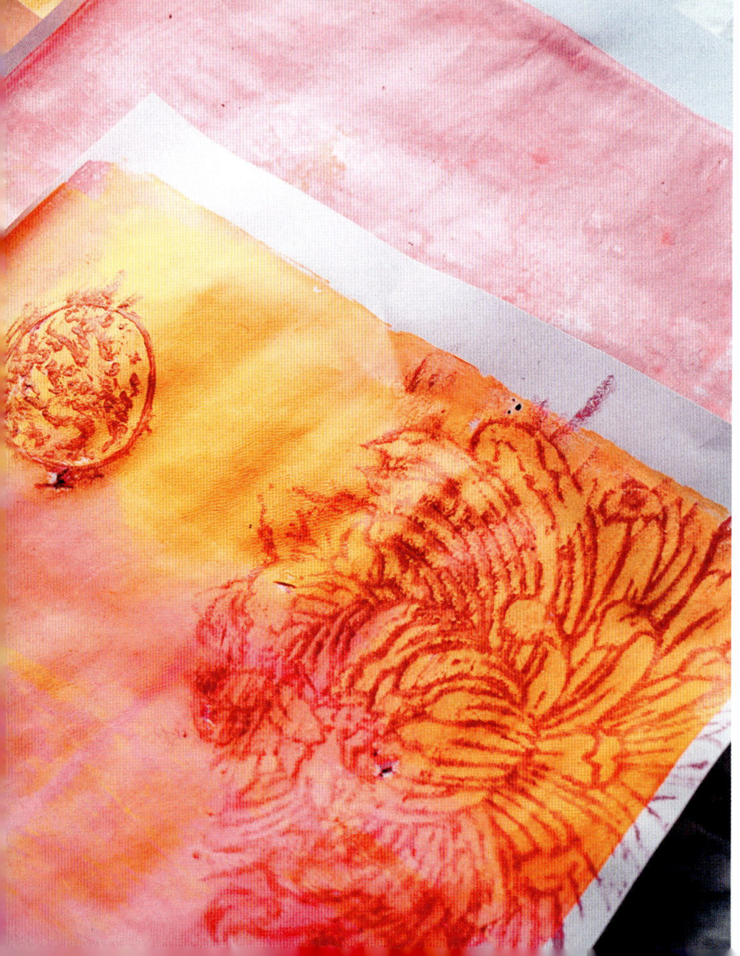

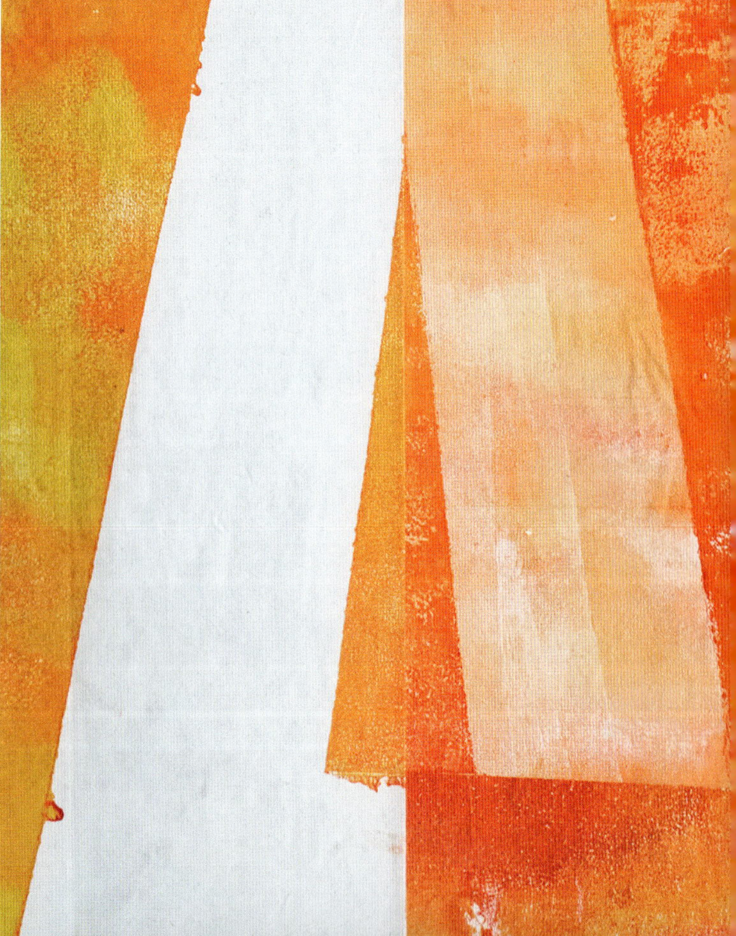

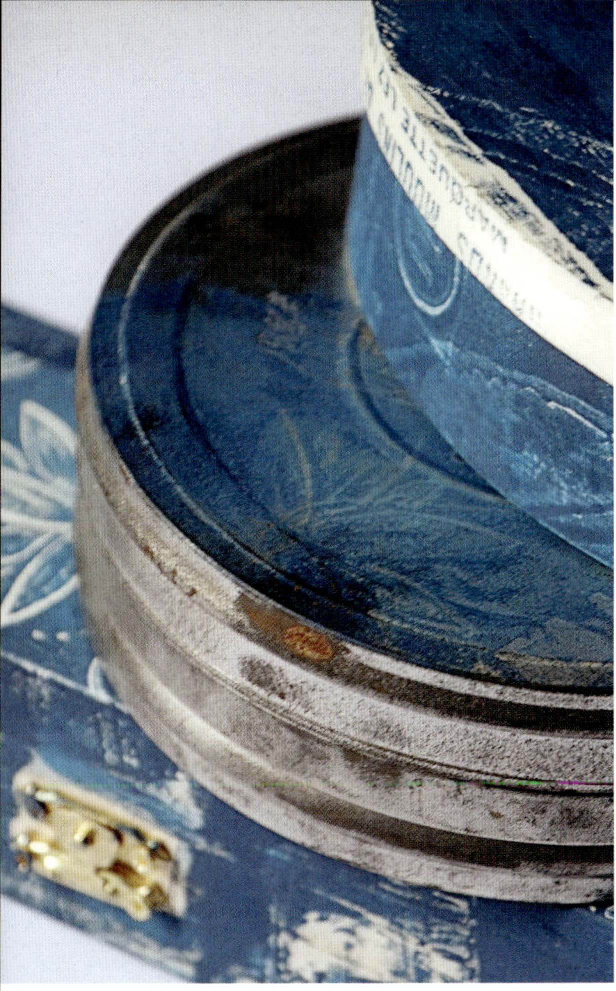

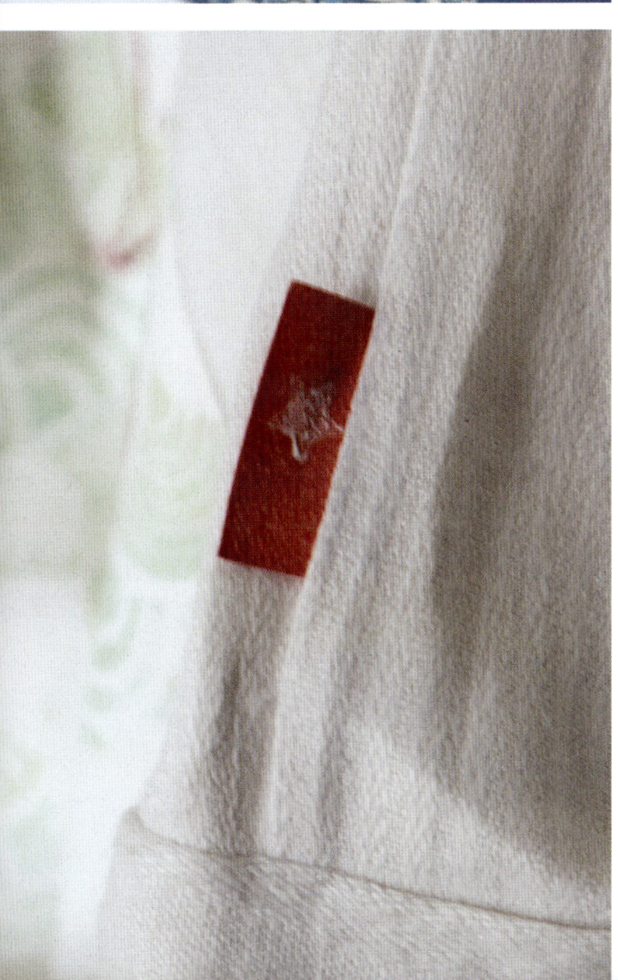

Design means, among other things, developing your own distinctive style. Over time, you will automatically develop your own style, depending on your favourite technique(s), colours, stamps and stencils. We have worked our way through the entire colour palette for this book; lots of projects have a touch of vintage or show our preference for typography. A professional finish is simply one step further on from experimental printing.

Speaking of experimental, when you make the step from paper to fabric or objects, there is another aspect that you can take from designers: the label. When you buy a bag or an item of clothing, there will be a label somewhere – inside or outside – that refers to the designer. We can do that too! We can print labels on our gelli plate. To do this, we created coloured strips from a material that is ideal for printing: vegan faux-leather, which is available to buy under the brand name SnapPap. It is relatively strong and bulky (it is easier to work with when wet, but should be dry for printing). It is stable, does not fray and is wonderful to print on. We also stamped a small star-shaped stamp on the coloured strips. If you sew the label into a fabric seam, it literally turns the finished item into a designer piece.

3

Projects

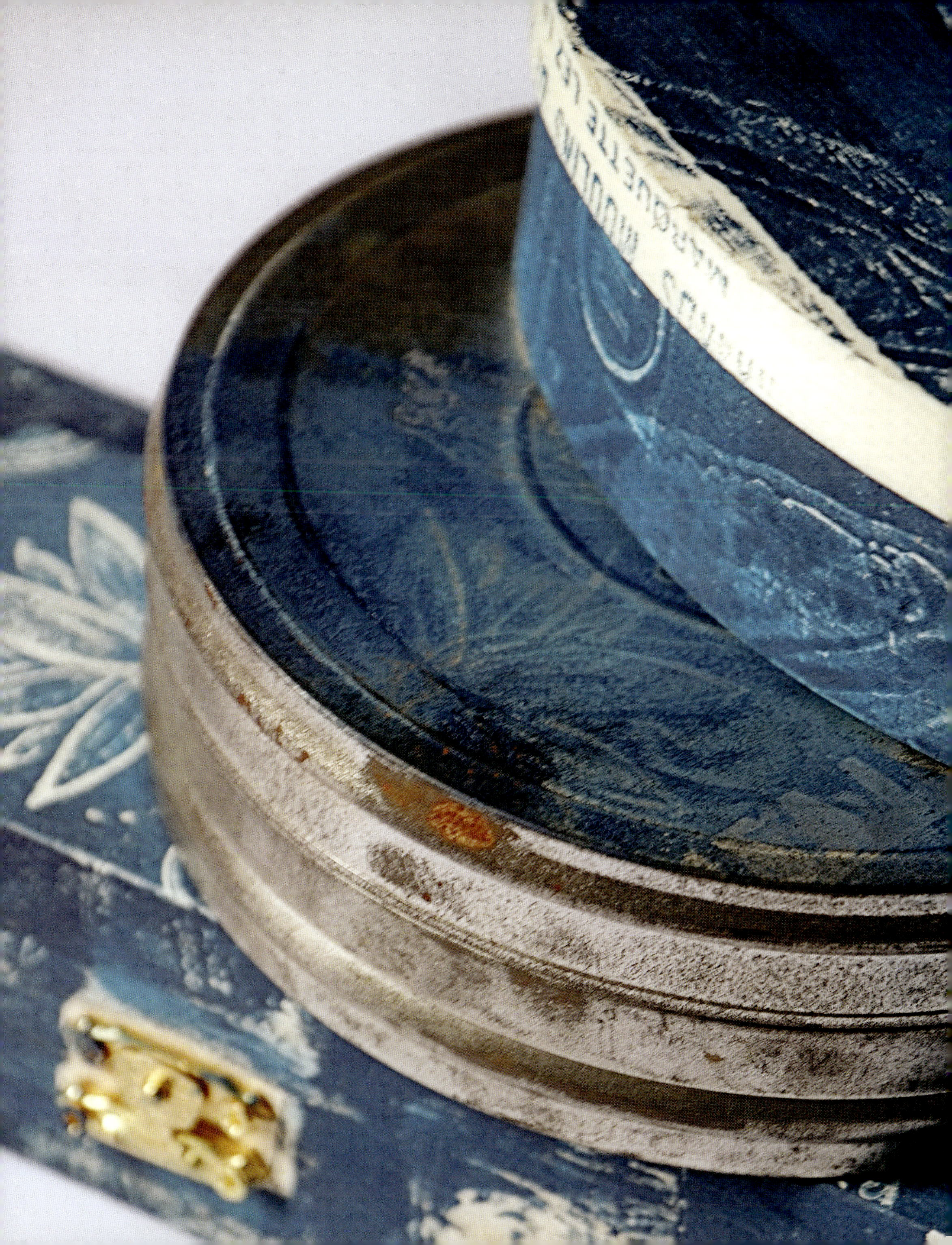

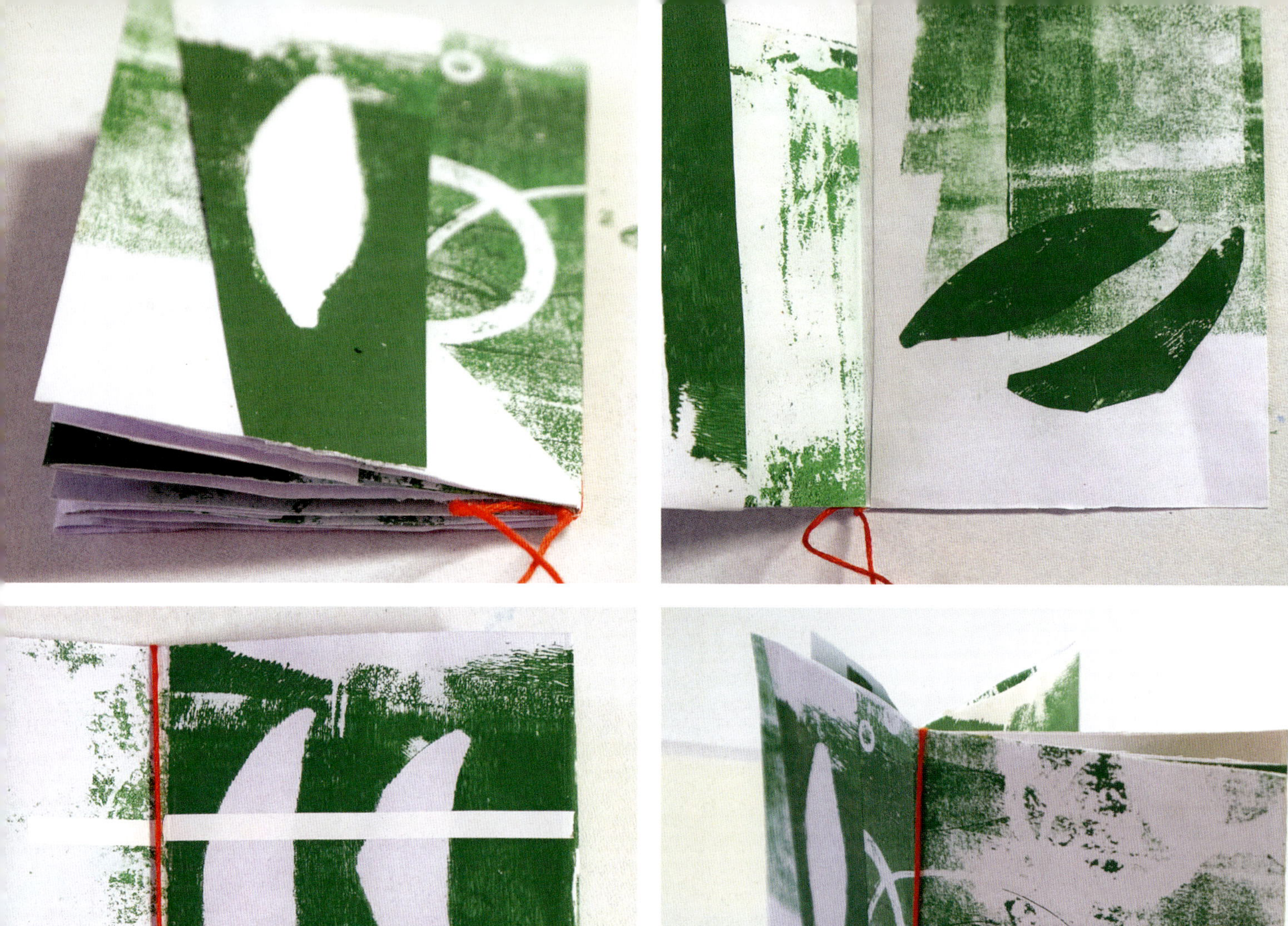

MINI BOOK

Fold a small book using the folding instructions on page 136. The larger the paper, the larger the book will be afterwards. Stick a collage of your printed papers inside the book.

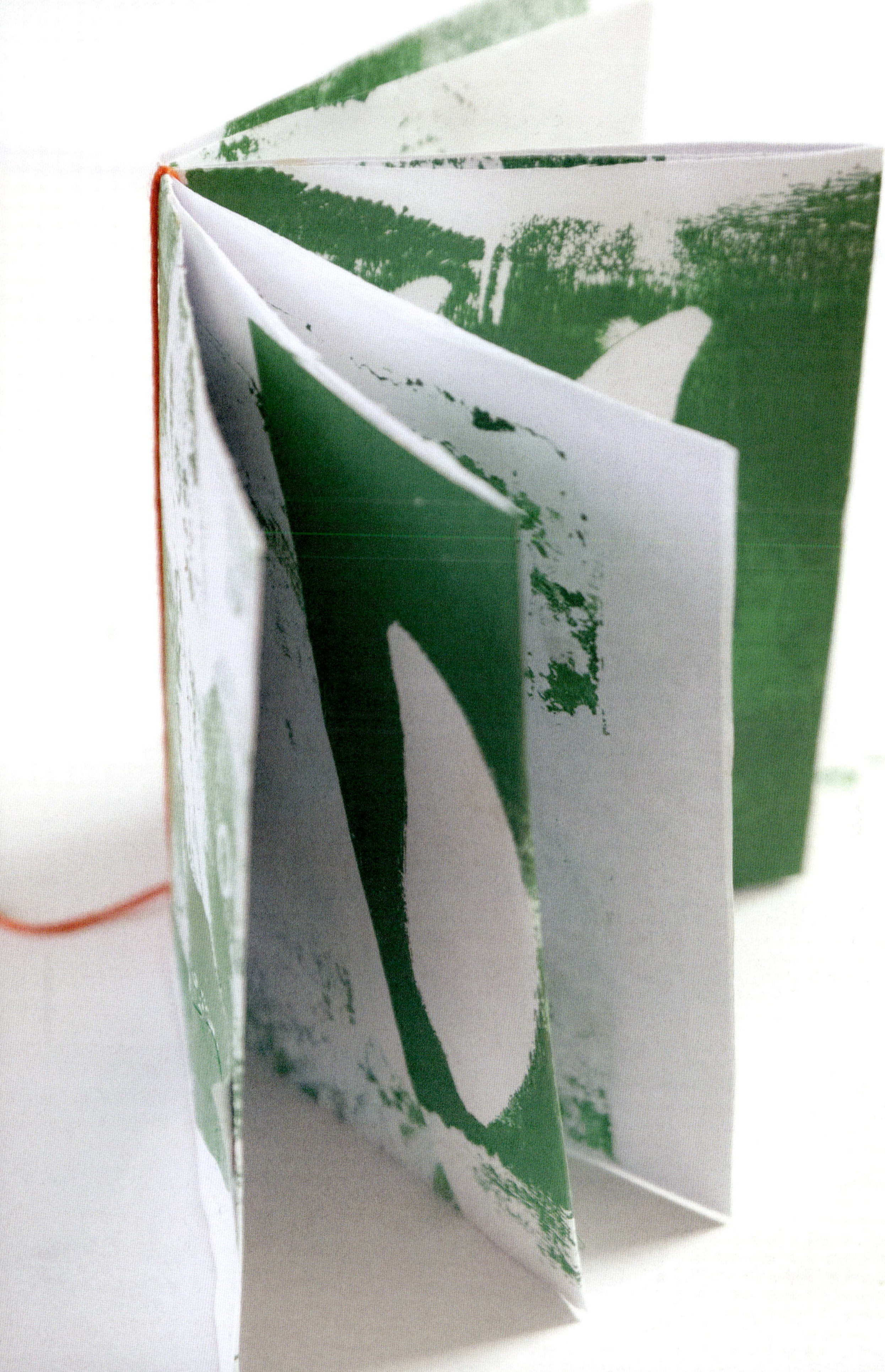

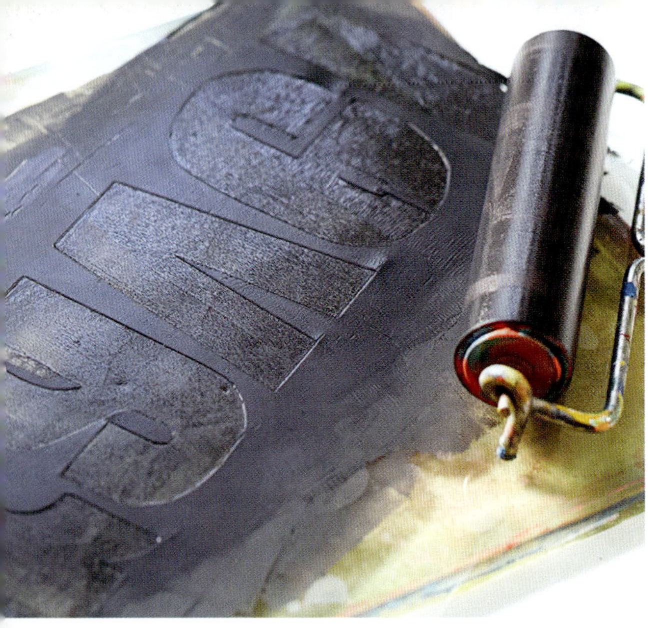

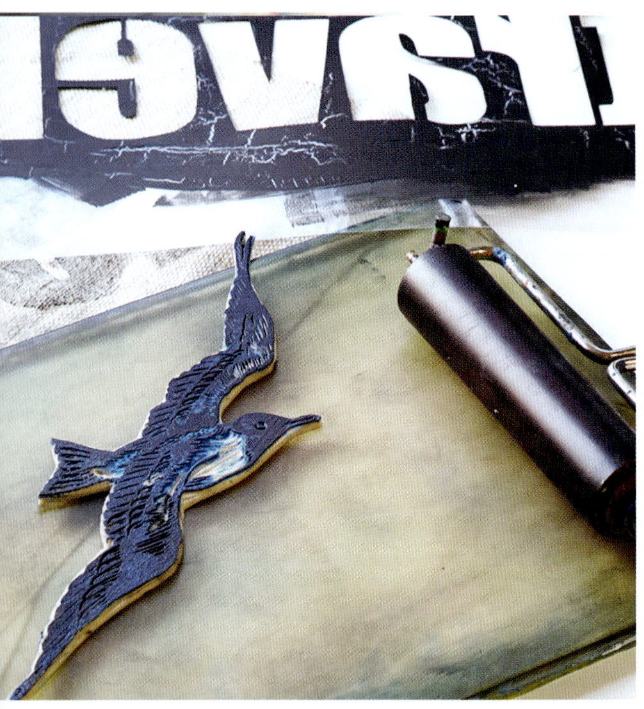

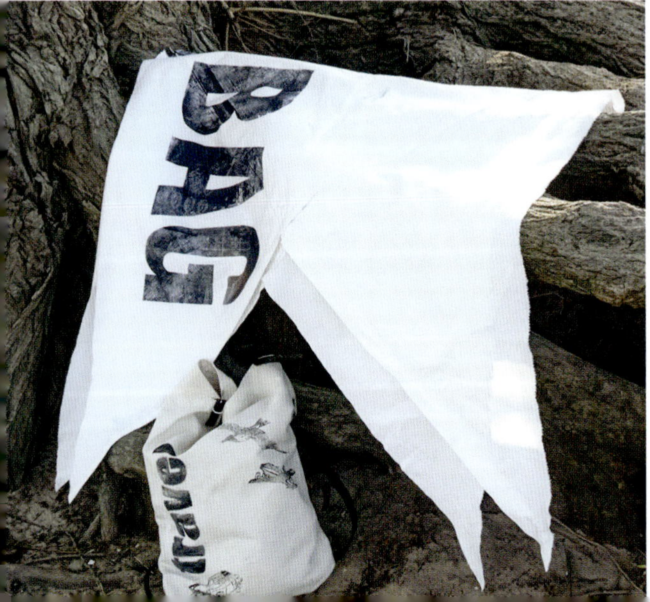

TRAVEL BAGS

Your designs don't always have to be colourful. In this case we have used fabric or linen for our typographic bags, so that they already have a 'base colour', and are not completely white.

We used a stencil, printing on fabric for the bags, but this time we didn't place the stencils on the gelli plate, but on the fabric. To be more precise: we stuck them on. We used self-adhesive transparent film for these stencils – this film is softer than overhead projector film or film for laser printers and is easier to cut, especially in curves. The grid pattern on the back of the adhesive film makes it easy to cut and fit.

We use the large lettering ('BAG') in two ways: we use it as a negative stencil for the giant bag, and, if you cut out the letters carefully, you still have the individual letters themselves. We used one of them for the backpack on page 101.

We used the gelli plate as a stamp, which we printed on to the stencil applied to the fabric. As a pure black surface would perhaps look a little heavy, we textured it with stamps and bubble wrap from used recycled packaging and padded envelopes.

You can find the patterns and stencils on pages 137–139.

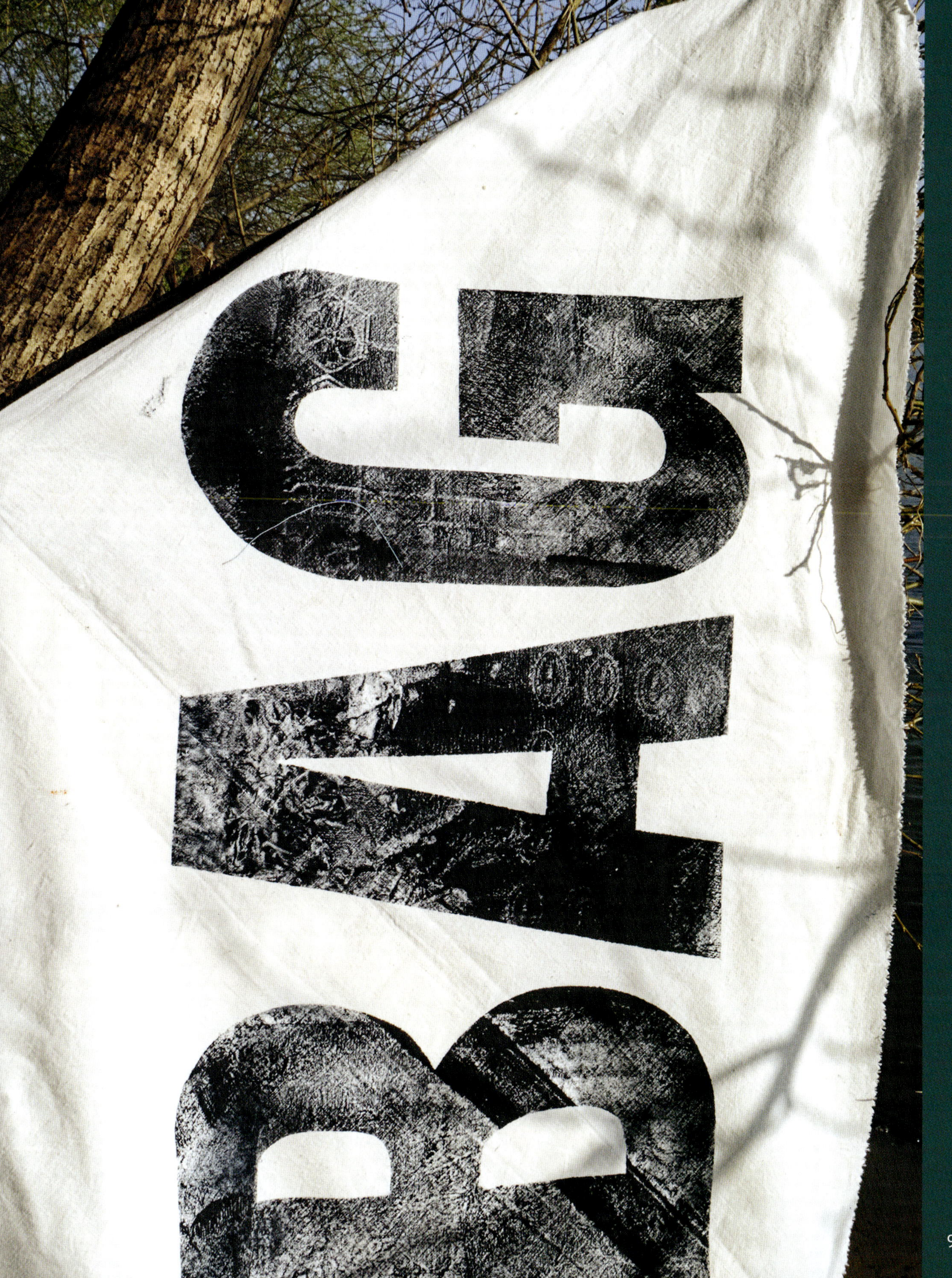
BAG

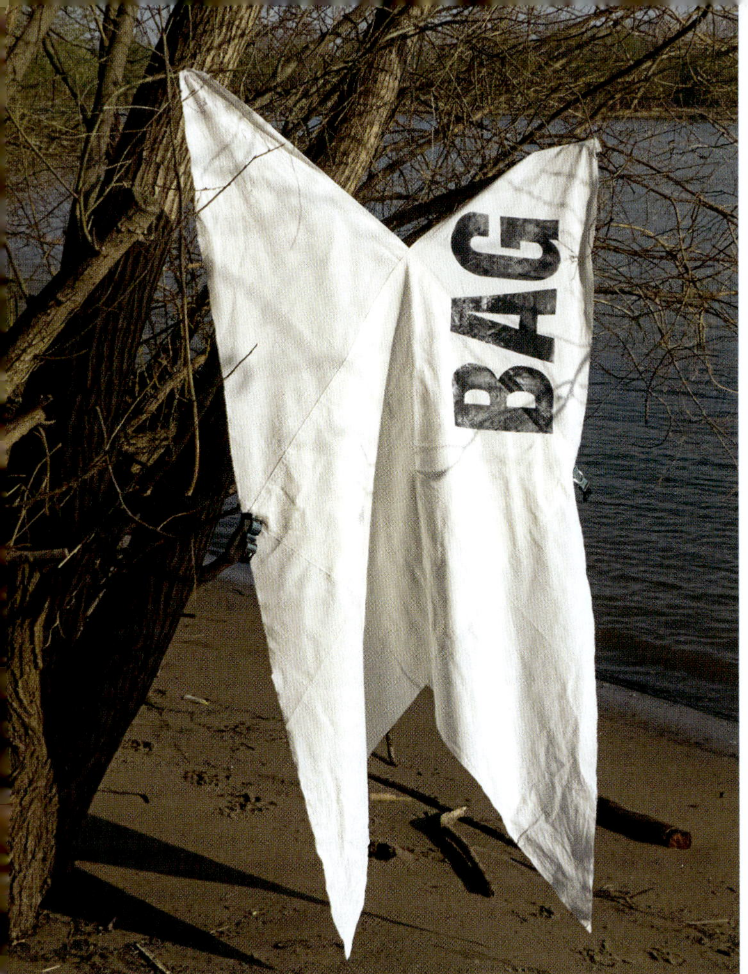

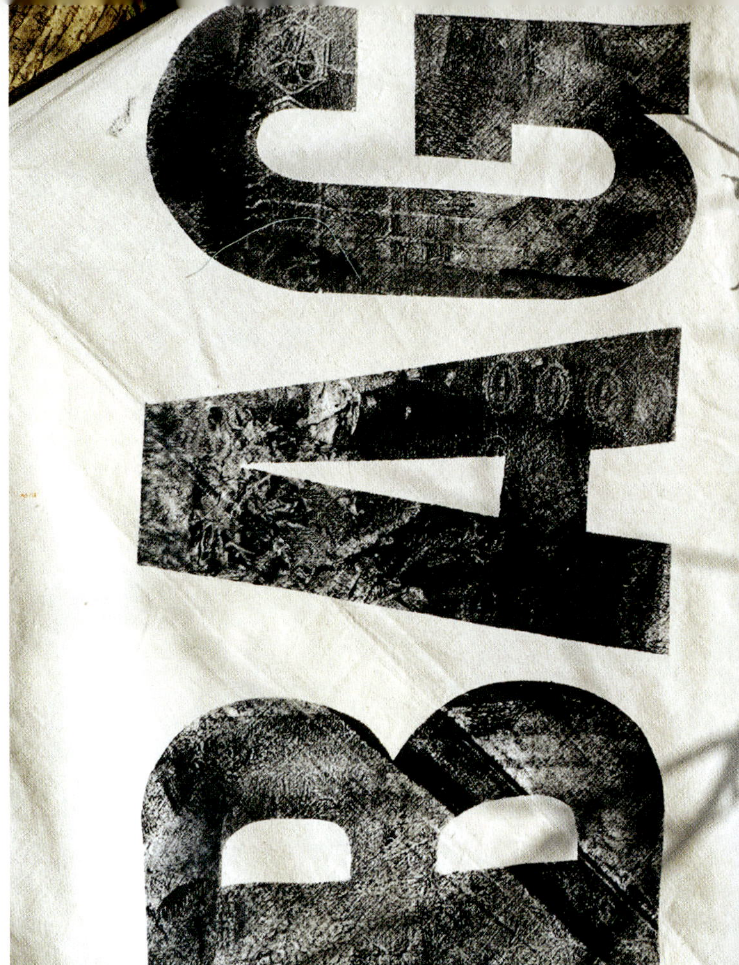

1. GIANT BAG

The basic pattern is the same as for our Japanese fabric bag with the eraser stamps (see page 58), only this time as big as an old sheet will allow. You can get away with only two seams: simply place the two triangles on top of one another and sew them together at the tips. You can also close the side sections with a seam, but we have chosen the version where you can unfold the bag completely. This way you can use it directly as a mat for a picnic or hang it up as a sunshade. Therefore, this cut works from small to huge.

To close the sides of the bag you can add a buckle fastener on each of the long sides (see picture above, left). You can buy these in sewing shops, but we repurposed the buckle from an old dog collar for our bag. You can either tightly knot the long ends of the triangles together around the contents of your bag, for example to make a pack that will also fit in a bicycle basket, or you could knot the lengths together at the top for a practical shoulder bag.

The bag was printed with a stencil (see page 138) stuck to the fabric, using the gelli plate as a stamp.

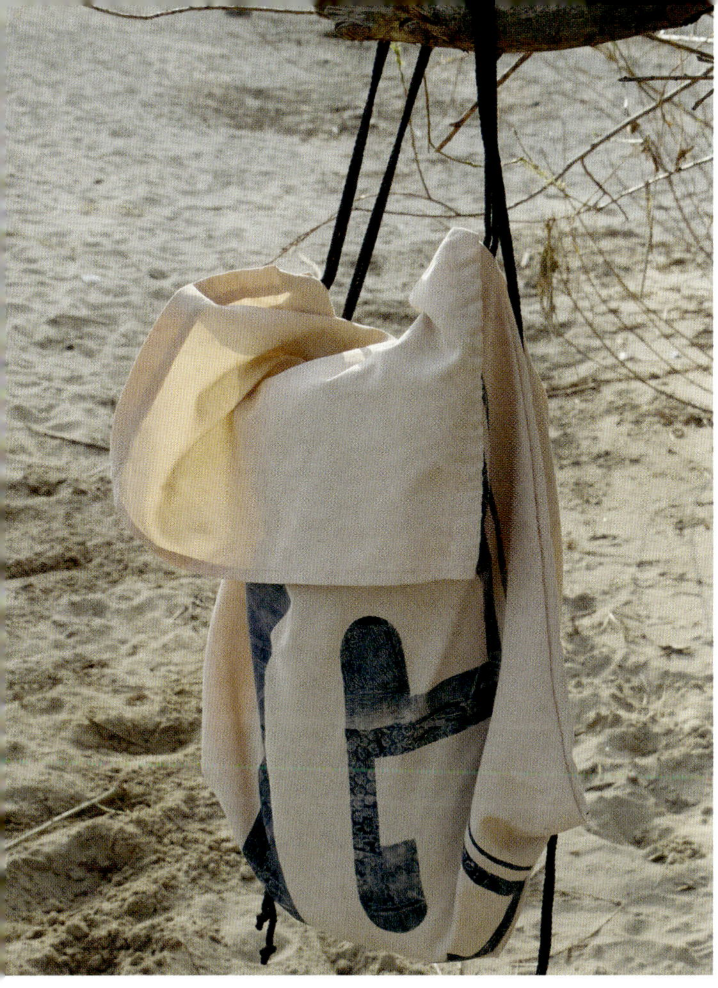

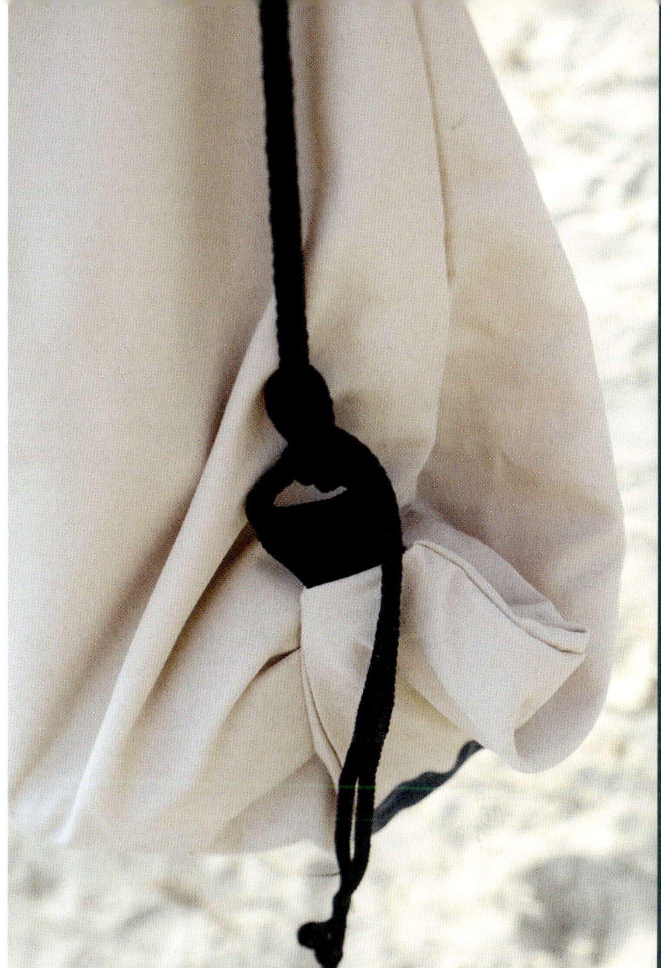

2. BACKPACK

This backpack is made from used pushchair/stroller sunshades. This is a special kind of recycling: the sunshade is practically cut to size. It tapers slightly towards the top and comes with the cords that will later be used as the backpack straps. Of course, you can also cut pieces of fabric to size.

The cords are doubled and attached to the side edges (see the illustration on page 137). For this purpose, we sewed two small pieces of black ribbon at the top and bottom, creating small loops into which the cords are knotted. Everything is completed with just two to four seams – it is super-lightweight as a travel backpack and made from very hard-wearing fabric.

For the printing, we rolled a gelli plate with paint, stamped on the textures and applied a cut-out letter before printing. The negative print creates a more dramatic effect than positive printing.

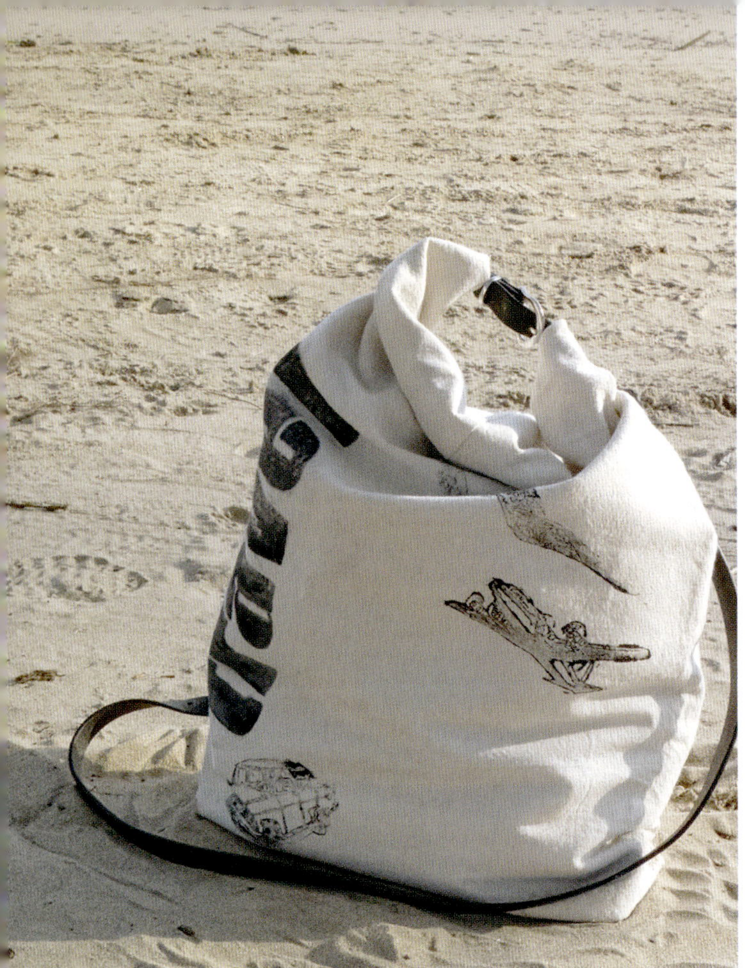

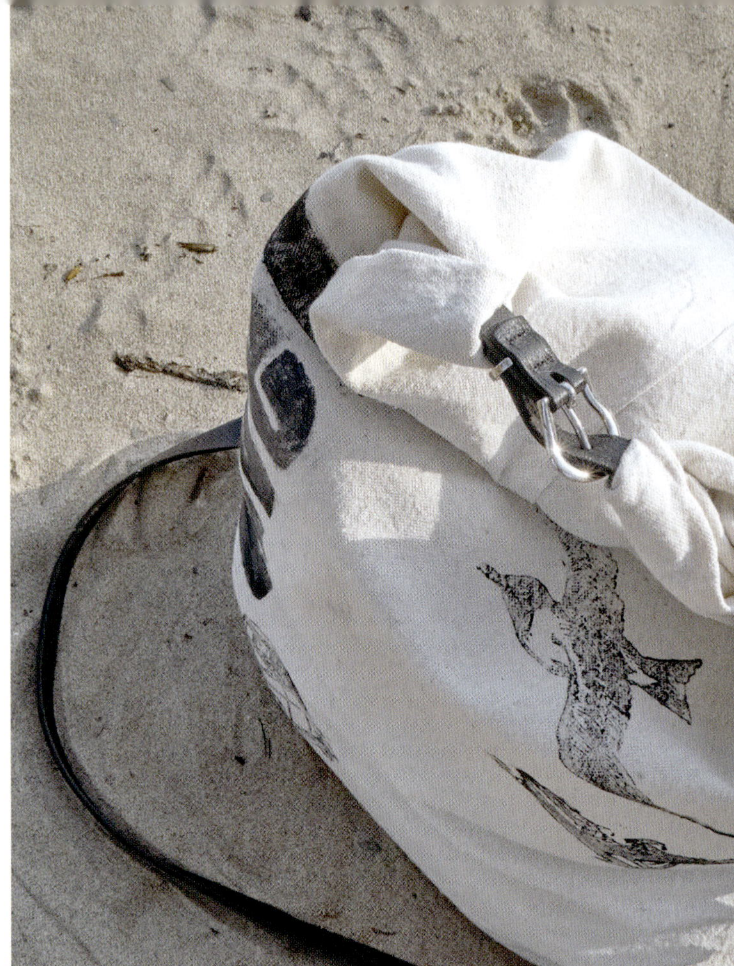

3. TRAVEL BAG

This bag variation is a backpack with the top folded over and rolled up (see illustration on page 137). To do this, sew an extra-long bag so that the upper part can be folded over. We used an old leather belt for the straps and fastening. The buckle and a piece from the other end of the belt with the holes form the fastening. The belt pieces are attached to the left and right sides of the top edge of the bag, which allows the edge to be folded multiple times and then secured with the buckle – the basic principle of messenger-style bags.

You can wear the bag as a shoulder bag – or, if the strap is long enough, across the chest. For the strap, simply punch two holes in the remaining piece of the belt so that it can be secured with a few rough stitches.

The 'travel' lettering was made using a stencil (see page 139), like the giant bag on page 100, and the black area was lightly textured. Do not take too much paint away at the edges, to ensure that the lettering remains clear and distinct.

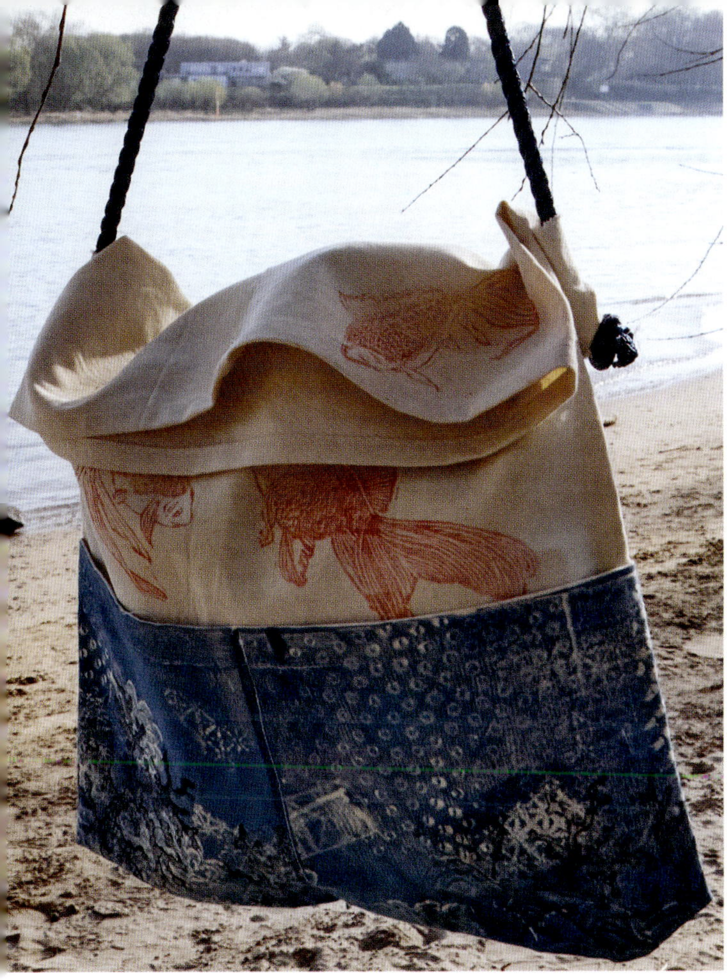

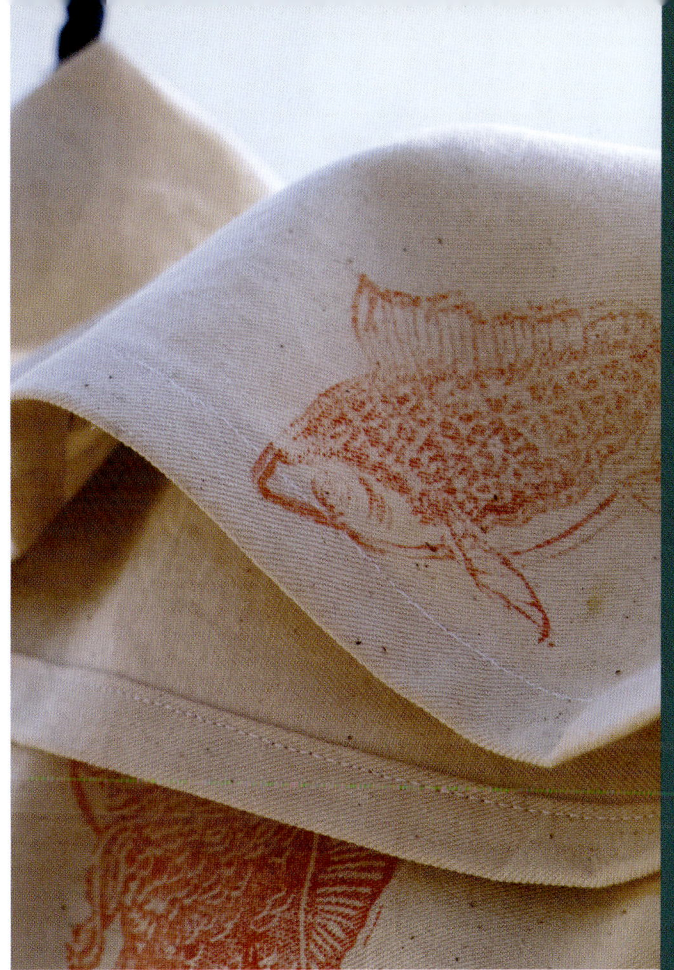

4. COLOURFUL BAG VARIATION

This bag style also works well in colour. Again, we sewed a bag from a thick linen fabric. If your fabric is not thick or strong enough, just double it!

This time we have also sewn a flat piece of fabric on the outside that has been gelli-printed in two colours, then divided it with a centre seam: we now have an outer pocket with two compartments. If you want the design to go right up to the edge, it should be printed before sewing.

We used blue rope from a DIY store as a strap. If you attach the ends to the top of the bag, you have a normal shopping bag. However, we have attached them a little lower so that the top of the bag folds down and the contents are more secure. As with the backpack on page 101, we have sewn two pieces of fabric as flaps when closing the side seam, but this time slightly wider and made from the same linen fabric. The fish design has been stamped on to the finished bag, so you can position the fish exactly where you want them.

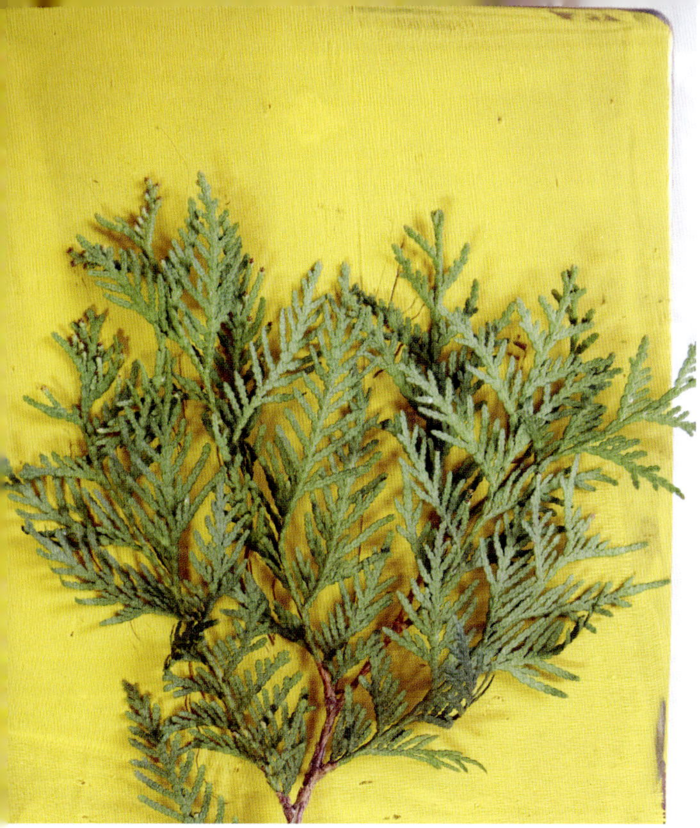

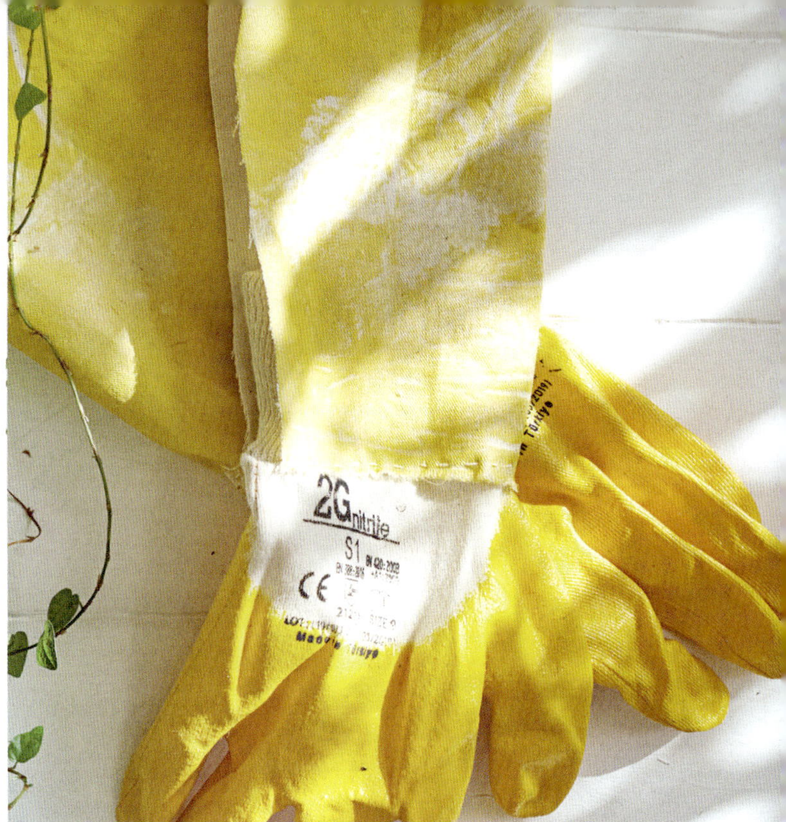

GARDENING GLOVES

We used the plant printing technique from pages 46–47 to print on gardening or work gloves. As these kinds of gloves are rarely washed, you can also use acrylic paint instead of fabric paint.

Print your design onto sturdy fabric, cut out two pieces and hand-sew them to the glove cuffs with coarse yarn. Make sure that the gloves still stretch enough at the wrist so you can slip your hands in afterwards.

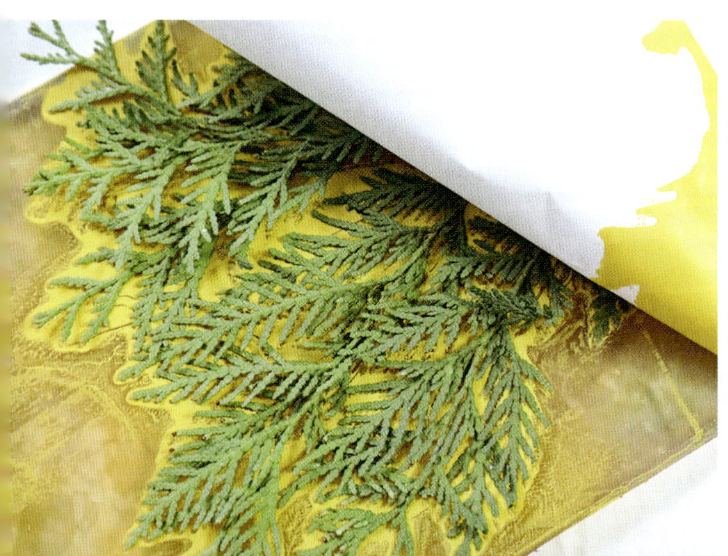

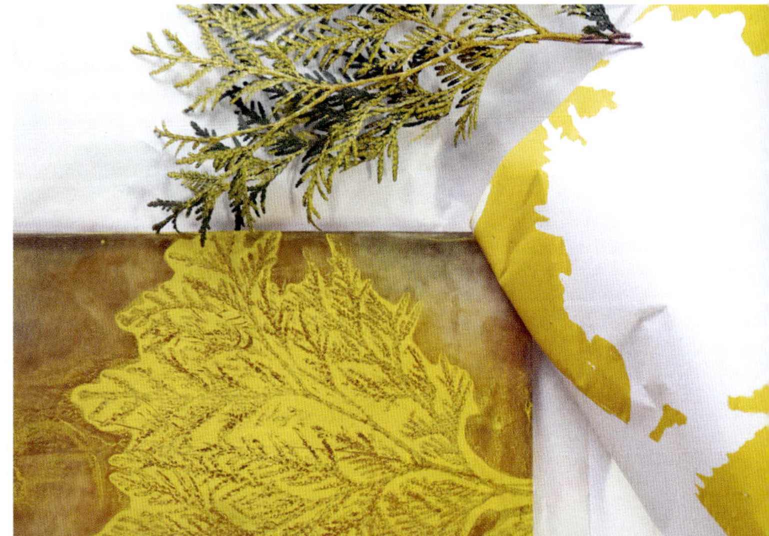

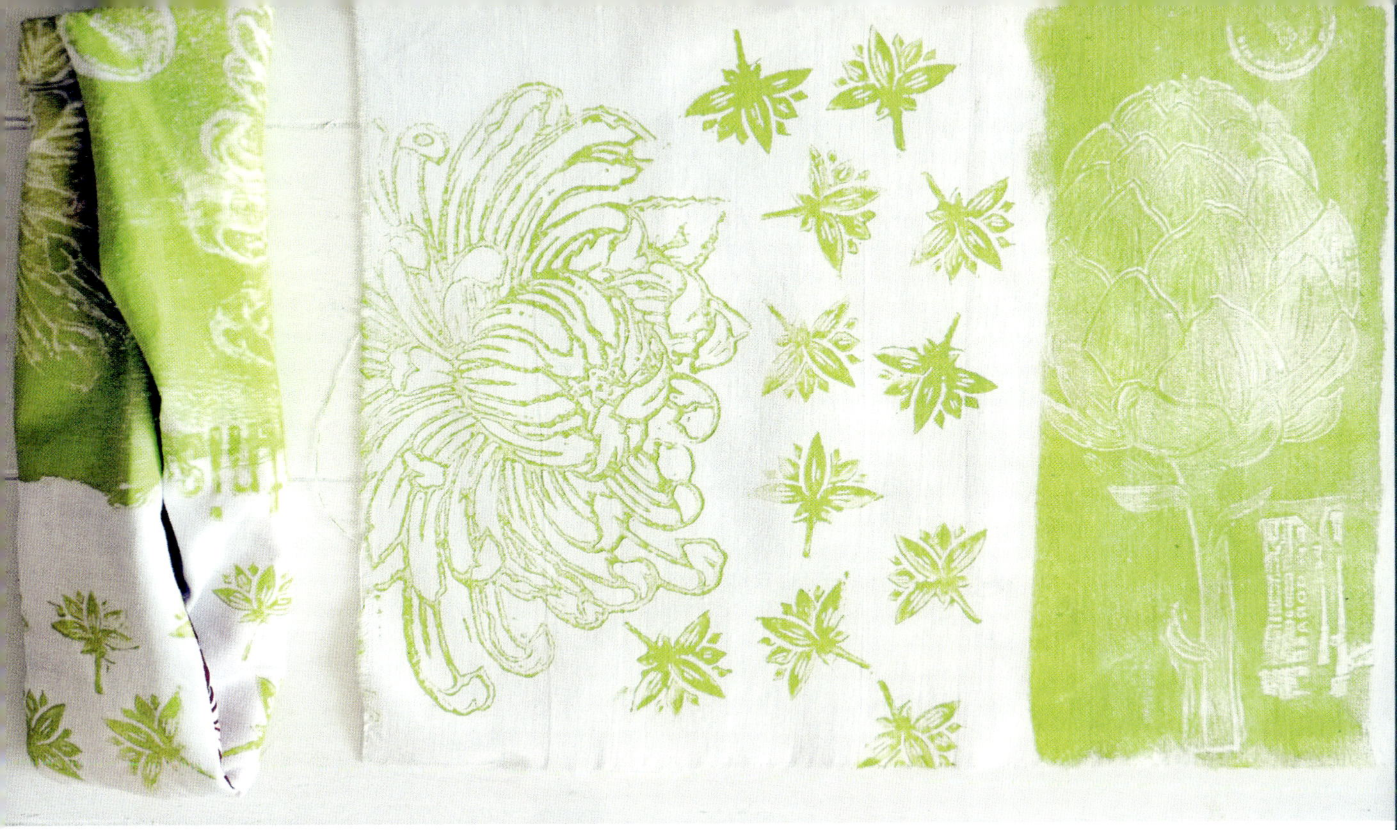

JAPANESE POUCH

These Japanese-style pouches can be sewn with four seams: place two fabric pieces, approximately 24 x 20cm (9½ x 8in), right sides together (we have used a piece of quilted fabric for the lining). Sew the longer sides together with a straight stitch along the edge, then turn the pouch the right way out.

Next, fold in the fabric piece twice, like a letter (with the future outer side on the inside) and sew together on one of the edges (see illustration on page 134). Fold the opposite side inversely to create the overlapping opening, topstitch, then turn inside out.

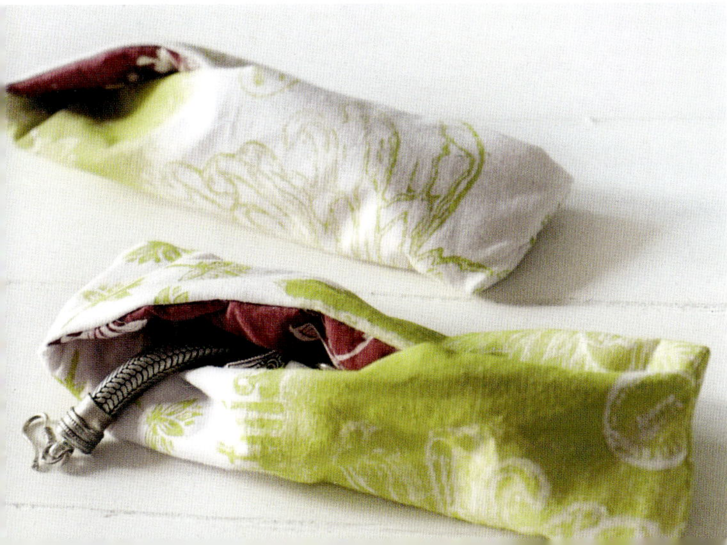

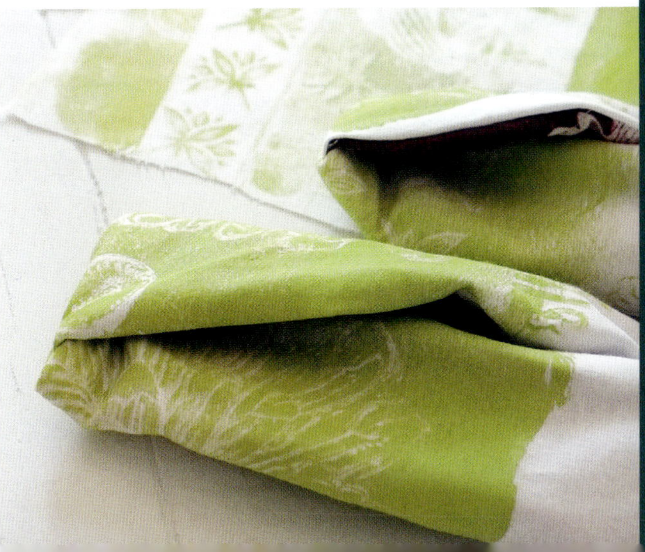

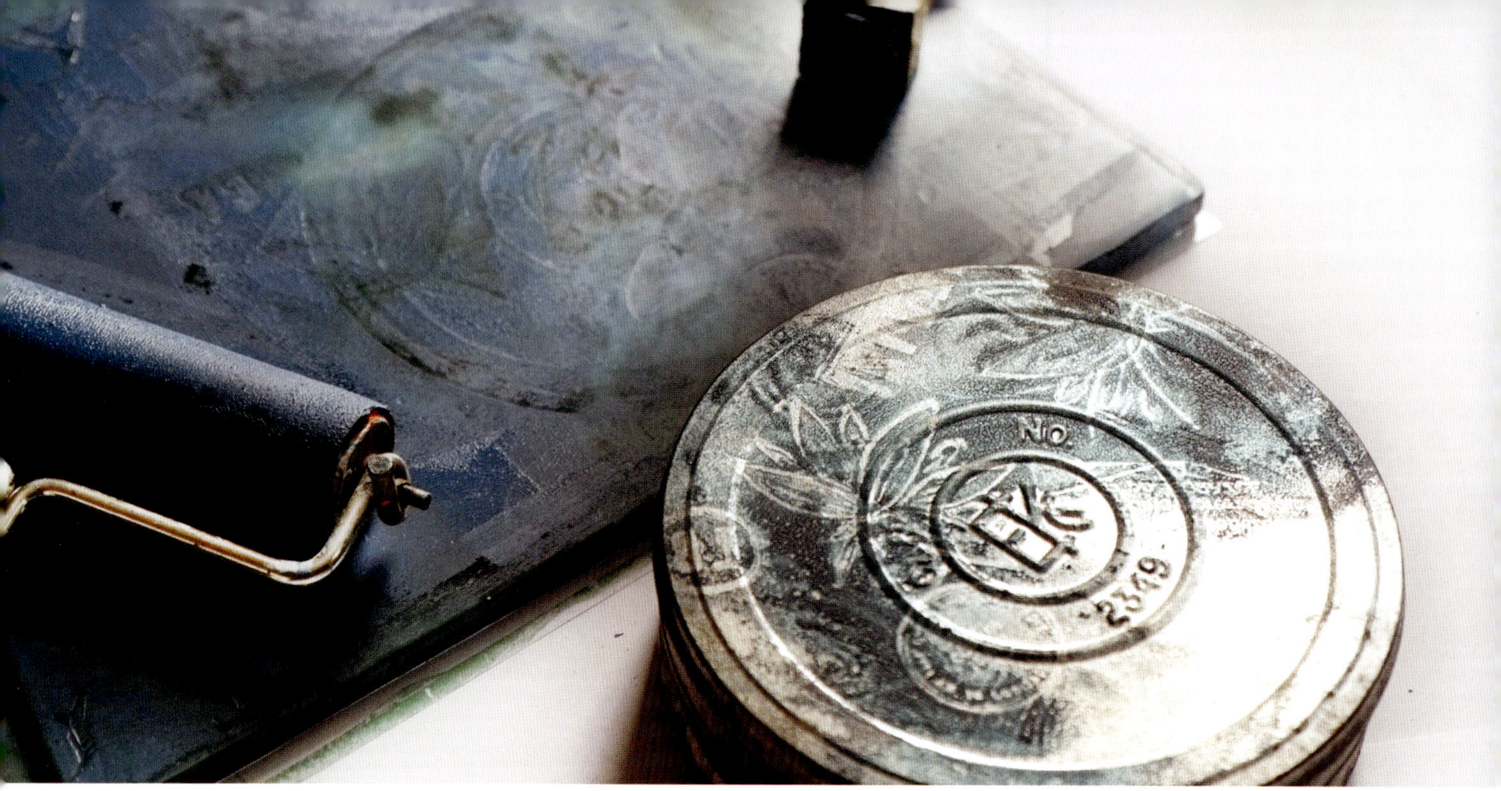

TINS, BOXES AND BOWLS

Since the gelli plates are flexible, you can also print on objects that don't have a completely flat surface. For this project, we have printed on tins and wooden boxes as well as a flat wooden bowl. When you print on objects that come into contact with food or that need to be cleaned often, you should use food-safe and long-lasting paints.

Depending on the object and the size of the gelli plate, you can press the objects on to the plate, rather than vice versa – this is how the wooden boxes were printed. The curved side of the oval box, for example, was simply rolled firmly over the gelli plate. Alternatively, you can stamp with the gelli plate – place the gelli plate on top of the object and press down – this is how the bowl was printed. If the objects are going to be used often, coat them with a clear varnish once the paint is dry to protect them.

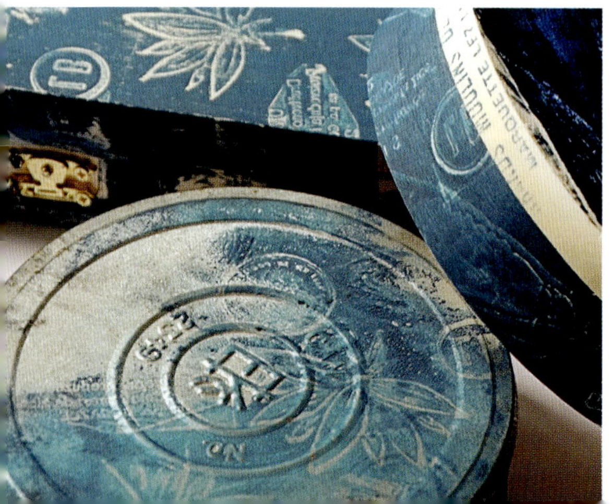

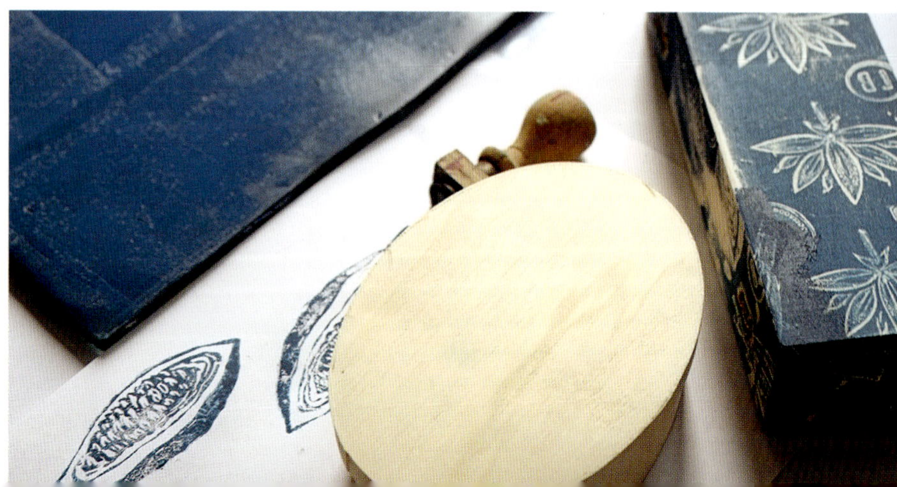

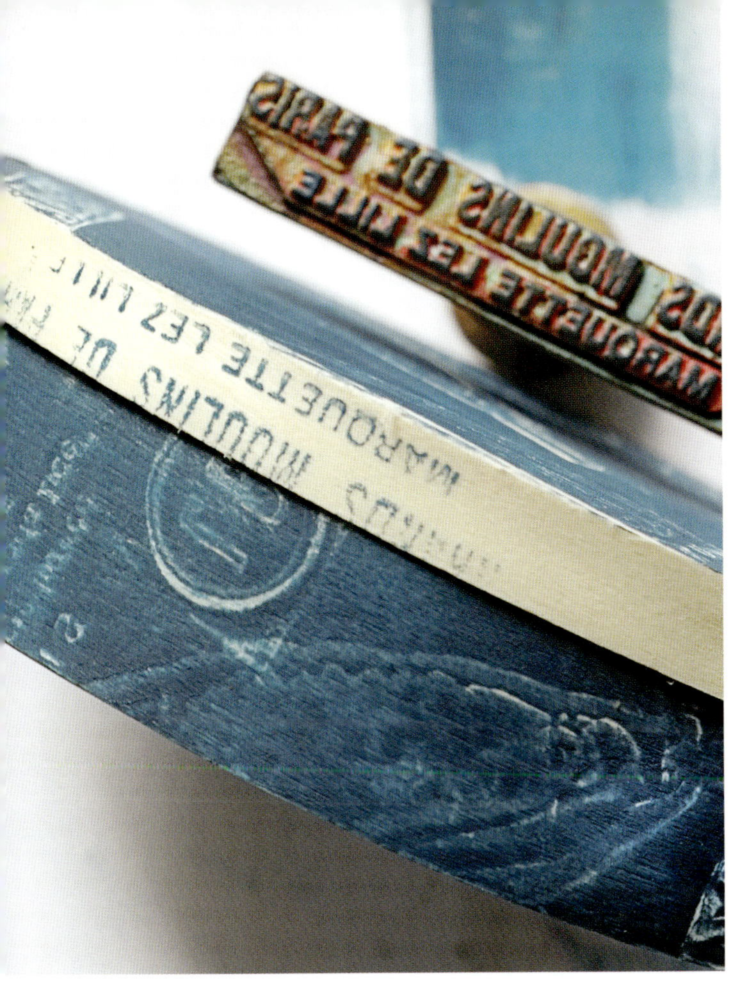
MOULINS DE PARIS
MARQUETTE LEZ LILLE

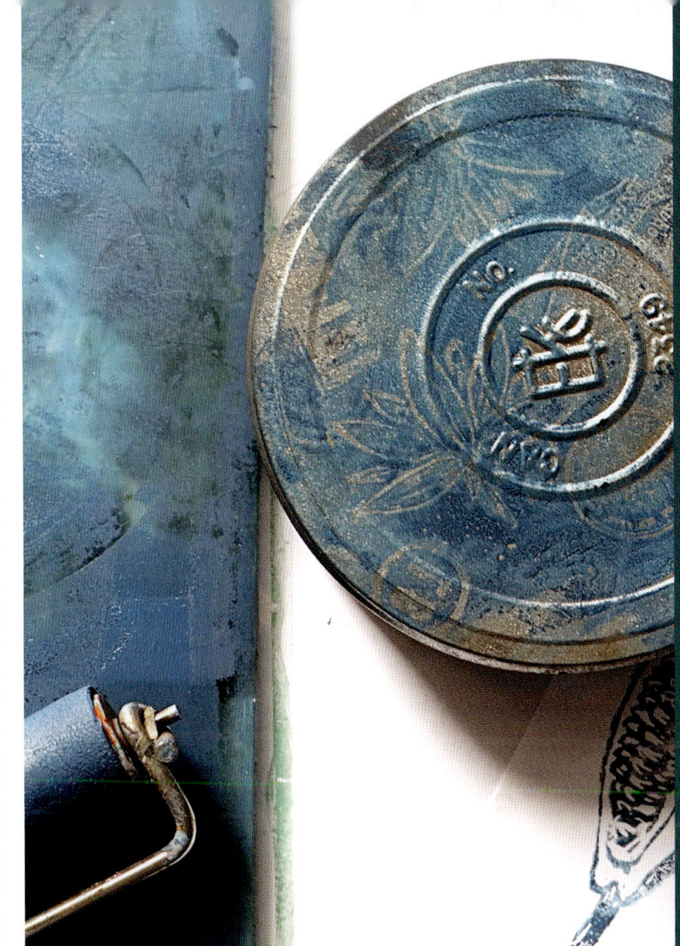

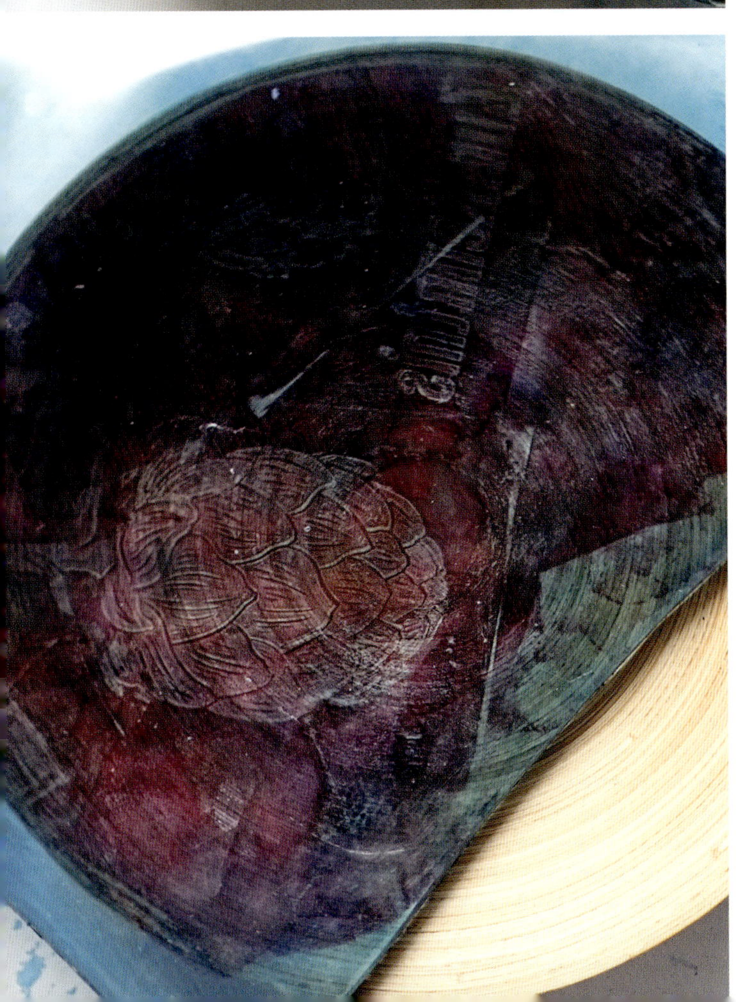

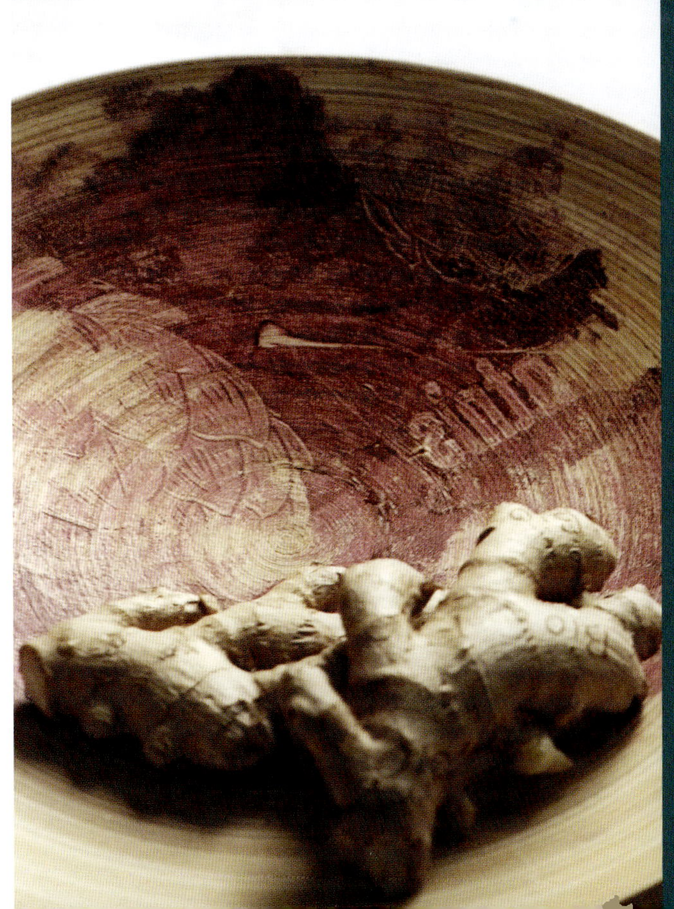

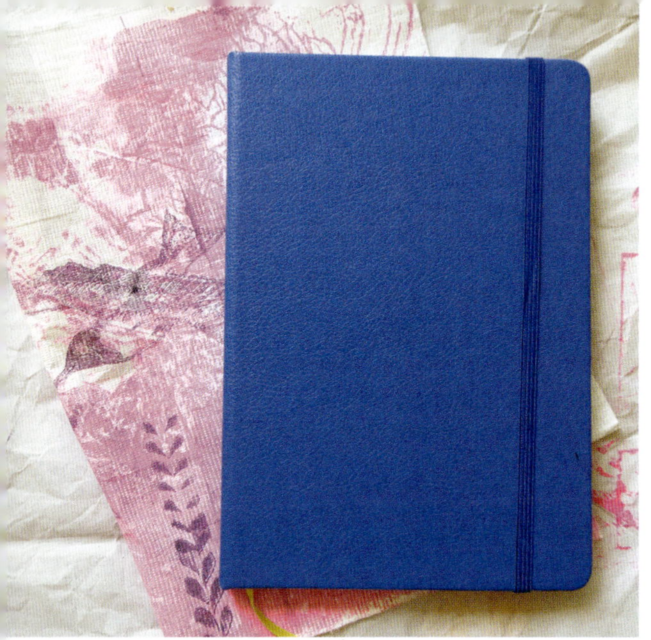

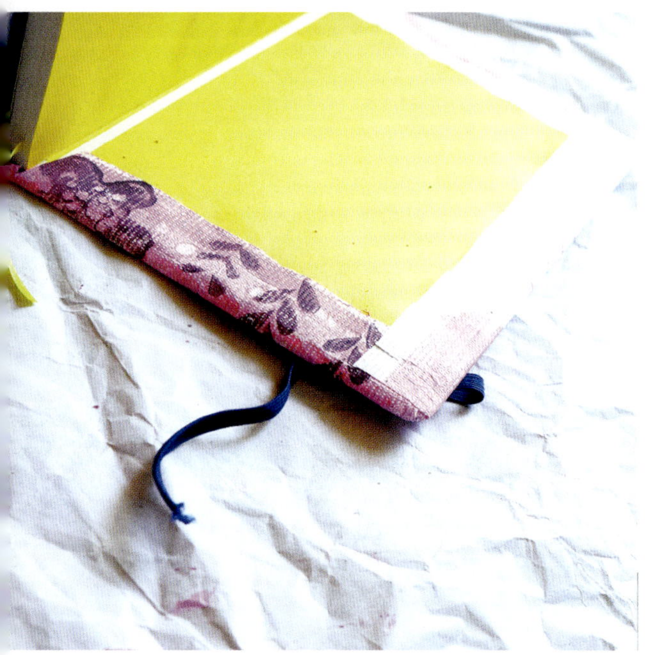

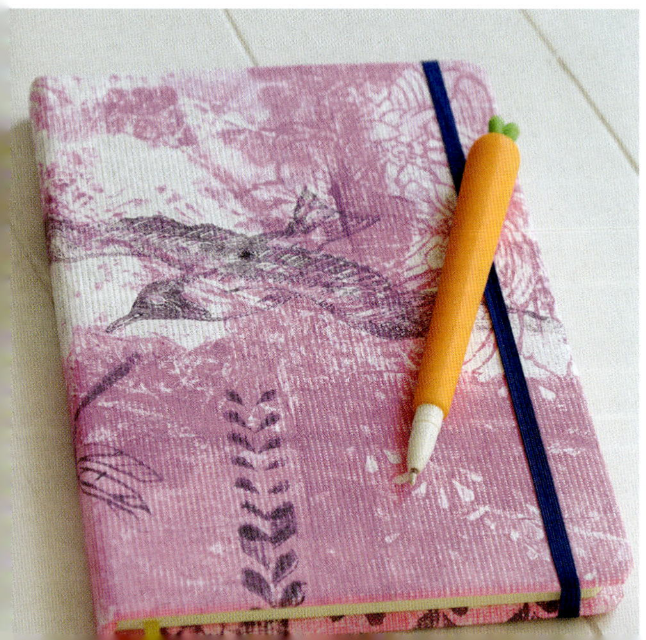

COVERING OBJECTS WITH TYVEK®

When you are transitioning from printing on paper to printing on fabric and objects, you may find yourself examining innocent household items for their printability. Unlike paper, you must consider the durability and texture of these surfaces – and, if they come into contact with food, their safety. If there is any doubt, acrylic paint can be used and then sealed to make sure the paint lasts. However, not all surfaces are suitable for printing; some may be uneven, too smooth or rough to take on paint.

A straightforward solution for many projects is Tyvek®, a material typically used in packaging or construction. It is available in hardware stores or online as a fabric, sold by length. Tyvek® is a very thin material that is wonderful for printing and is also waterproof. It has a slight texture but is as easy to print on as paper. Tyvek® is lightweight and durable and has another advantage: it is tear-resistant, which is particularly useful for printing. The longer you leave paper or fabric on wet paint, the more paint will be transferred. However, there are limits with paper; if left too long on the gelli plate, the paper fibres dissolve and stick to the paint. With Tyvek®, you can rub the print and even leave it on the gelli plate until everything is dry. This results in an even stronger paint application.

Tyvek® withstands frequent use, making it a suitable covering for notebooks or sketchbooks. Paper would be too delicate for this purpose, and fabric not sturdy enough. Tyvek®, on the other hand, can be easily wiped clean, while fabric tends to preserve stains. Be careful, though: you cannot iron Tyvek®.

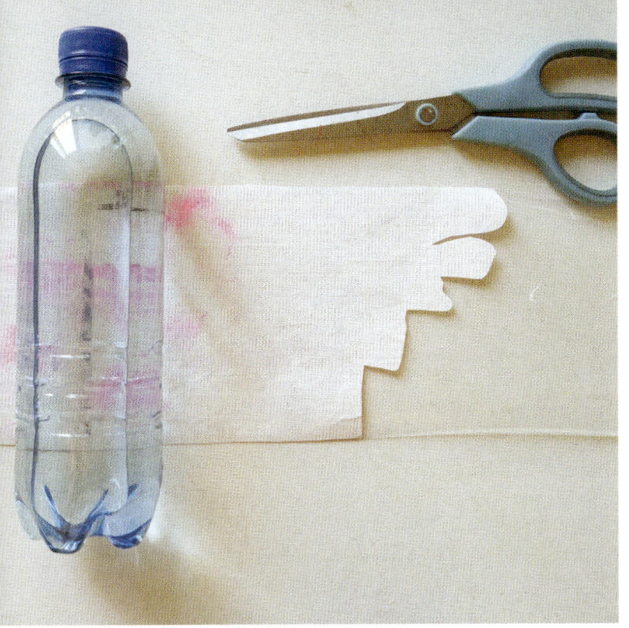

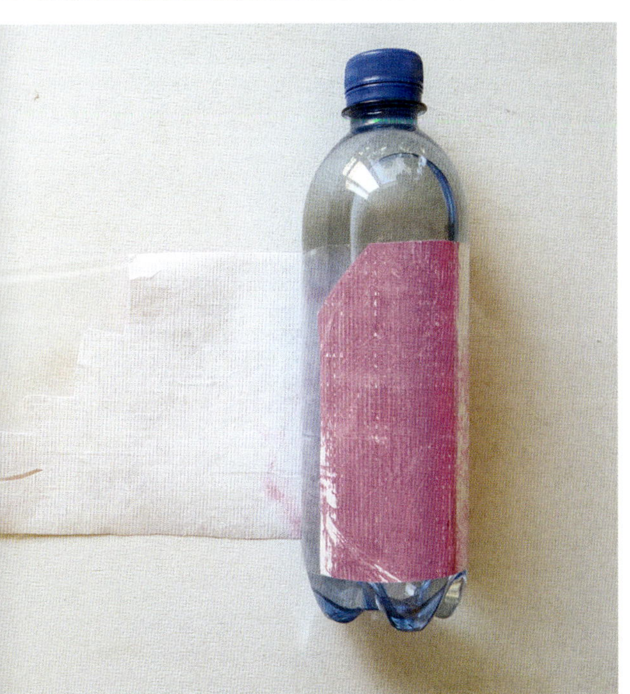

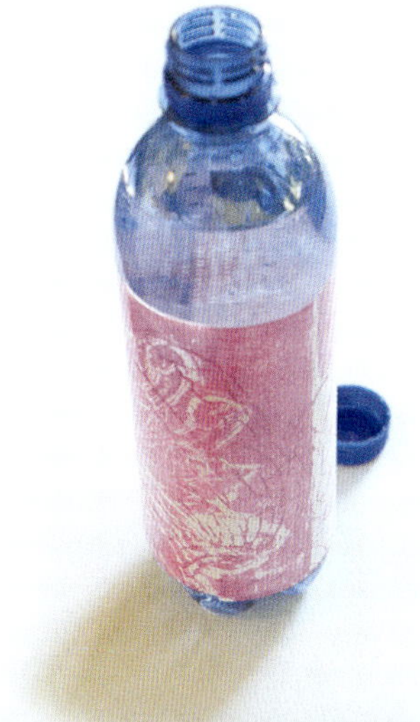

NOTEBOOK

Opposite we have covered a ready-made notebook, but it's even nicer if you bind an entire notebook yourself. This makes the advantages of Tyvek® evident: it's easy to work with, forgiving of mistakes and so thin that it barely adds bulk.

Cut the Tyvek® slightly larger than the notebook, brush the book with bookbinding glue, and smoothly pull the Tyvek® over it. Tyvek® doesn't fray, so incisions, such as for the elastic band, can be made perfectly. Place the covered book between two heavier books to weigh it down, and leave to dry.

WATER BOTTLE

Round and extremely smooth surfaces can't be printed on? That's true in principle. But with Tyvek®, we can create a type of cover. To make it all a bit sturdier and more water-resistant, we stick a piece of printed Tyvek® on to self-adhesive transparent film. If you let the film extend beyond the edges, you don't need additional glue to secure it. To create a smoother transition, we didn't use a rectangular piece of Tyvek®, but cut the overlapping edge along a floral motif. Finally, wrap it around the water bottle and firmly press the film down.

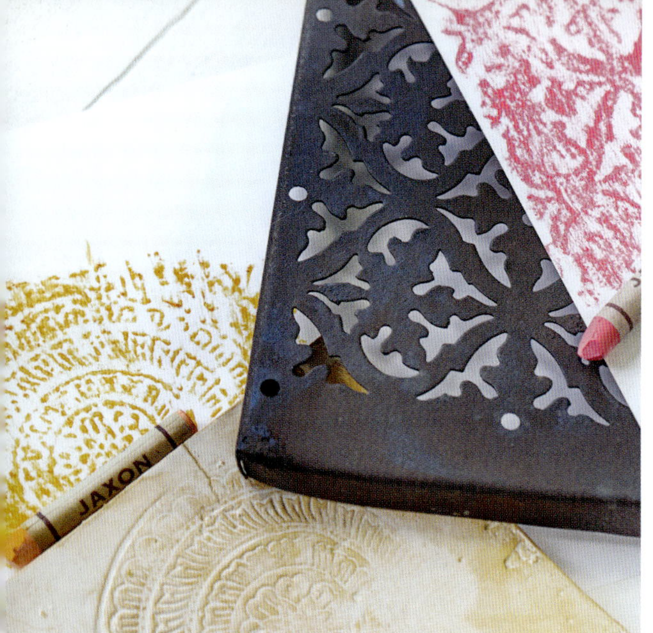

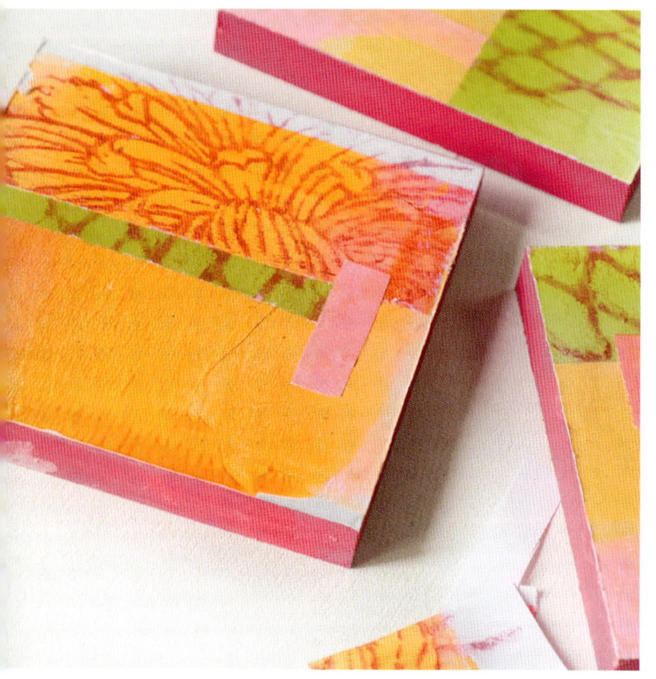

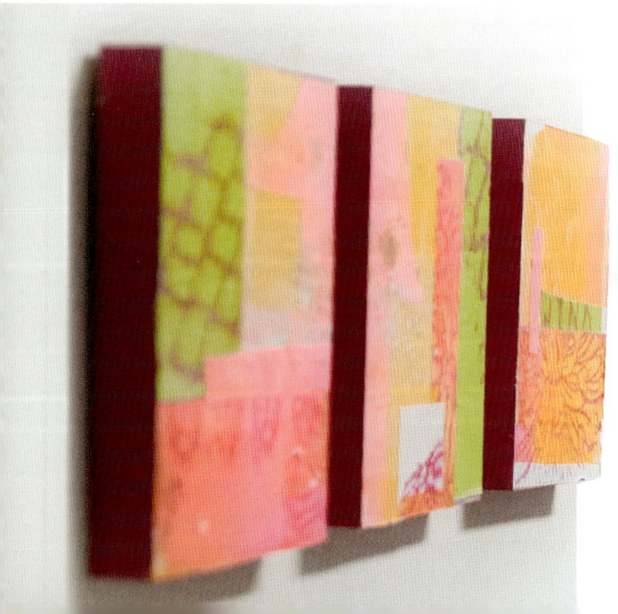

WALL ART

The wax resist technique from page 62 can be varied further. The technique of rubbing over objects to transfer textures is called frottage. Instead of developing your own motifs, you can quickly and easily use existing objects – from household items such as placemats or trivets to stamps. You can use anything that is relatively flat and has an interesting texture that is not too fine.

Again, prepare some motifs before you start printing. The more detailed the motif, the less clearly it will appear in the print afterwards. However, this is not necessarily a disadvantage; with this variation, the goal is to create papers in different colours with interesting textures.

The procedure is the same as with the hand-painted motifs in the wax resist technique, except that this time the paper is placed on a textured surface and rubbed with wax crayons. This transfers the texture on to the paper, which is then placed on the gelli plate to pick up the paint.

We then arranged the prints into collages to create small works of art. To do this, you can cut cardboard to your desired size or, as here, MDF board (or engineered wood) from a hardware store, 12 x 12cm (4¾ x 4¾in) and 16mm (¾in) thick. Then, brush the collages with bookbinding glue or diluted white PVA glue and stick them on.

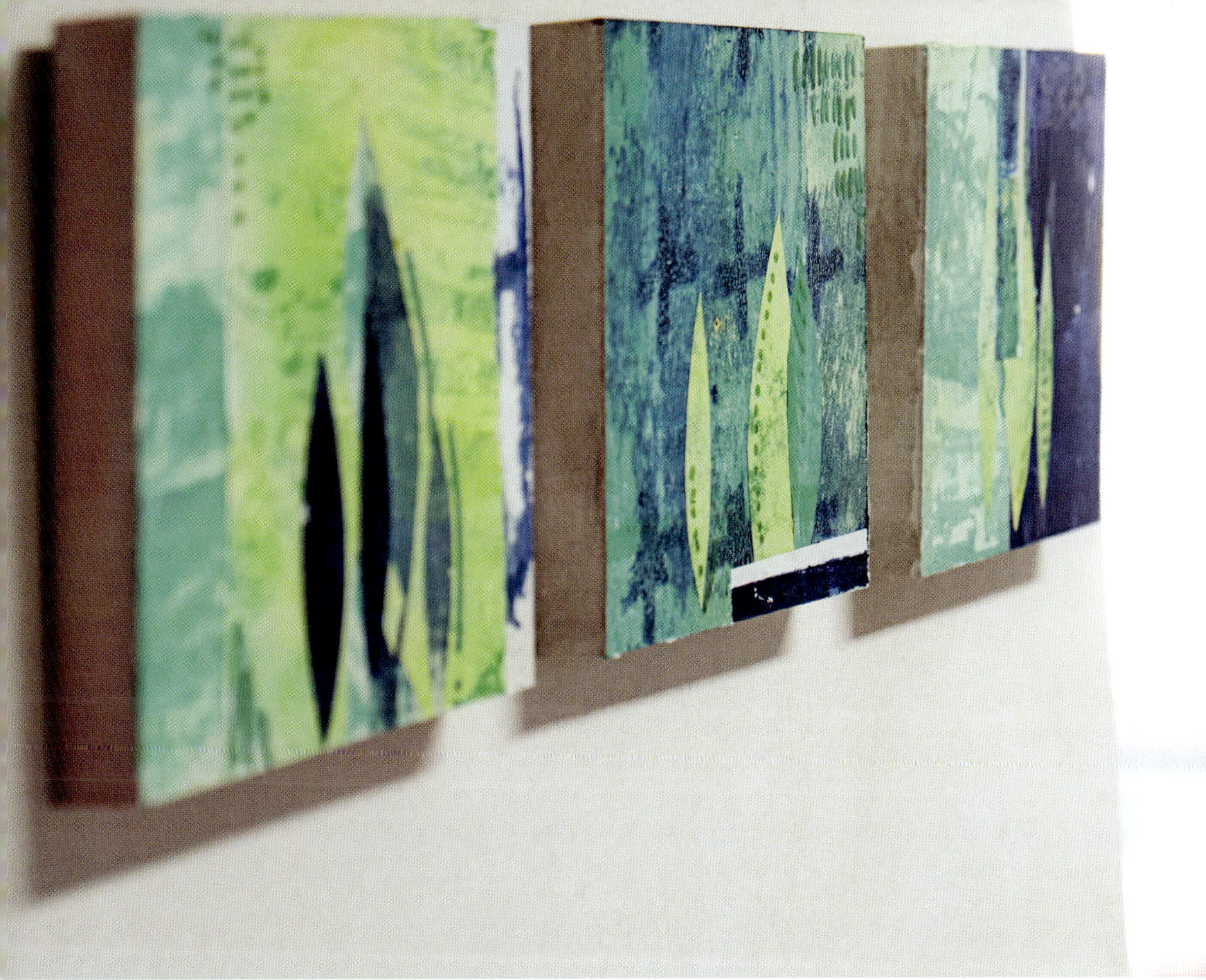

If you want to colour the edges of the boards, it is best to paint them before covering (to be honest, it is easiest to do this directly with your finger, even if it involves a certain amount of paint blotting).

You can, of course, also print directly on to the cardboard or wooden blocks (which is a little more difficult than printing on to paper and then mounting it). You should then prime them white beforehand to give a nice base for printing.

If your MDF blocks are thick enough, you can carefully drill a hole in the wood from behind for easy, invisible hanging, but do not drill all the way through.

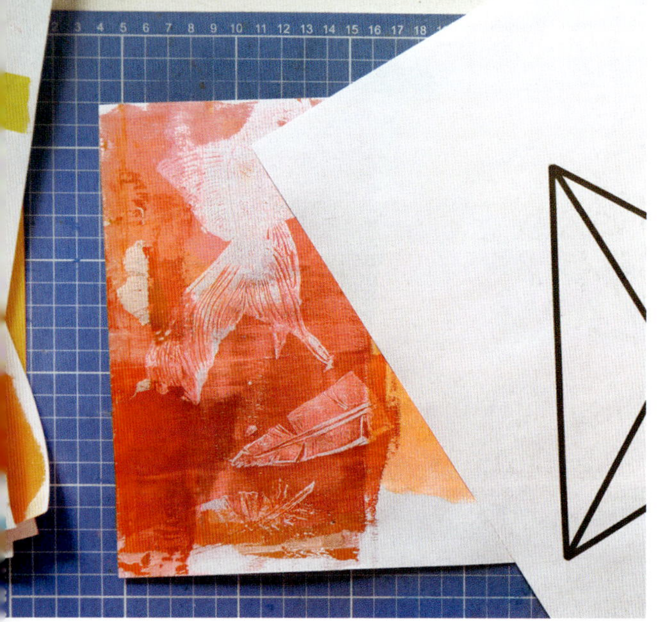

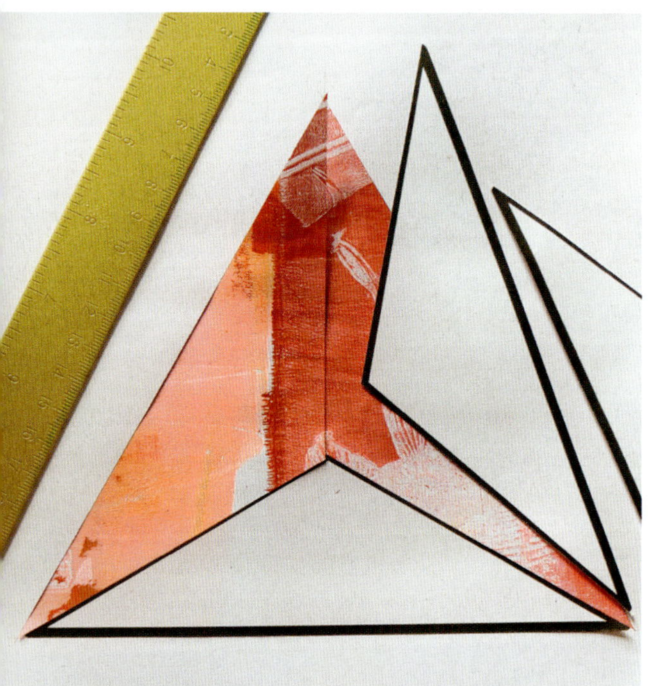

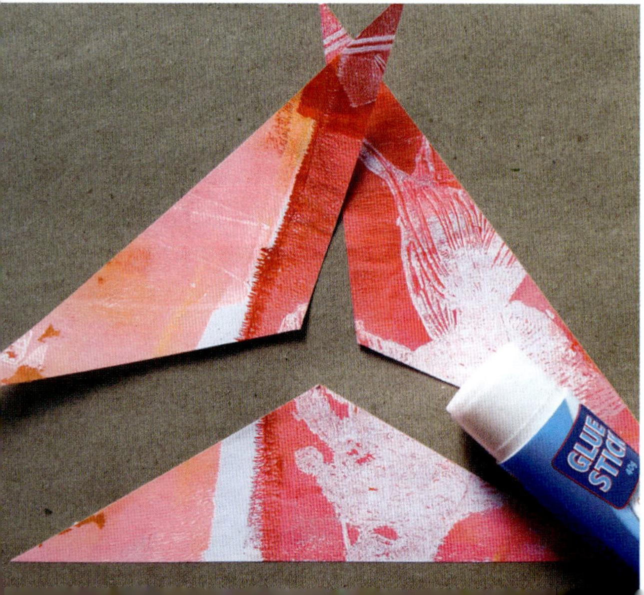

GEOMETRIC SHAPES

You can make quick and beautiful pictures with geometric shapes made from gelli prints. You could frame them or glue them onto wooden blocks or coloured backgrounds.

1. Scan the stencils from page 141, print them out and cut out the shapes.

2. Select your paper that has already been gelli-printed, and place one of the stencils over it. If you hold both papers up to the light or a window, you can see exactly where the stencil outlines are and adjust your print to where you want it within the shape. Alternatively, take leftover pieces from other projects and make a colourful mix. Fix the two pieces of paper together – use a glue stick or a dab of glue in the area outside the lines of the geometric shape. Cut through both sheets along the lines. It is advisable to cut out the shape from the inside to the outside, so that the shapes slip less.

3. Lay out the paper on which you want to stick the shape. Select a printed piece of paper that is to be glued parallel to a page edge and draw in an orientation line on the background paper.

4. Carefully coat the piece of paper with a glue stick (so that the paper does not curl, again preferably in strokes from the inside outwards) and attach it to the background. Then stick on all the other pieces of paper with a slight gap between them.

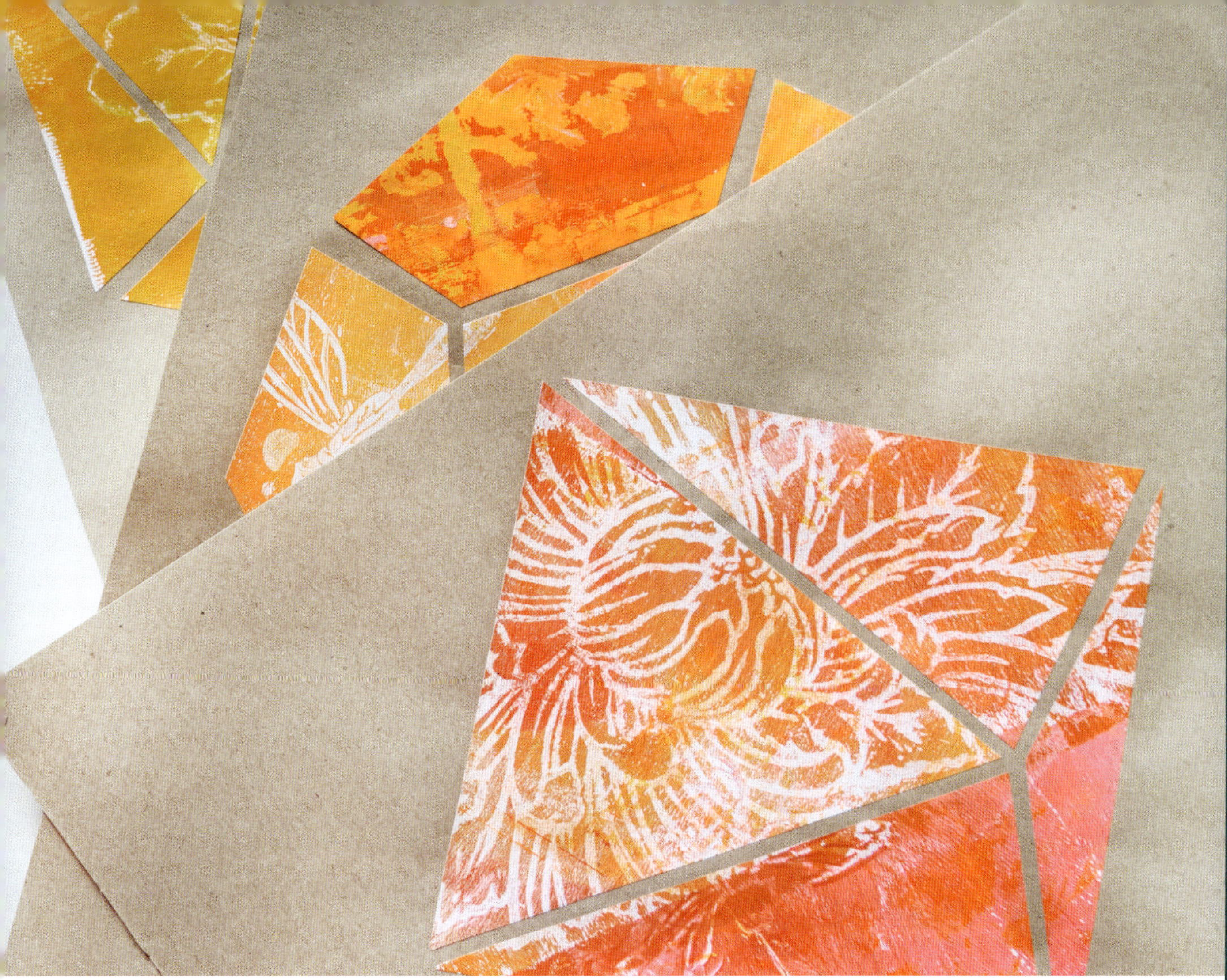

These geometric shapes look best when they are positioned side-by-side. Incidentally, these geometric shapes were referred to as 'platonic solids' by Plato, the Greek philosopher, and are symbols for symmetry and harmony.

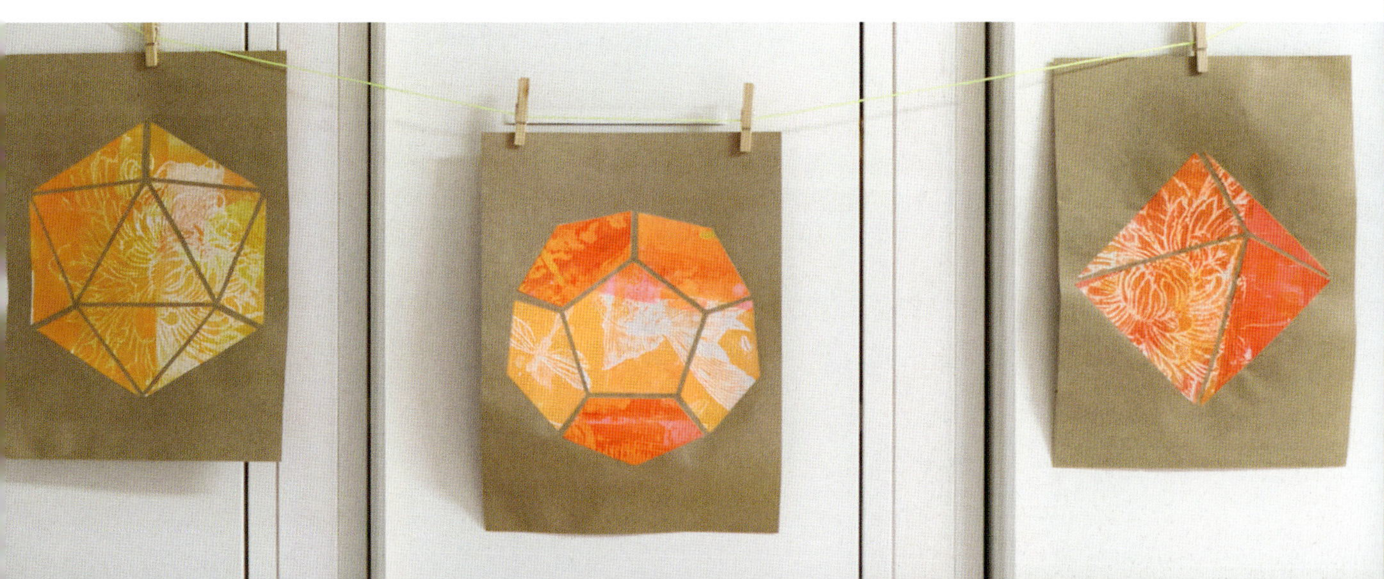

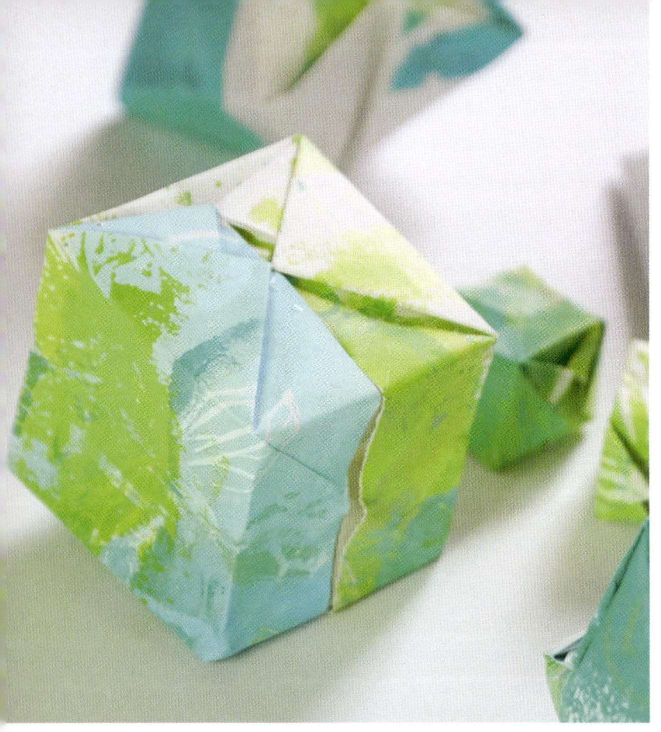

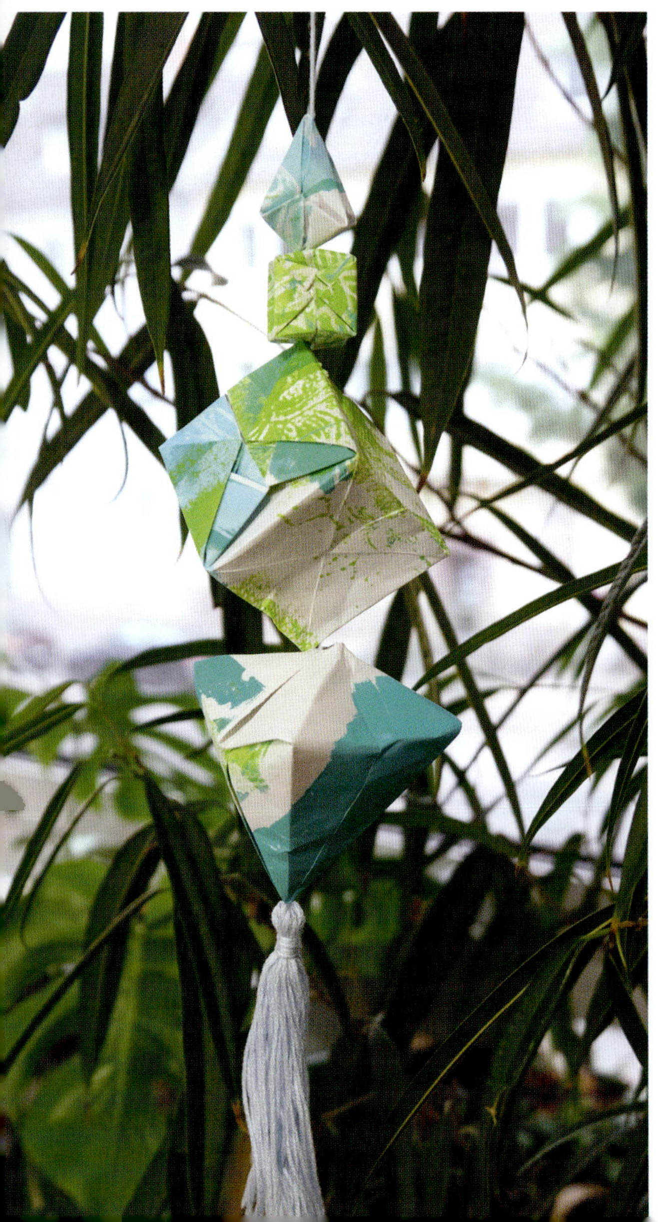

3D GEOMETRIC SHAPES

We can create another variation of geometric shapes simply by folding finished gelli prints. Here, we've designed a small pendant using four shapes and adding a tassel.

The simplest way to fold three-dimensional shapes comes from origami. Please search online for tutorials on the classic origami shapes, such as the cube, pyramid or diamond. Fold your shapes from gelli-printed paper, and secure some of the corners with a liquid glue, if necessary, to help the folded pieces hold their shape.

For our pendant, we chose four shapes in complementing sizes. When making the tassel (there are also tutorials for this online), leave a long piece of yarn hanging and thread it onto a long needle. We pierced the needle from one corner through to the opposite corner for the large cube and through the centre of the side for the small cube. You can choose to tie just one shape with a tassel if you like, and use it as a gift tag, or you can also add beads...

After threading, make a loop at the end of the yarn and hang the object in a suitable place.

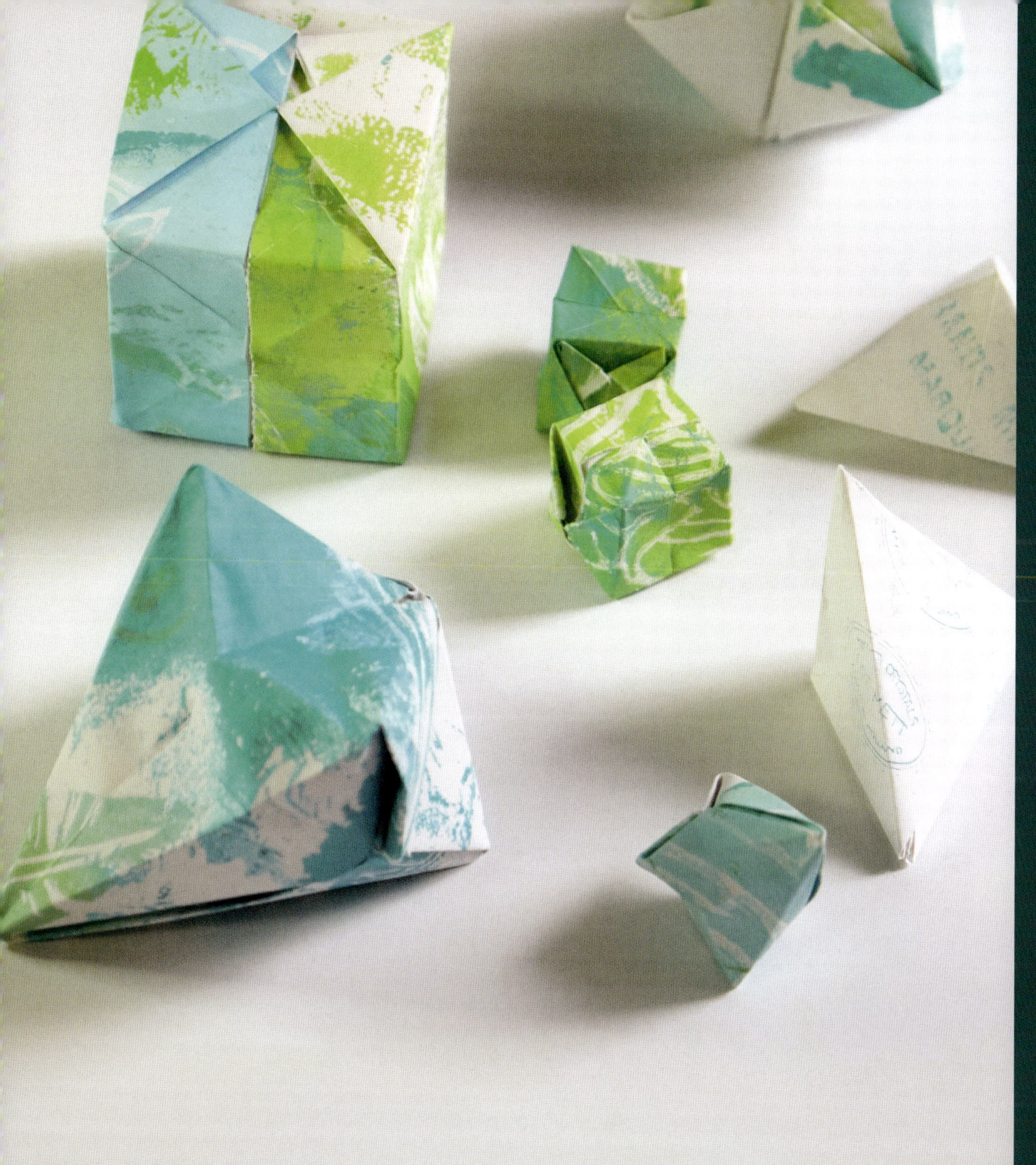

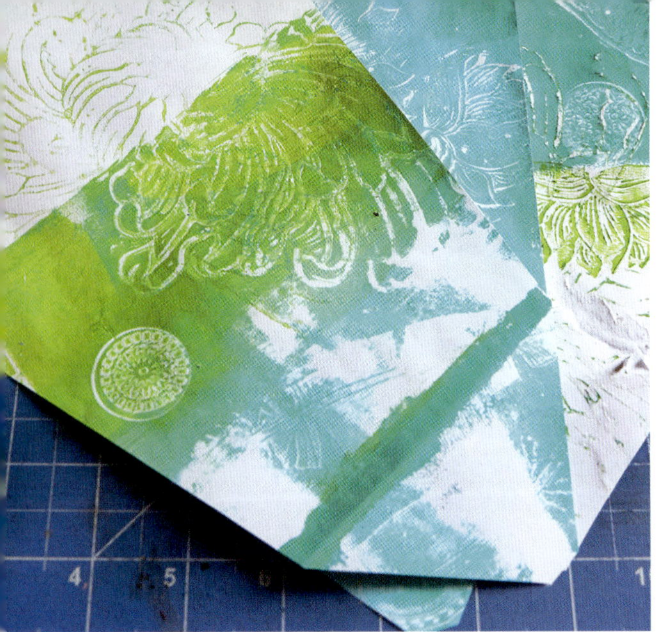

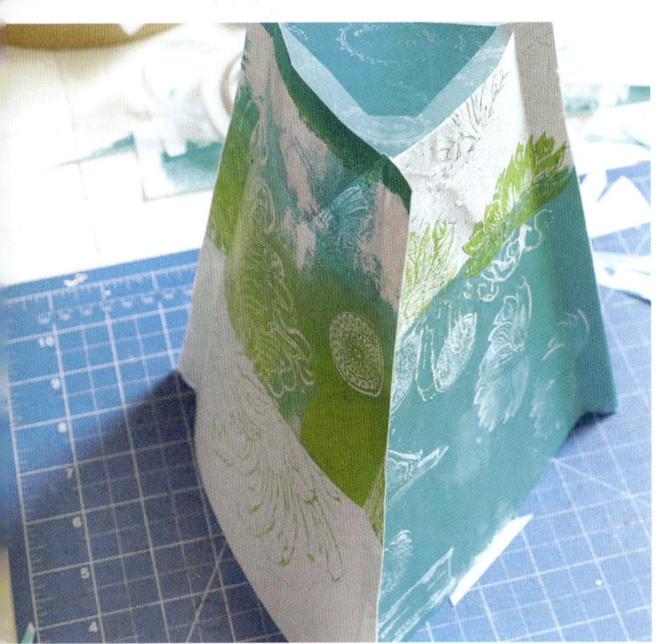

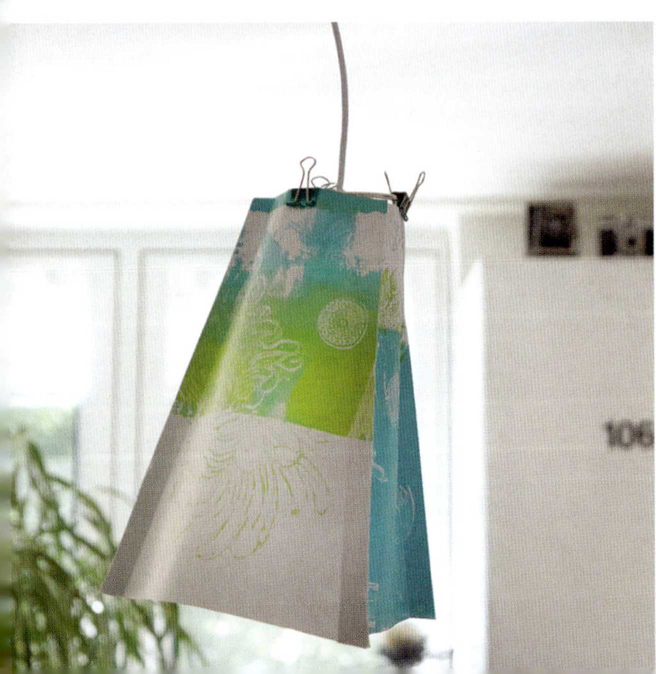

LAMPSHADES

PAPER SHADE

You can make a lampshade out of ordinary paper: cartridge paper works, but thicker paper is better. As paper is stiffer than fabric it almost brings some shape with it, and more so when multiple sheets are glued or sewn together, as shown in this example; the last layer adds a decorative element. Overlapping layers provides reinforcement, and you can create sturdy shapes using three or more layers of paper. Of course, you can also cut out and join four or more pieces.

For our lampshade, we cut out three pieces of paper that taper outwards slightly towards the bottom. We folded the upper edge inwards to reinforce it. A ring serves as the hanger, secured with three coloured clips from the craft store. Cables and fittings can be attached using a simple trick: cut a cardboard circle slightly larger than the top of the lampshade. Cut from the outside to the centre, then cut out a small circle with the approximate diameter of the lamp cord. Clamp this ring around the cord and pull it through the lampshade from below. This secures the cut-out circle inside the lampshade. If the light is to shine upwards through the lamp opening, cut the circle from thicker transparent film. Alternatively, holders can be bent from wire, a thin twig or braided tubing.

Opposite, we show you another variation for a lampshade.

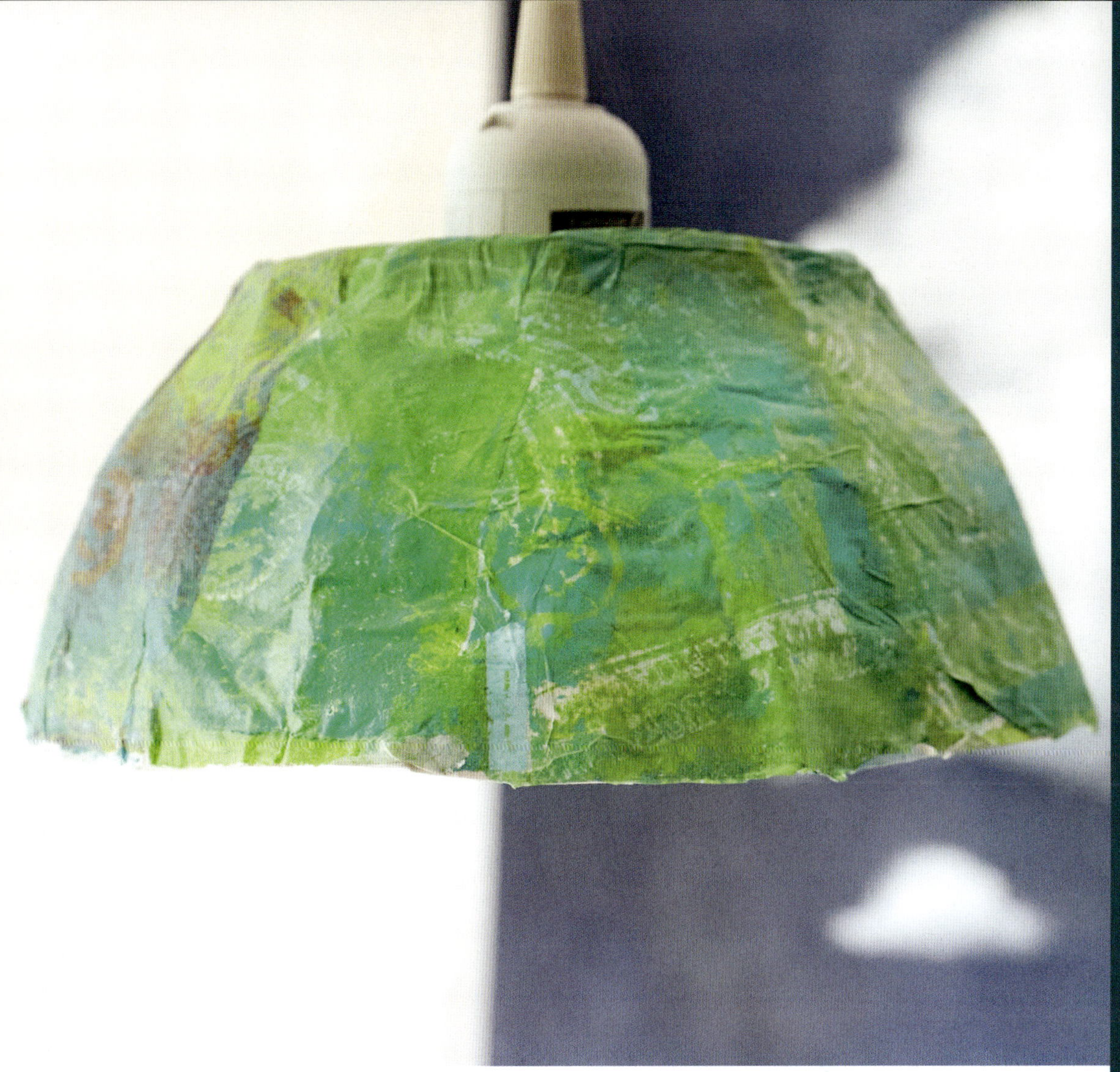

COVERING WITH PRINTED TISSUE PAPER

For this project, we create paper moulds using papier-mâché by lining basins or bowls of an appropriate size with strips of paper.

1. To make it easier to later remove the paper moulds from the bowls, first cover them with a layer of thin plastic film: you can use plastic food wrap from the kitchen or clean plastic bags for this.

2. Tear elongated strips of cartridge paper that taper outwards slightly at the bottom and that are slightly longer than the distance from the interior of the basin to the rim.

3. Mix some thick wallpaper paste or dilute white PVA glue that dries transparently. Your paste should be easy to spread and not contain any lumps.

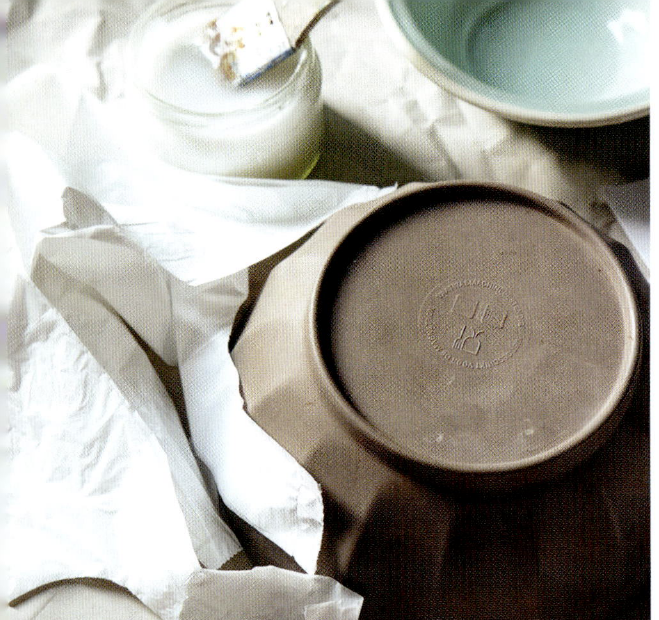

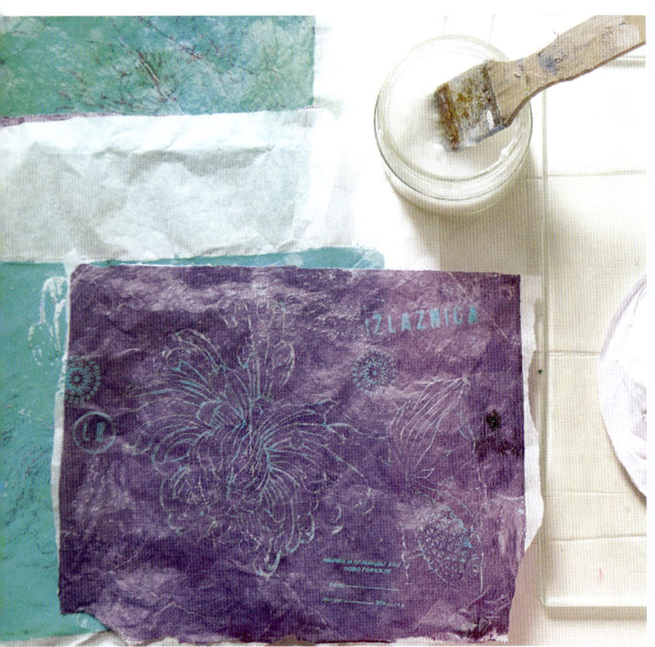

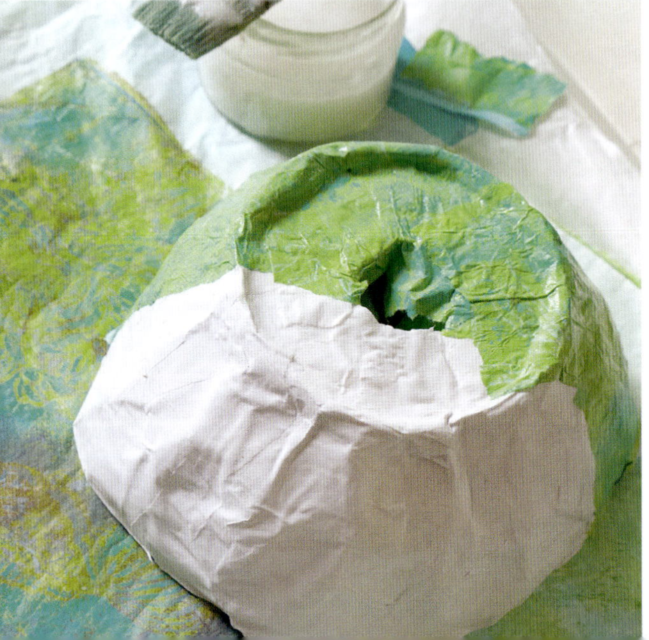

4. Turn the bowl for the lampshade upside down and glue it from the outside. Spread adhesive over part of the bowl or plastic wrap using a wide brush. Then, place a strip of paper on it and brush a layer of adhesive over it. Continue to apply the other strips in the same way, slightly overlapping them – with a total of at least three layers of paper on every area, so that the finished item will be sturdy.

5. Leave the shape to dry well, preferably overnight. Carefully lift it off the bowl – the form does not stick due to the film. If it is not completely dry yet, let the inside air dry. If possible, place in or over the bowl so that it keeps its shape.

6. Theoretically, you can make the top layer of paper from printed papers. However, a more uniform image is obtained if we use printed tissue paper (see page 79) because it is thinner and therefore more flexible. This allows it to be glued on to the bowl in slightly larger pieces. The tissue paper layer should be applied with a little adhesive, which has been diluted once again. This will dry so quickly that the paper shape does not soften and distort.

   When being stuck on to a round shape, the tissue paper may slightly warp, but folds can be quickly smoothed out with the brush. It is best to use 'freestyle printing' here and not a regular, repeat pattern.

7. You can also cover the inside of the paper shape with printed tissue paper, or paint it with a matching colour. For a lampshade, keep in mind that light colours reflect the light source better.

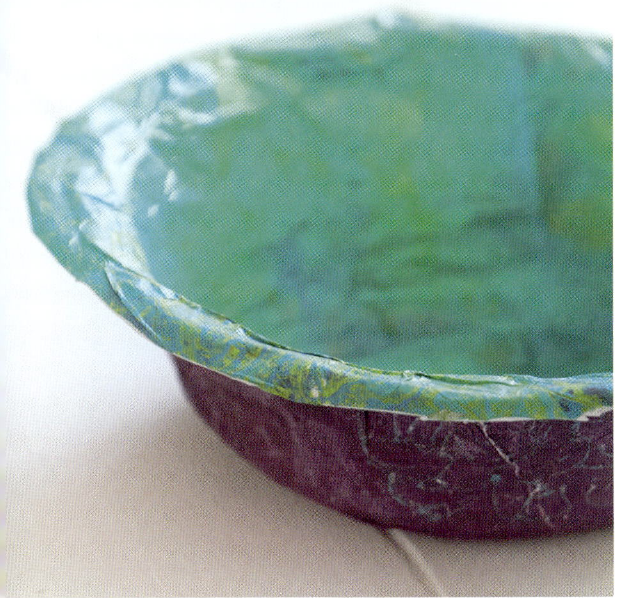

8. Leave the tissue paper to dry thoroughly and then trim the edges. You may need to re-glue the paper layers at the edges to seal them. When the whole thing is dry, you can paint the edge with a gel or gold marker if you like – this also applies to the entire lampshade if you want to add further decorative detail.

9. To make the lampshade more durable, apply one or more layers of clear varnish afterwards. The lampshade will not be waterproof, but it can be gently wiped clean with a damp cloth.

10. To complete the lampshade, you just need to cut a hole for the fitting, then screw it in from both sides.

It does not have to be lampshades either. This technique works just as well with other objects, such as the rectangular tray in the pictures to the left.

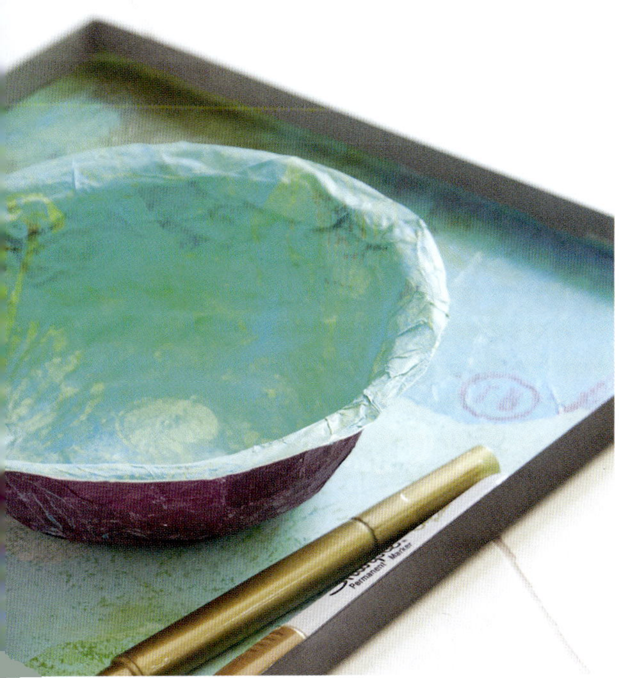

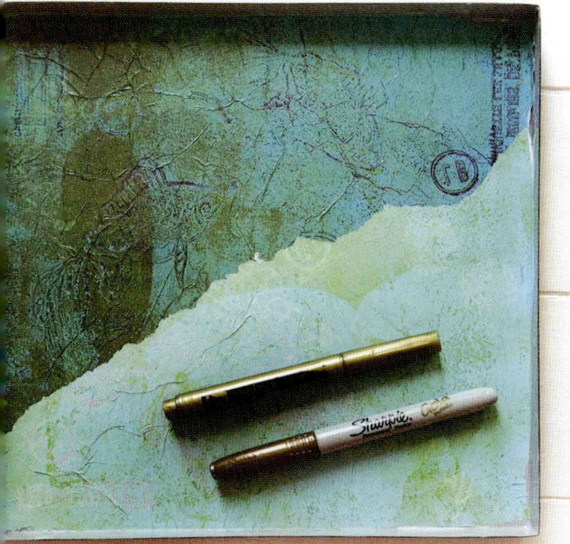

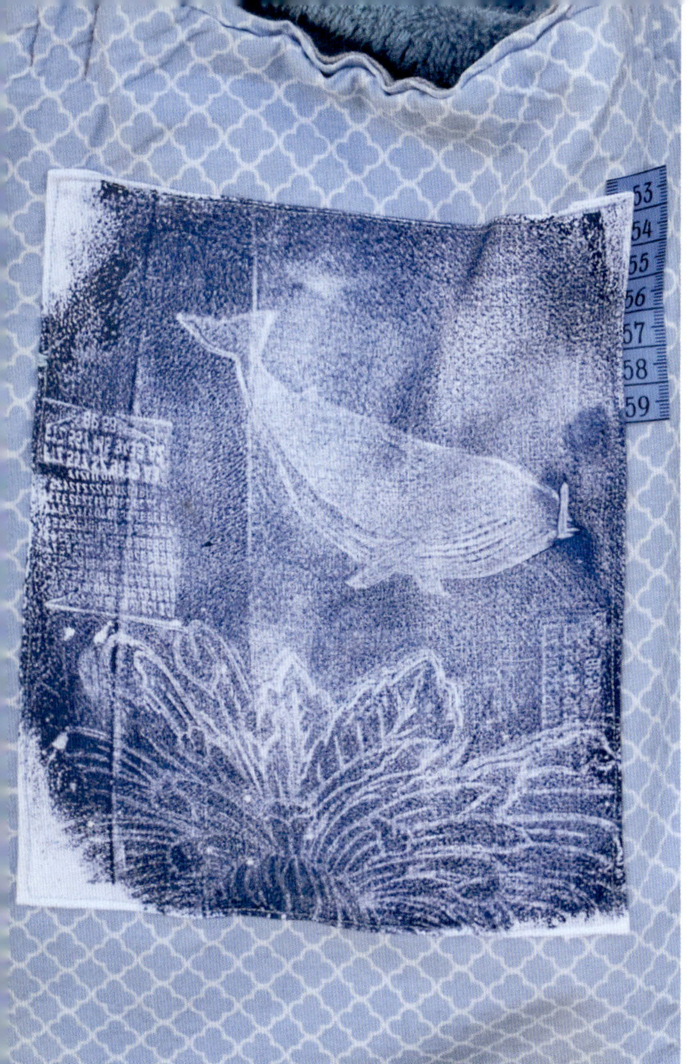

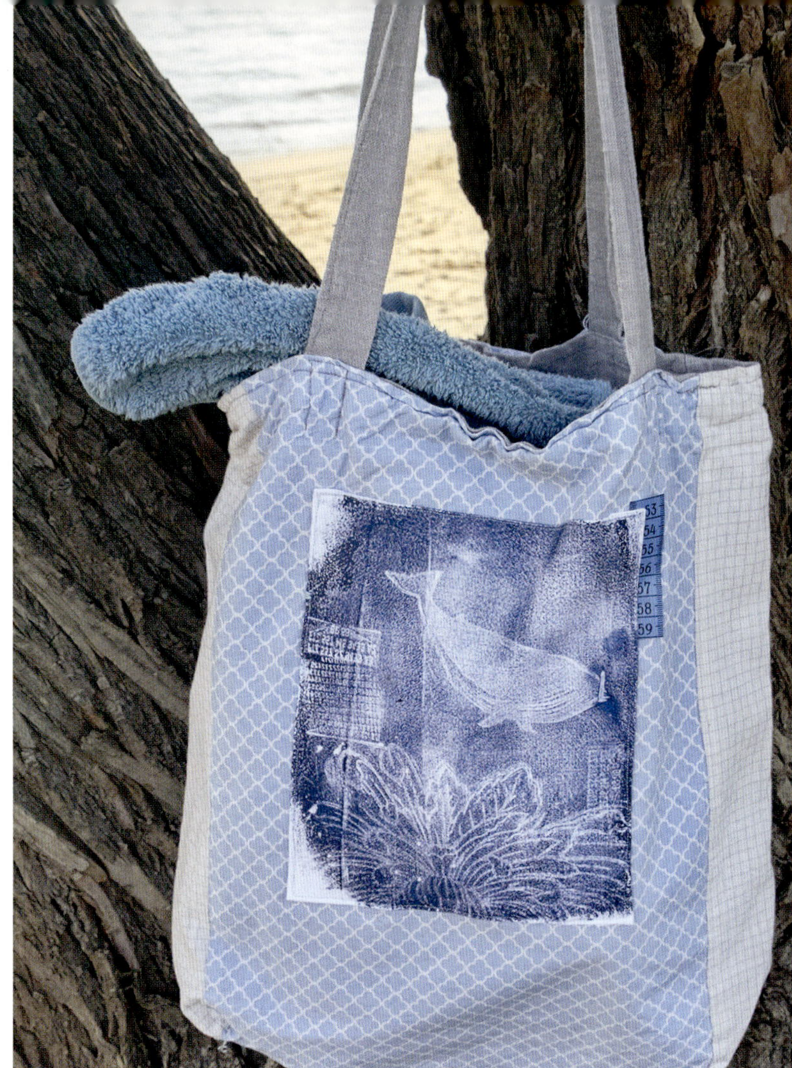

SHOPPING BAG

A simple way to start with fabric projects is to embellish existing objects with a piece of gelli-printed fabric, like the hand-sewn shopping bag shown here.

BUNTING

Another beginner project is bunting. It can be made out of fabric, Tyvek®, or even paper for indoor use. Have a look to see which tests and misprints you can use for this.

1. Take a cord, some cotton yarn, or a ribbon from your craft or sewing supplies and decide how long you want your bunting to be. Consider two factors:
   a. Over what distance do you want to display the bunting, and how low do you want it to hang?
   b. How much extra ribbon do you need to attach the bunting at the ends?

2. Cut out a triangular bunting shape from paper. Fold the paper lengthwise and cut out a triangle (the fold will make the bunting symmetrical). The smaller you want the bunting to be, the smaller the triangles should be.

3. Lay out a few paper or pre-cut fabric triangles side by side to determine the spacing of the bunting. Cut all the required triangles in the same way, plus two or three extras as spares in case of misprints.

4. If the bunting will hang freely, it's best to print on both the front and back.

5. Attach the dried triangles to the cord or ribbon: options include sewing, gluing, stapling or eyelets inserted into holes.

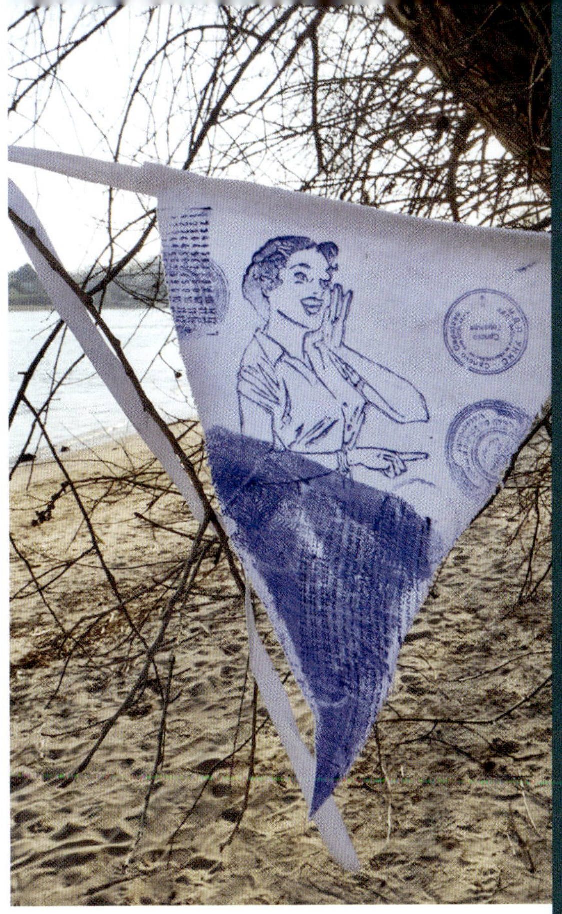

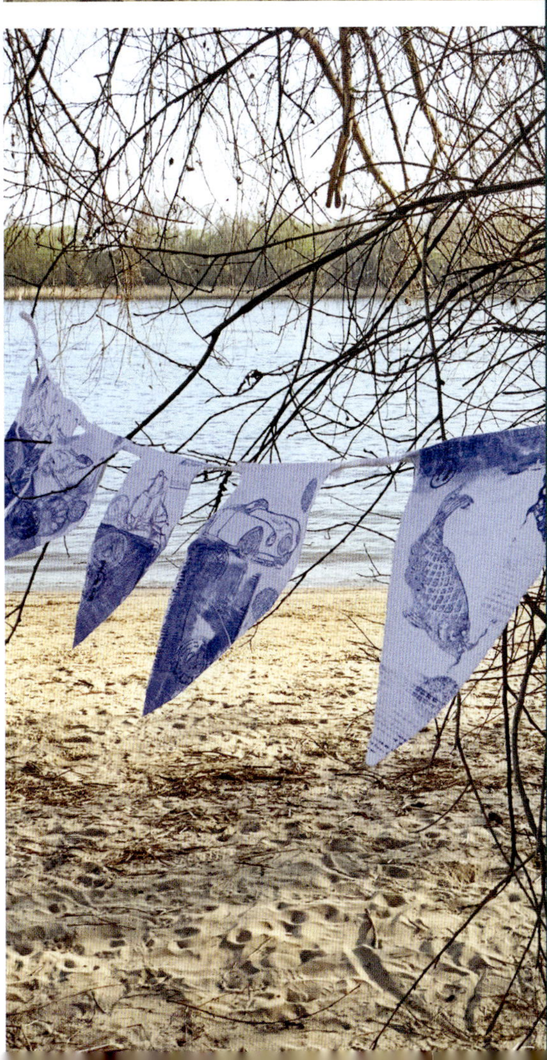

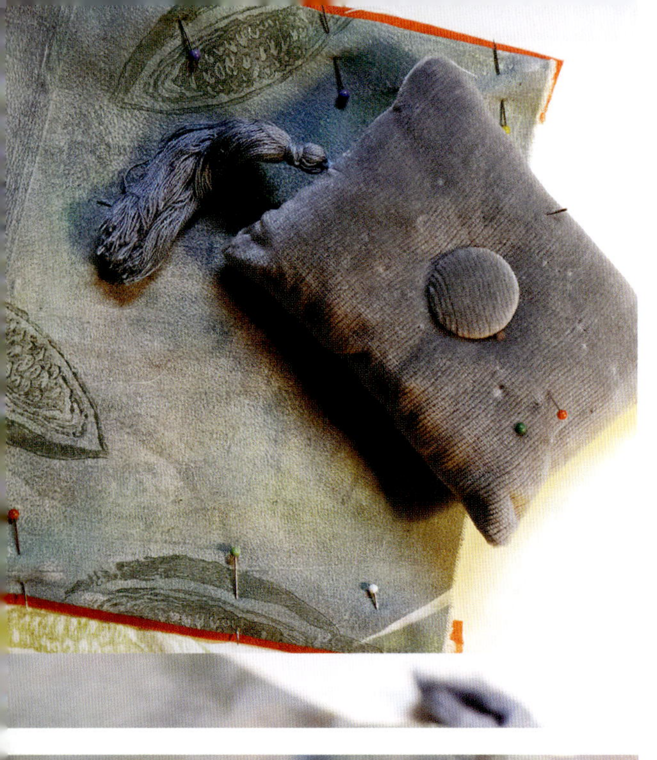

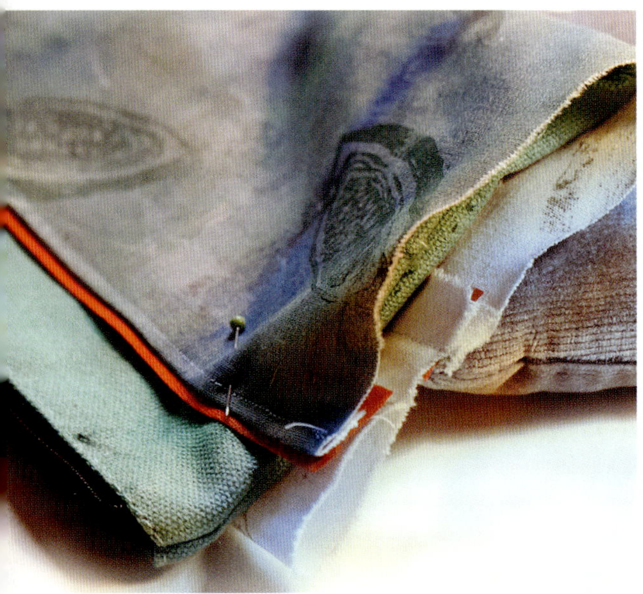

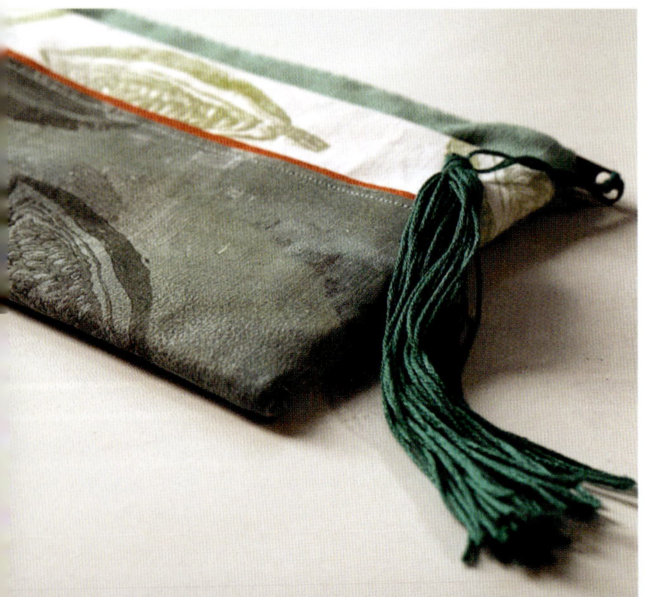

ZIPPED BAG

You can create surprisingly elaborate-looking projects with items you already have at home and without any sewing experience – in this case, a zipped bag with a tassel. For this project, we used a shop-bought mint-green pouch, which is the size of a cosmetics bag.

Then we developed a mini collection of two light and dark complementary fabric variations. All you need for this is white fabric, fabric paint in a light and a dark shade, and a single stamp. We used a hand-carved stamp with a cocoa bean motif.

1. Print light green gradations on the white fabric.

2. Mix some light and dark green fabric paint to create a medium green and then print evenly over the rest of the fabric with it in one go, covering the entire surface.

3. Then stamp the motifs on to both fabrics using a slightly darker and a very dark green (as with the freestyle technique on page 76).

4. Sew the two pieces of fabric together. If you like, add a small trim or a piece of matching fabric between them. Here, the red of the ribbon brings out the green as a complementary contrast.

5. Fold both the top and bottom edges of the fabric inwards, tucking the fabric around the pouch. Carefully unpick the side seams of the pouch, insert the printed fabric, and then sew the seams closed again.

If you prefer not to sew, use fabric glue to stick the folded fabric edges to the pouch. Unpick the side seams of the pouch and insert the fabric. You can either sew the sides by hand from the inside or staple them together.

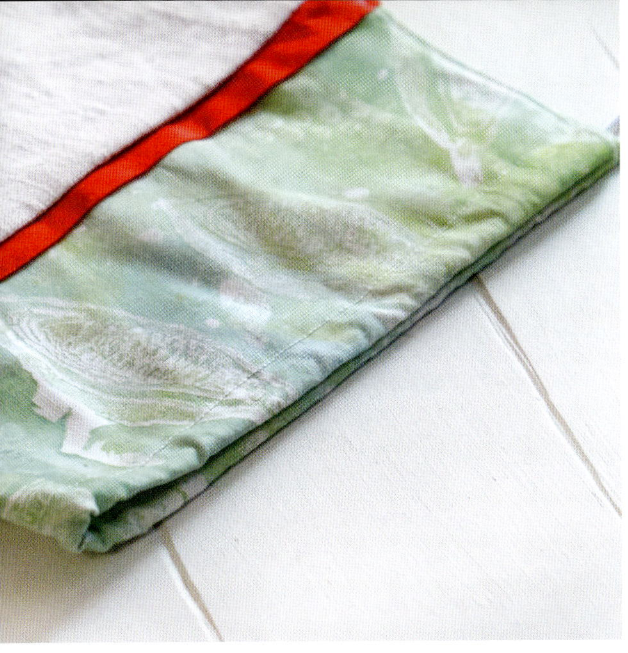

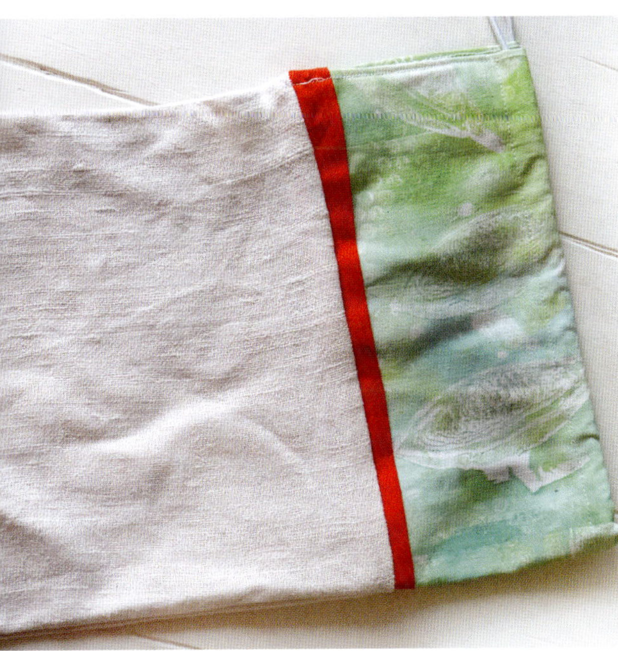

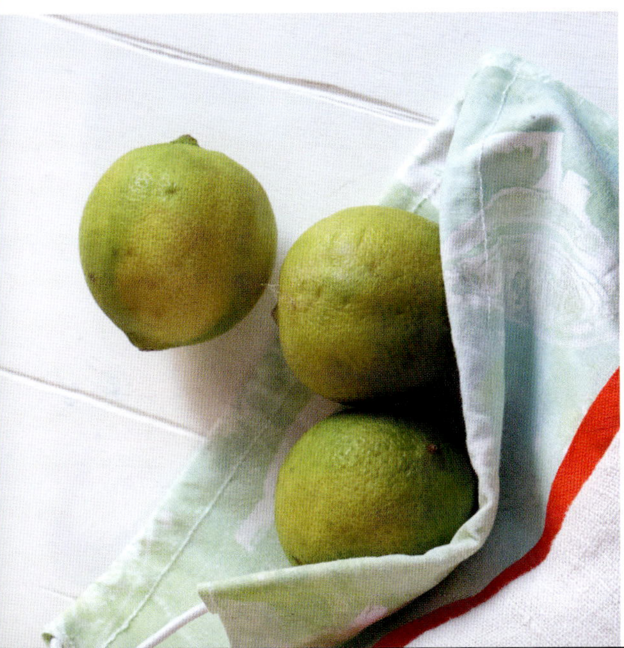

VARIATION: BAG

We sewed a bag with a self-designed fabric border from some old linen fabric. You can never have enough bags in various sizes – ideal for storing everything from cosmetics to sports gear. There are ready-made, unprinted bags, as well as aprons or pouches, available in craft stores, waiting for your gelli-print decoration!

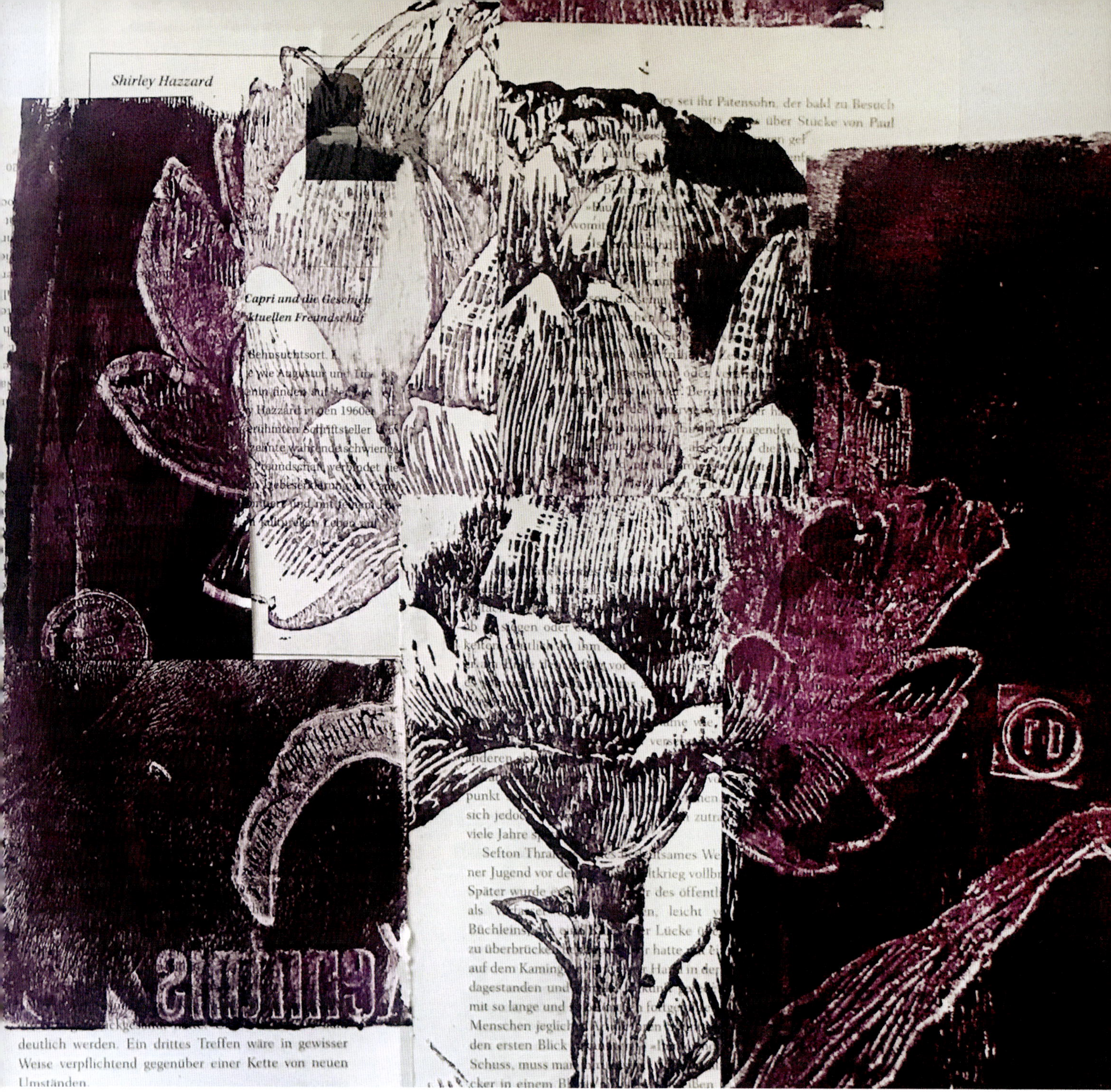

COLLAGE

You can experiment with printing and still work towards a goal by creating several prints and then assembling them into larger images. This is a good way to get started – to not only create lots of random prints, but also to combine them to create a finished project.

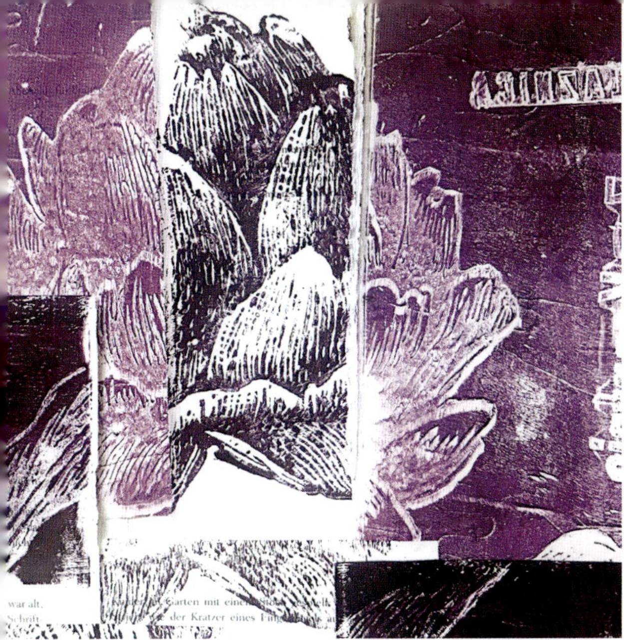

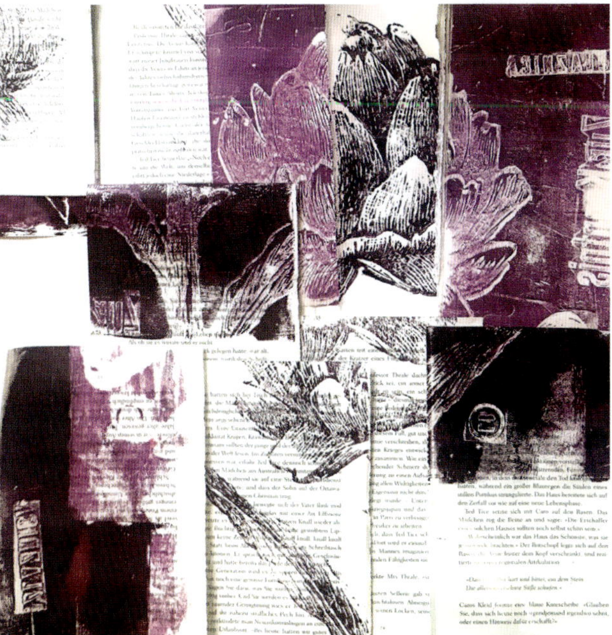

Here, we are making use of the positive and negative prints created with stamps on a gelli plate. If you print on pages from recycled books (you'll find plenty at recycling centres and book exchange stations), you are not only working in an environmentally conscious way, but you are also bringing an additional design element into play through the printed lines of text.

The end result is a collection of large-format images that can be framed or mounted on a wooden board (see page 110). To achieve a large format, there are two options, depending on the size of the printed motifs:

a. For a single large motif – applied using a stencil or, as shown in the pictures here, with a large, hand-carved lino stamp with an artichoke motif – the image can be composed of various parts of a motif that are printed together without fitting exactly. When positive and negative prints are arranged slightly offset, the result is a slightly abstract motif.

b. If you don't have a large-format stamp to hand, you can line up many smaller motifs. This does not result in a single recognizable image, but by arranging similar prints, you can create a format of any size, which takes on its own character through the repetition.

These techniques are also used by artists: Andy Warhol is known for his use of repeated motifs, and David Hockney has created huge compositions from multiple small photographs.

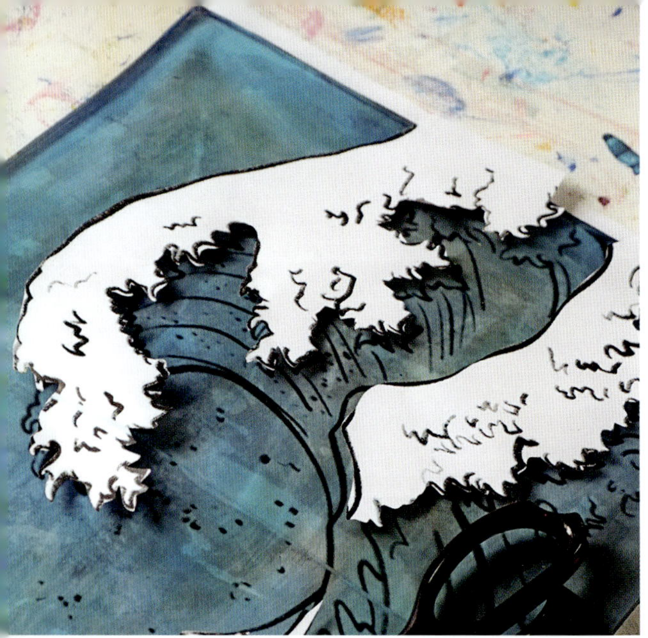

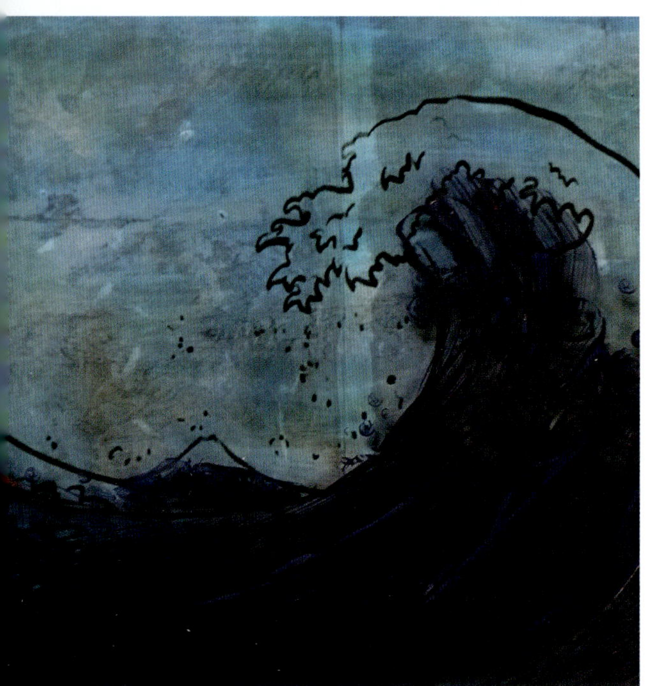

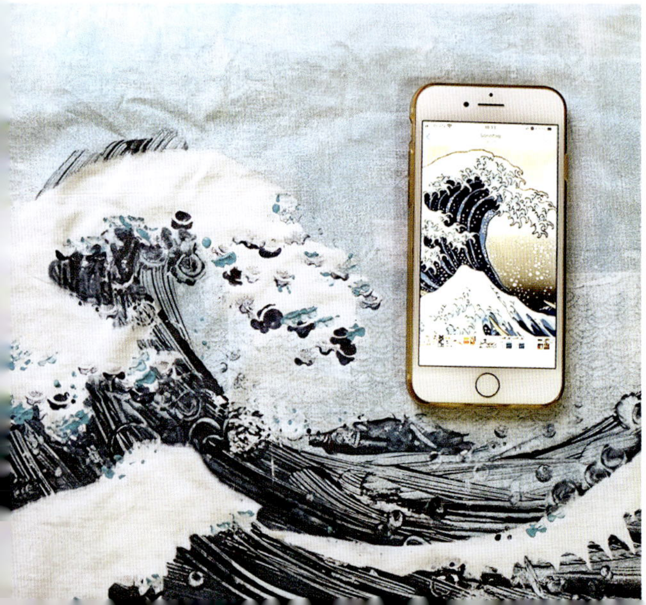

KIMONO

You can take inspiration from an object or work of art and try to achieve similar effects using gelli printing techniques.

This was the principle we used for the prints with household objects (see page 34), where Japanese patterned bowls served as inspiration. The whole thing can also be made a little more sophisticated. For this kimono, we took a well-known woodcut as our starting point: Hokusai's print *The Great Wave off Kanagawa*. Woodcuts and Japanese patterns are generally a great source of inspiration.

1. A quick analysis of the image showed that we needed a stencil to cover the white crests of the waves, but otherwise we could work with a few colours and textured areas. As gelli plates are transparent, printed motifs can be placed under the plate so that the design elements can be accurately positioned.

2. First, draw or trace the motif in a simplified form (you will find our version on page 140), resized to fit the gelli plate, and print out or copy it twice. Place one copy under the plate, then cut out the stencils for the crests of the waves from the second print.

3. Before starting to print, organize your materials. If you want to print in multiple colours, you need to consider the sequence of colours and motifs. The first layer on the plate – the dark blue waves – will be the top layer of the print, so we apply it first. Once it's dry, we roll the background over it and texture it. The stencils for the white areas are only applied just before printing, to cover the colour underneath and to create precise lines or blocks of colour.

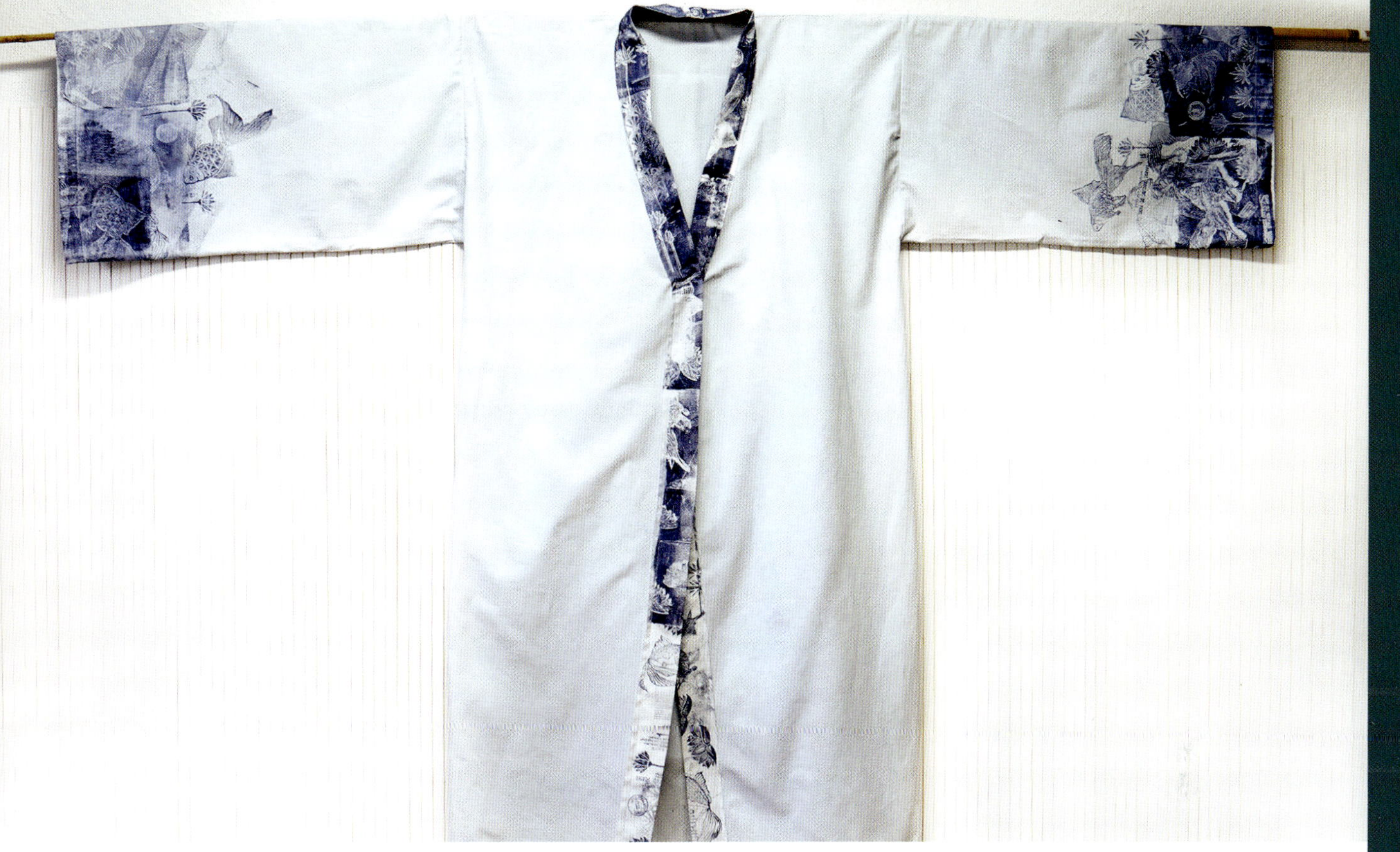

If you want to take your time with the design elements, leave each layer of paint to dry, and then activate them for printing with a thin layer of white paint. The colour sequence in this case would be: dark blue (waves), light blue (sky), turquoise (wave details, which can also be stamped on at the very end) and white (an invisible background to activate the paint). With gelli printing, you don't need to be too precise in the way you apply colours over each other; you can instead capture everything in a single print – just make sure to rub the paper or fabric on well.

If you're working with fabric, you can lightly dampen it with a spray bottle, which will also activate the paint.

It's best to conduct test runs beforehand with the materials you plan to use.

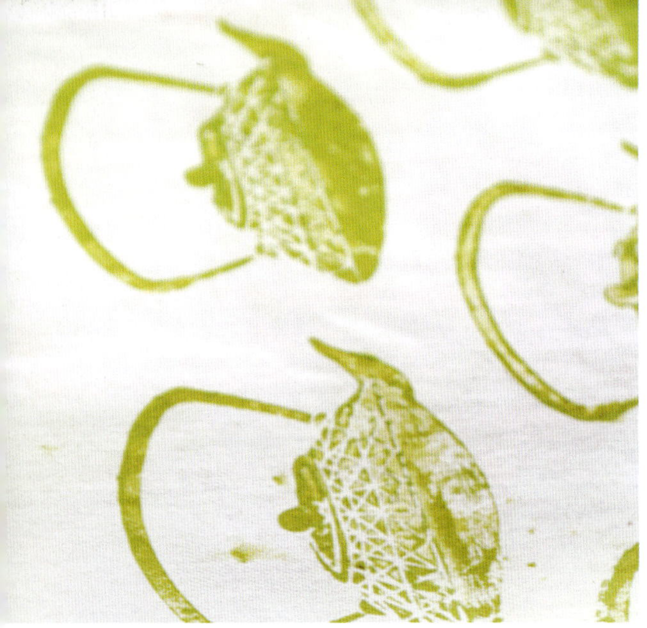

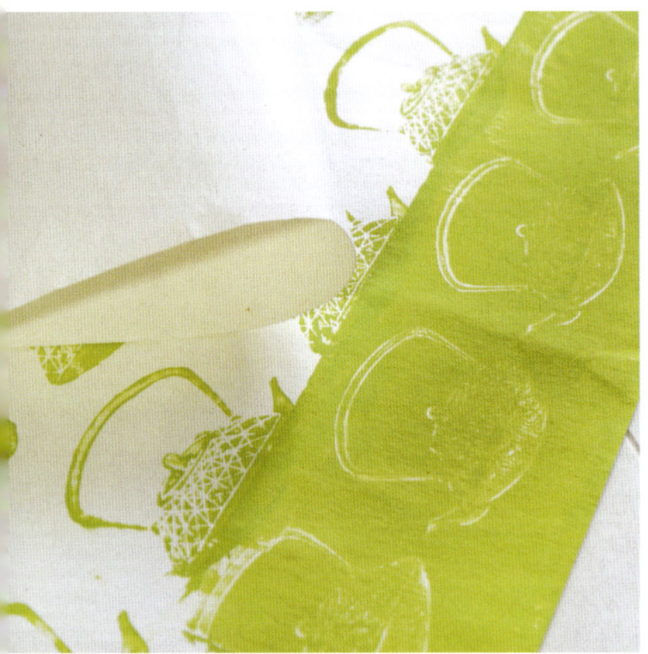

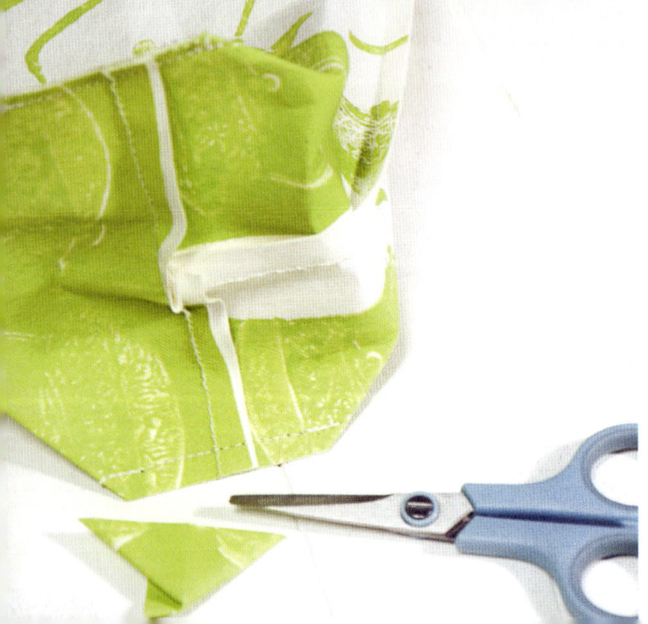

LUNCH BAG

SnapPap (see page 93) is a robust vegan faux-leather similar to Tyvek® that is wonderful for printing on, but compared with Tyvek® it is significantly thicker and quite stiff when dry. For this reason, if you sew it instead of gluing, it is best to work with it slightly damp. SnapPap is very suitable for bags, wallets and pouches (sewing instructions are available online).

1. We made a lunch bag from SnapPap. As you don't have to trim the material, we kept the seams visible on the outside as an additional design detail. Start by sewing the short edges of your rectangular fabric toegther – this makes the seam for the back of the bag.

2. At the base, close the bottom seam so that the side seam runs centrally on the back. To make the lunch bag three-dimensional, pull the bottom corners outwards, then sew and trim the triangles at the corners. The larger the triangles, the wider the base surface.

The same principle can be used to sew storage caddies or flowerpots (use a waterproof pot inside).

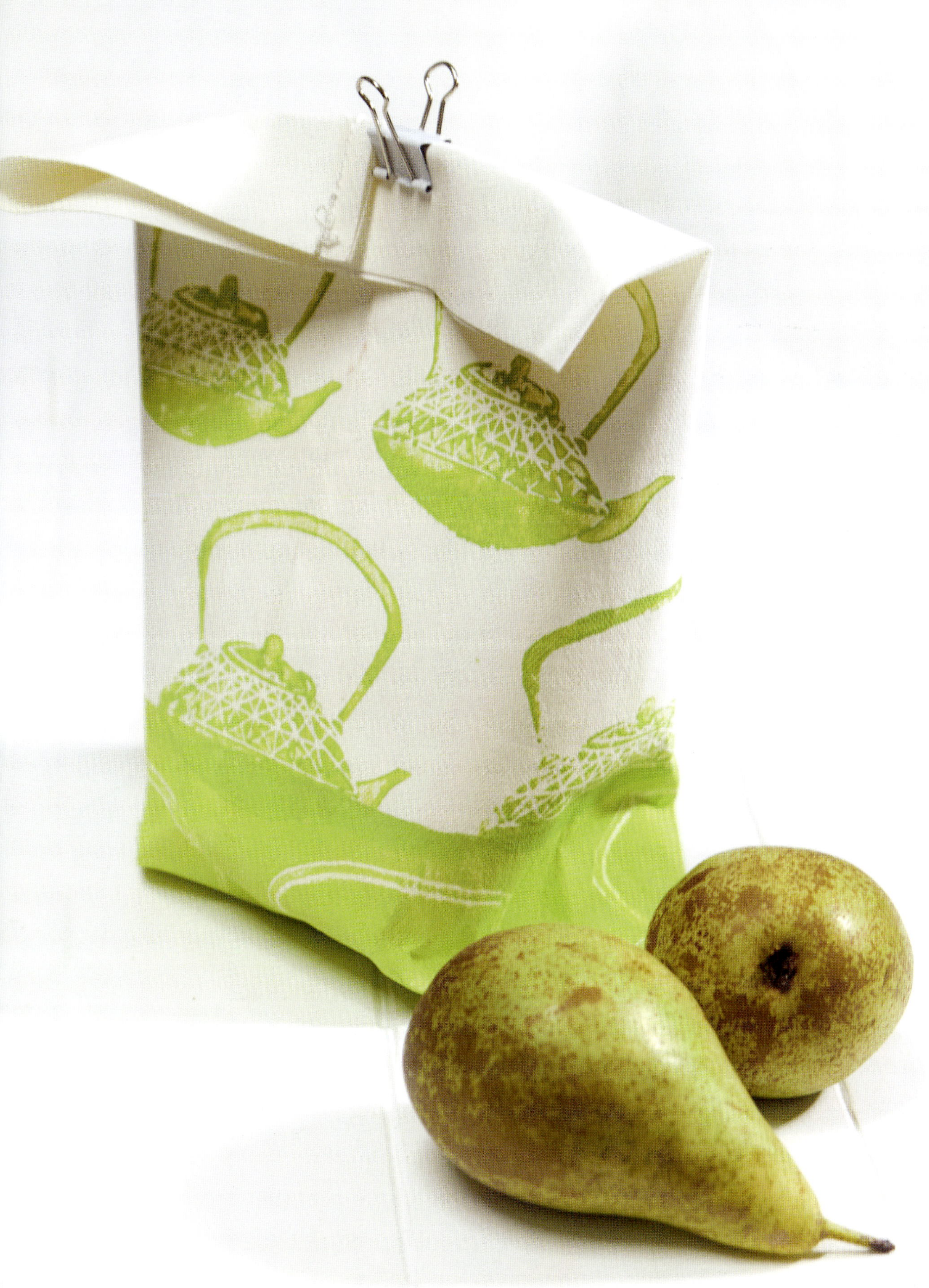

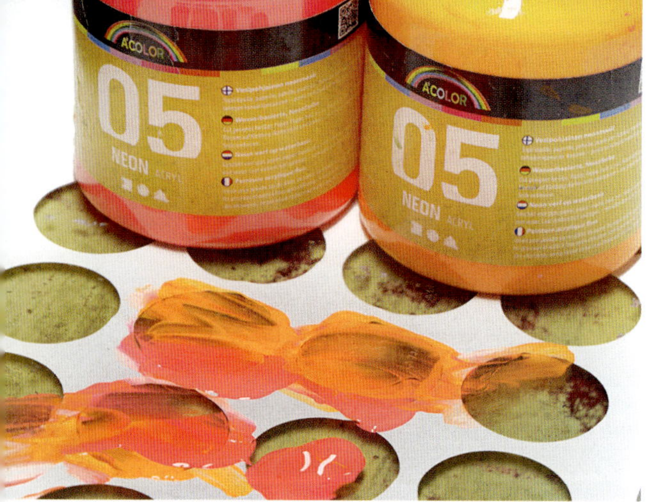

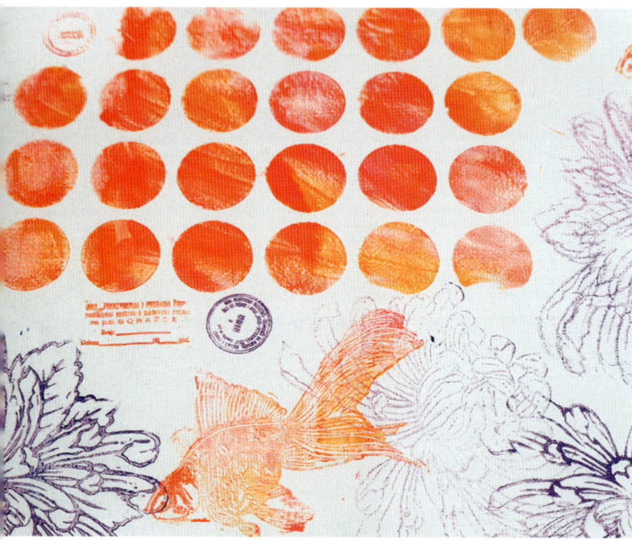

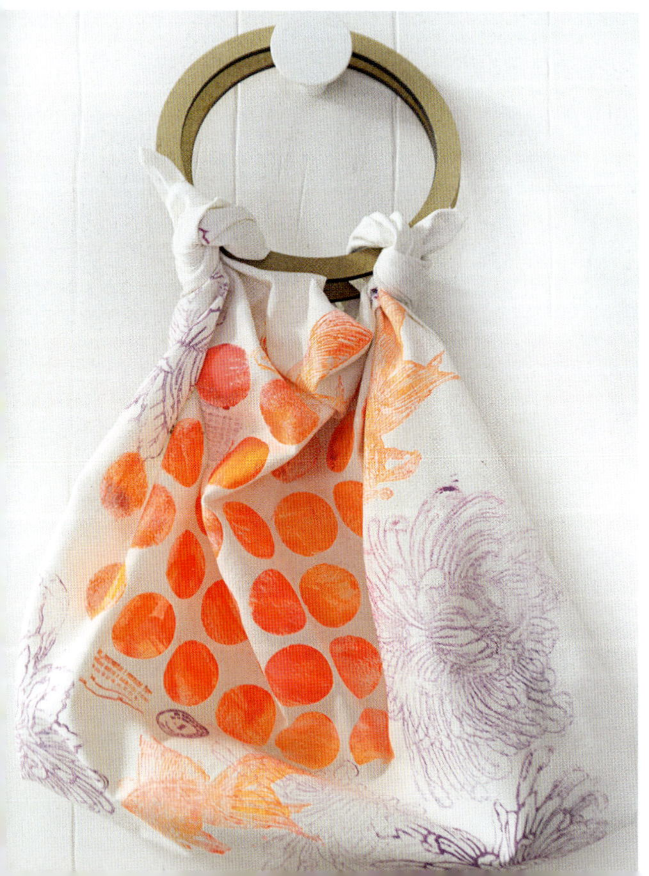

BAG WITH HOOP HANDLES

If the printing needs to be done quickly or you need a thin layer of paint, there's no getting around the need for a brayer. But when it comes to creating interesting areas of colour, our fingers are also wonderful tools. However, they are more suitable for smaller areas, and as the paint is applied quite thickly and irregularly, fabric is easier to print on than thin paper.

Here, we have used an adhesive film with punched circles. Round self-adhesive labels, available from stationery or craft shops, are well-suited to printing – except that we don't use the labels themselves, but the adhesive film around the holes, as a negative stencil.

For this technique, it's better to use only two or three contrasting colours. The effect is barely noticeable with similar colours.

Dab the paint on with your fingers and smear the different shades together.

To make a quick Japanese-style bag, we bought wooden hoops from a craft store, and tied the printed piece of fabric with two knots around each hoops.

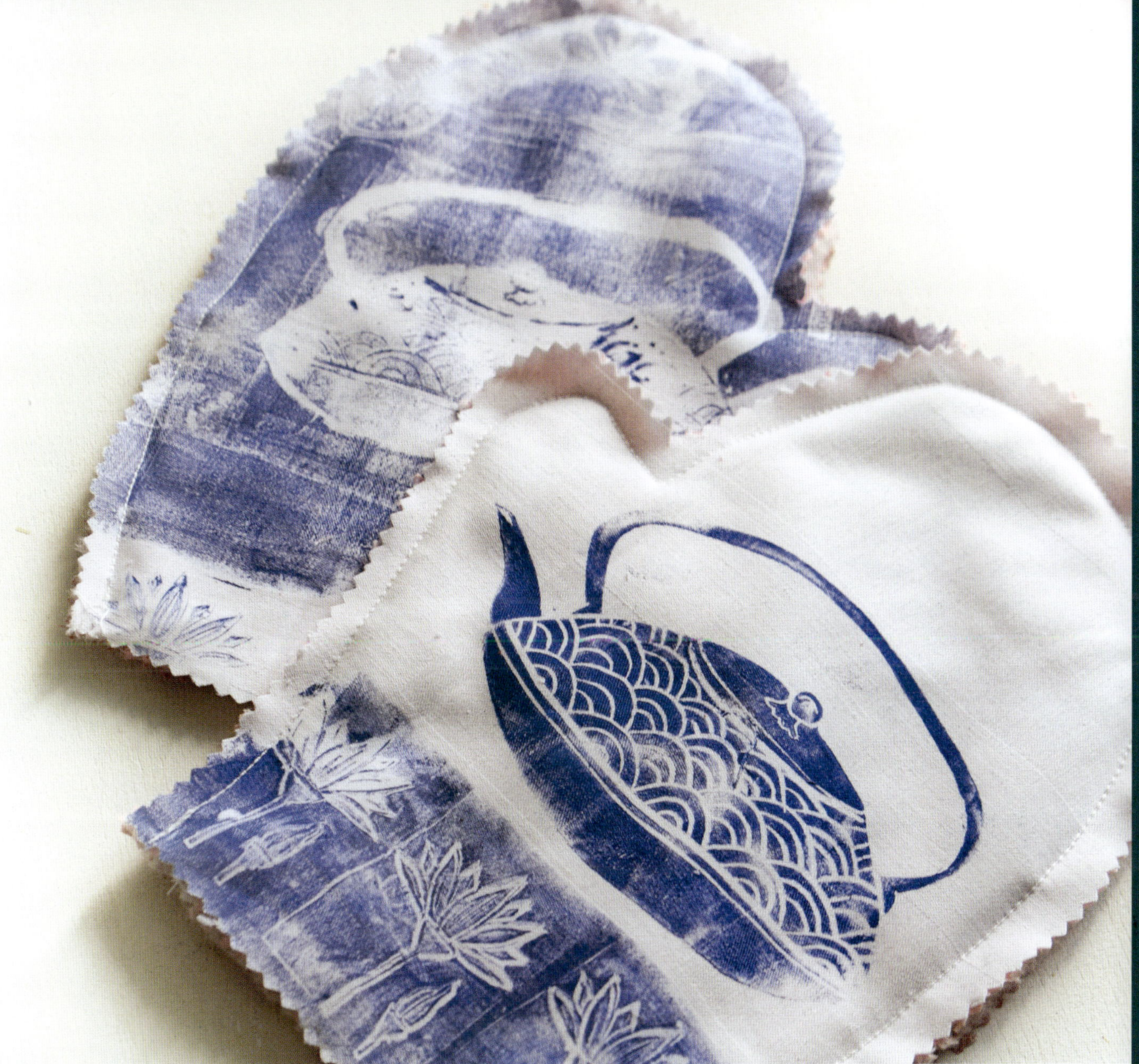

OVEN MITTS

Oven mitts are another quick project. They need to be thick to protect your hands from heat, so you should use sturdier fabric and either reinforce it with iron-on interfacing or – as we have done – use a piece of an old cotton quilt as the underside.

To get the right shape, place one hand on a piece of paper and draw the outline with a thick pen, leaving a gap around your hand. It is important to have a wide enough cuff at the bottom so that you can comfortably slip your hand inside (you will find a template on page 142, which you may need to resize for your own hand). Transfer the template to your printed fabric, sew the edges together with the right side facing outwards, and trim with pinking shears.

Templates

These templates are also available to download free from the Bookmarked Hub: www.bookmarkedhub.com. Search for this book by title or ISBN: the files can be found under 'Book Extras'. Membership of the Bookmarked online community is free. The templates can be scaled to suit your own project.

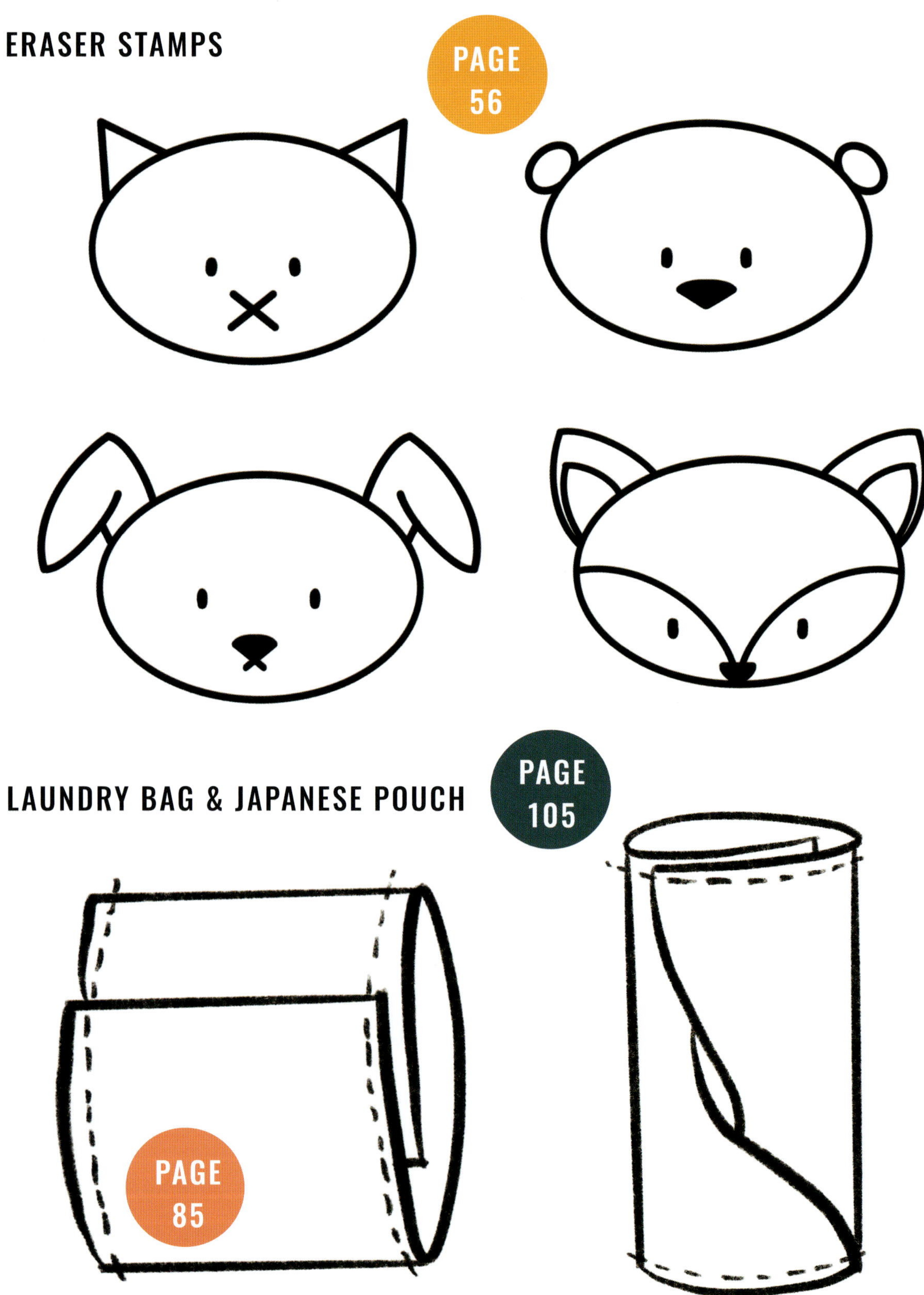

JAPANESE FABRIC BAGS

(resize as required)

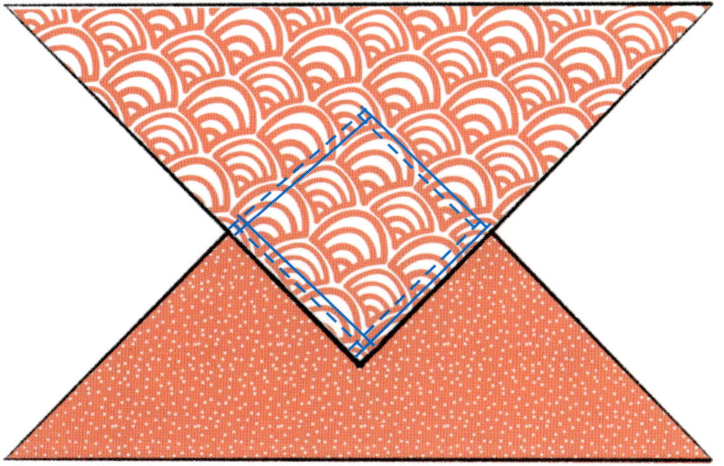

STORAGE BAG OR PURSE

(sew or knot the side seams)

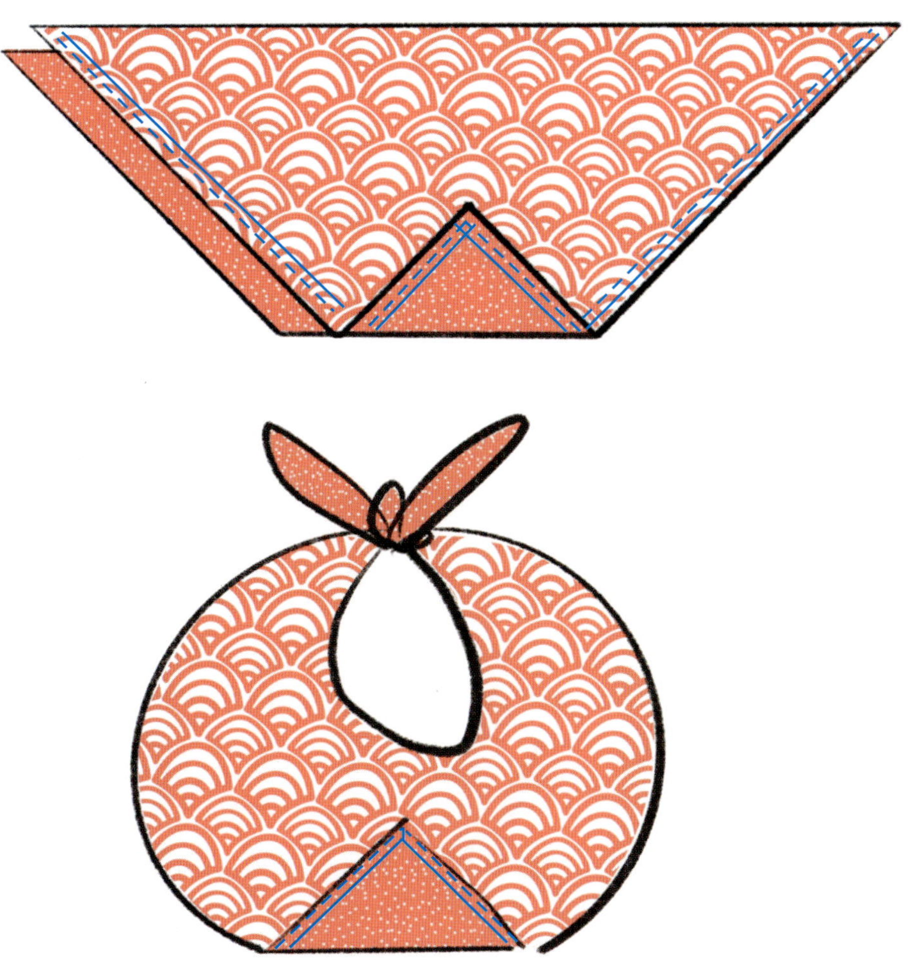

MINI BOOK FOLDING INSTRUCTIONS

PAGE 96

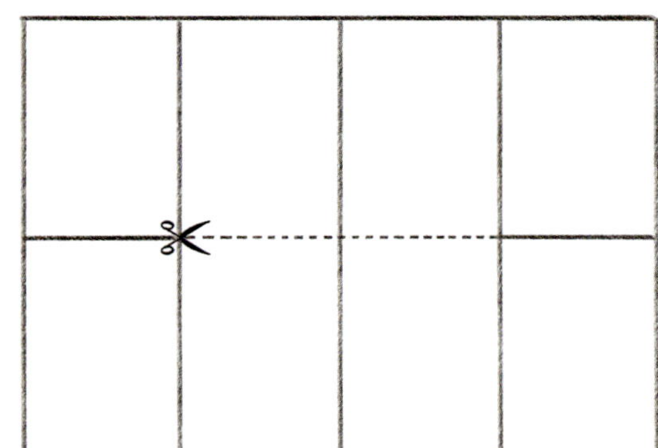

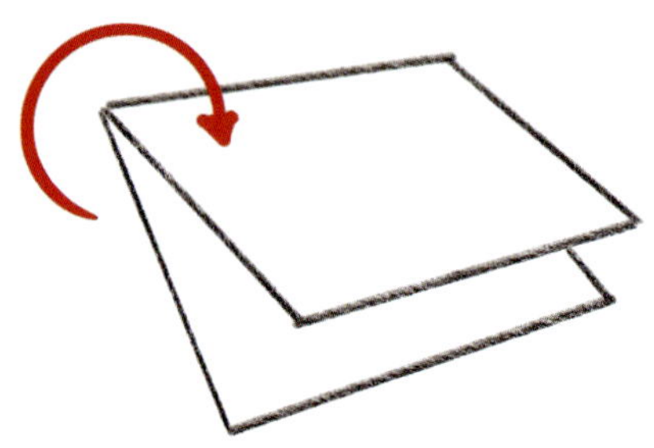

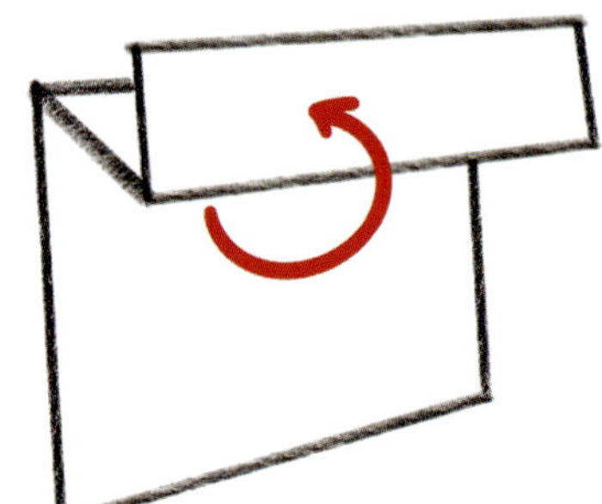

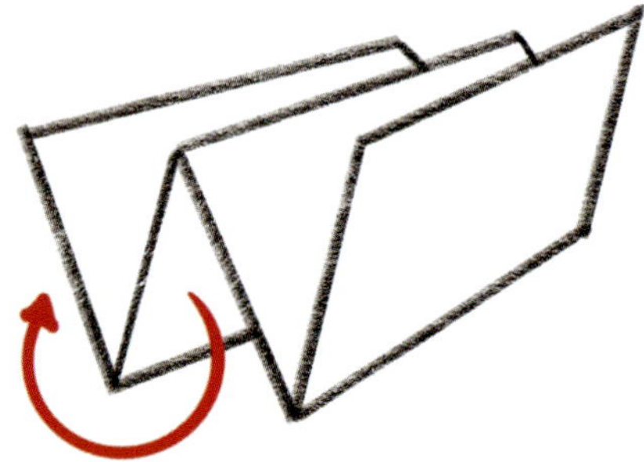

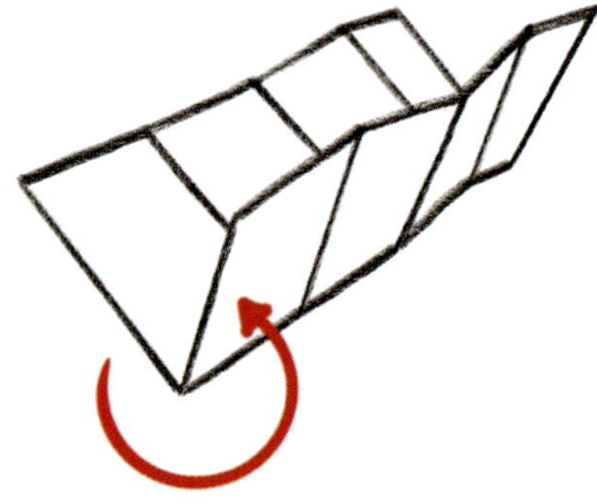

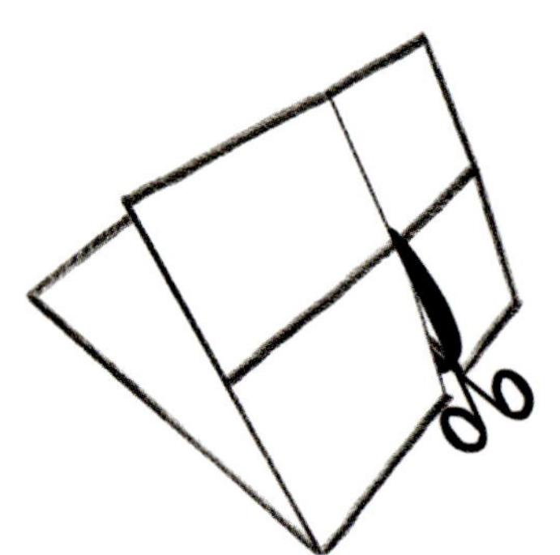

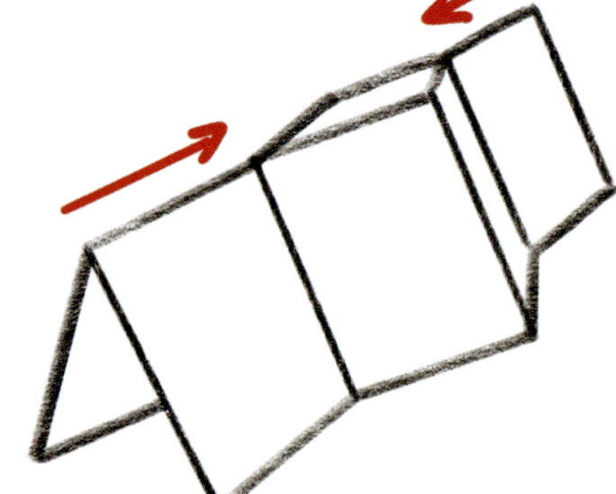

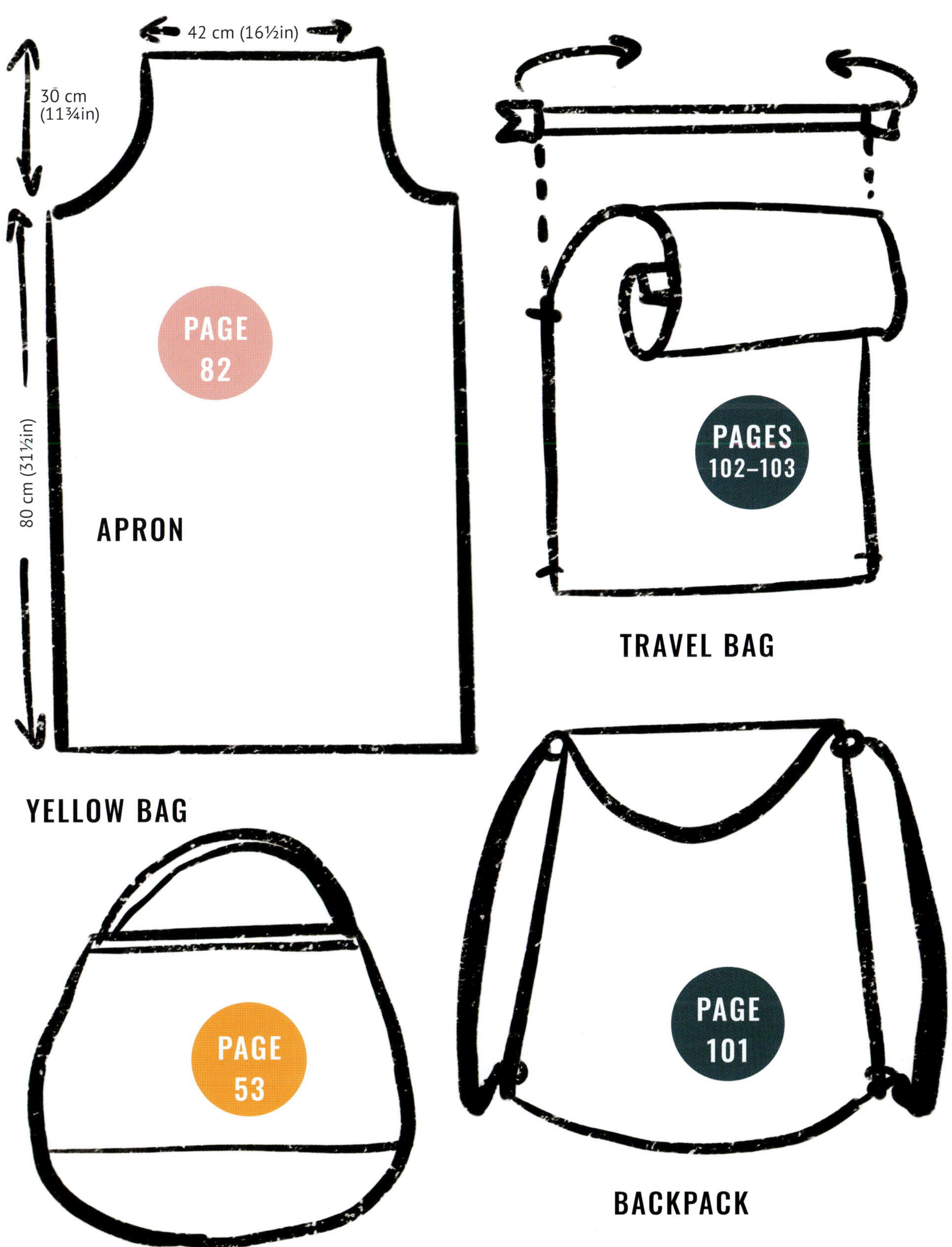
42 cm (16½in)
30 cm
(11¾in)
80 cm (31½in)
PAGE
82
APRON
PAGES
102–103
TRAVEL BAG
YELLOW BAG
PAGE
53
PAGE
101
BACKPACK

GIANT BAG & BACKPACK

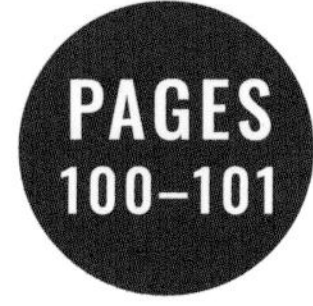

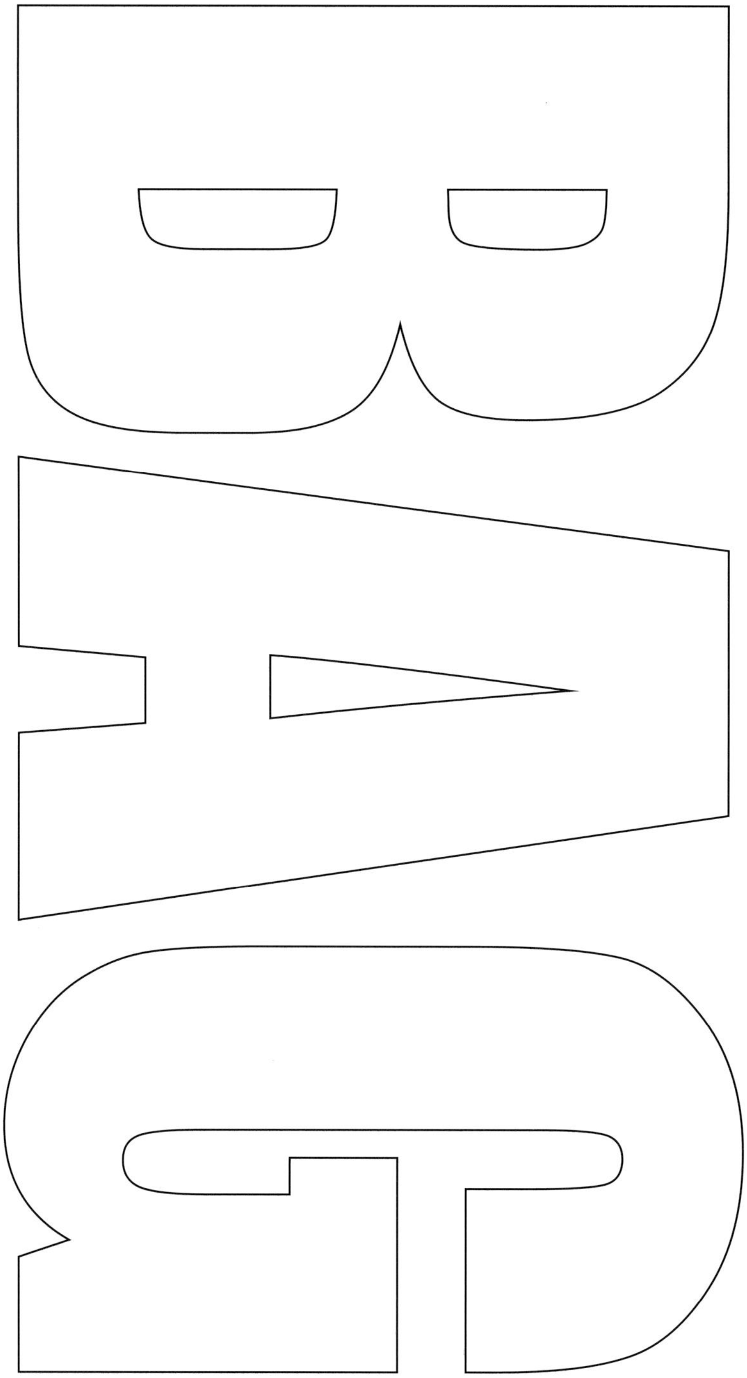

TRAVEL BAG

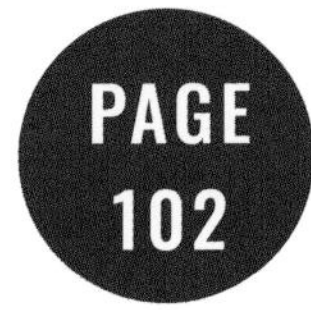

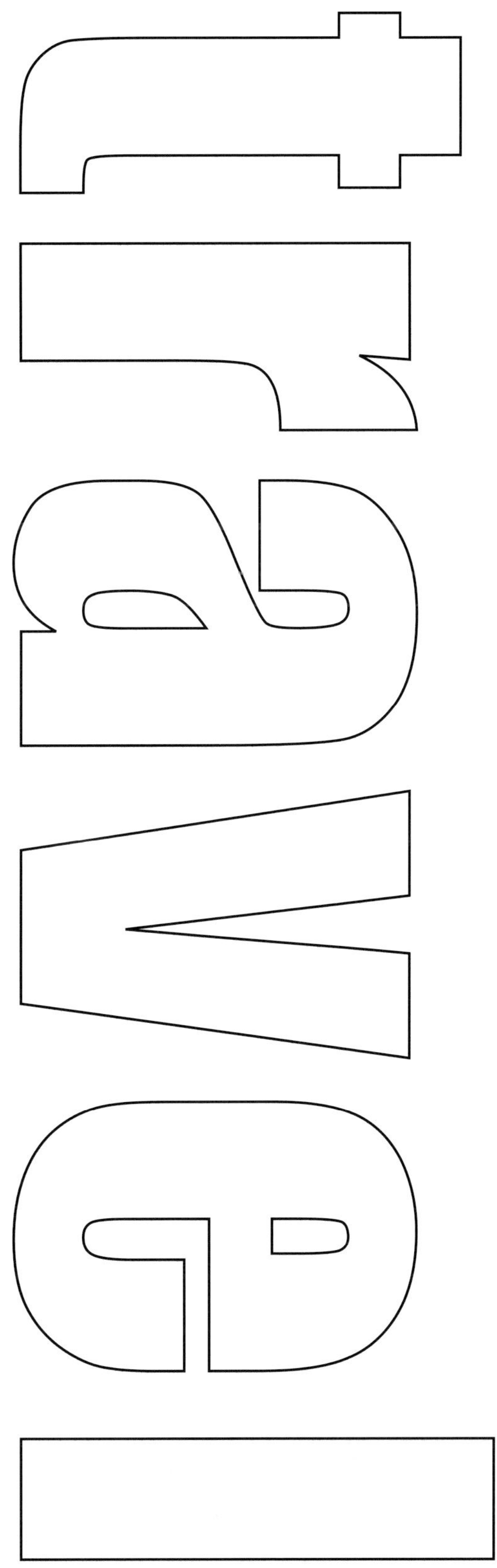

KIMONO

PAGE 126

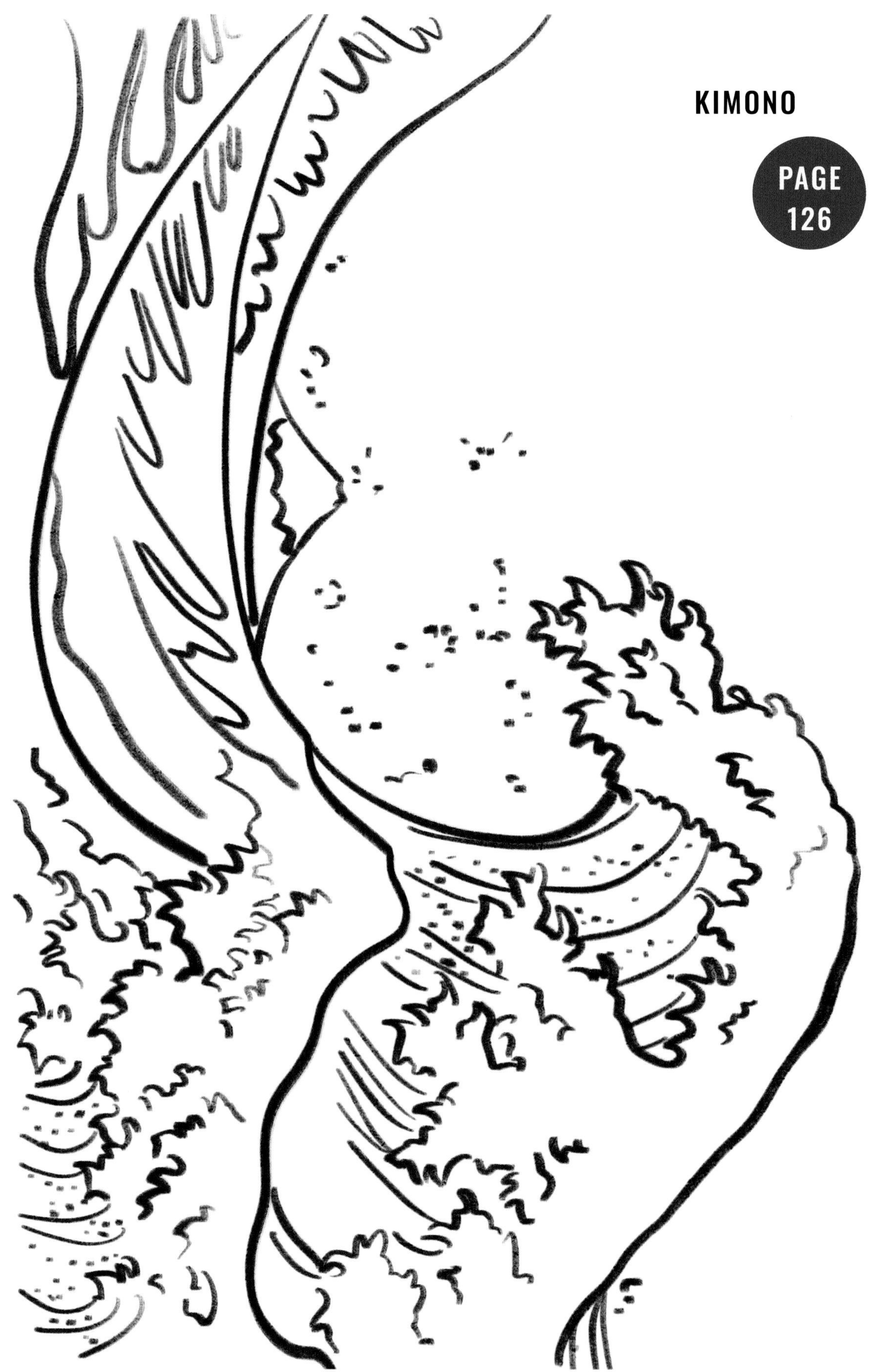

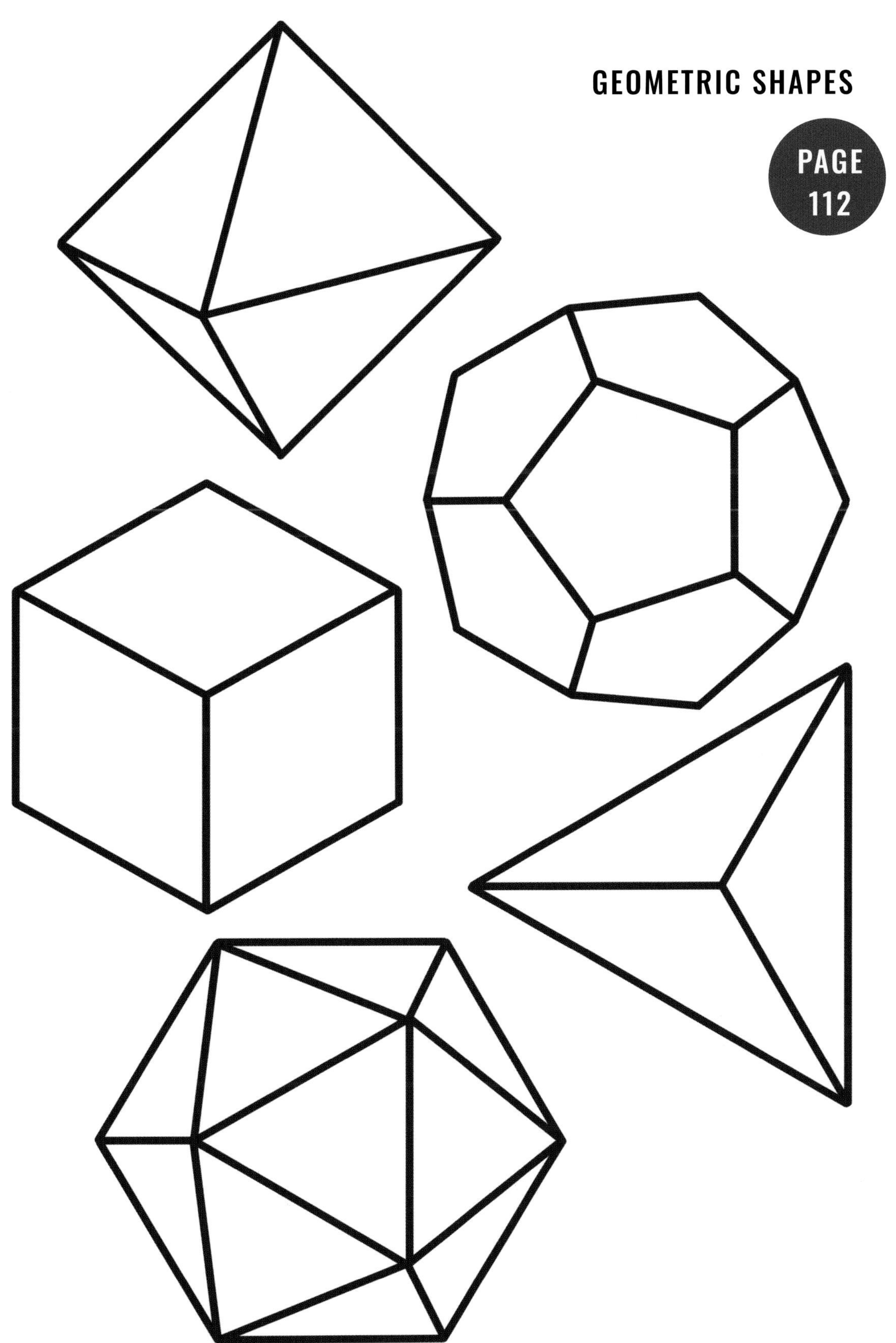

GEOMETRIC SHAPES

PAGE 112

OVEN MITTS

PAGE 131

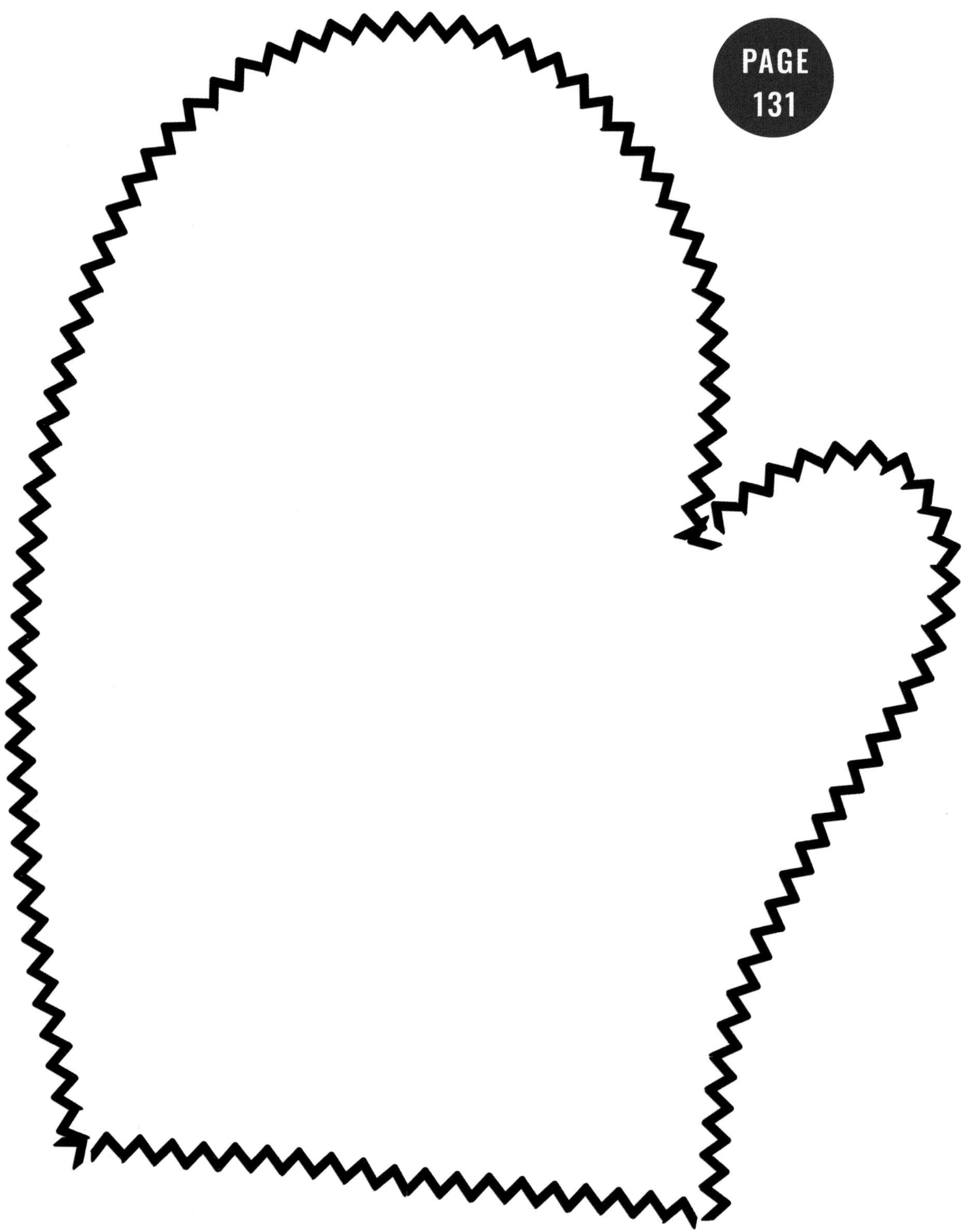

PRINTED APRON

PAGE 82

Pasta la vista Baby!

First published in Great Britain 2025 by
Search Press Limited
Wellwood, North Farm Road
Tunbridge Wells
Kent TN2 3DR

Originally published as *Gelliprint: Unikate drucken auf Papier, Stoff and Holz*

English translation by Tankerton Translation Services

Original edition:
Cover design: Katrin Klink and Sabine Ickler
Photography and illustrations: Katrin Klink
Layout and typesetting: Sabine Ickler
Editing: Antje Krause

ISBN: 978-1-80092-321-8
ebook ISBN: 978-1-80093-307-1

Suppliers

If you have difficulty in obtaining any of the materials and equipment mentioned in this book, then please visit the Search Press website for details of suppliers: www.searchpress.com

The projects in this book have been made using metric measurements, and the imperial equivalents provided have been calculated following standard conversion practices. The imperial measurements are rounded to the nearest ¼in for ease of use. Always use either metric or imperial measurements, not a combination of both.

Bookmarked Hub

Extra copies of the templates are also available to download free from the Bookmarked Hub: www.bookmarkedhub.com
Search for this book by title or ISBN: the files can be found under 'Book Extras'. Membership of the Bookmarked online community is free.

You are invited to find out more about the authors and their work:

Collaborative work:
@artlaboratorium3 on Instagram

Katrin Klink:
www.katrin-klink.de
@katrin.illustrates on Instagram

Sabine Ickler:
www.sabine-ickler.de
@herzfrisch on Instagram

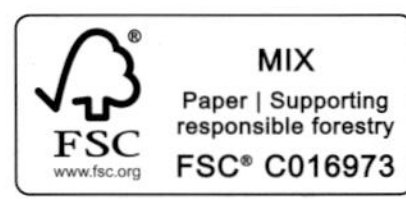